The Kidnapping and Murder
of Little Skeegie Cash

# The Kidnapping and Murder of Little Skeegie Cash

## J. Edgar Hoover and Florida's Lindbergh Case

ROBERT A. WATERS and ZACK C. WATERS

THE UNIVERSITY OF ALABAMA PRESS
Tuscaloosa

Typeface: Caslon and Corbel

Cover photographs: Background photo, J. Edgar Hoover in his office (courtesy of the
Library of Congress); foreground photo, Skeegie Cash just weeks before his abduction
and murder (courtesy of the FBI).
Cover design: Michele Myatt Quinn

∞

The paper on which this book is printed meets the minimum requirements of American
National Standard for Information Sciences—Permanence of Paper for Printed Library
Materials, ANSI Z39.48-1984.

Library of Congress Cataloging-in-Publication Data

Waters, Robert A., 1944–
The kidnapping and murder of Little Skeegie Cash : J. Edgar Hoover and Florida's
Lindbergh case / Robert A. Waters and Zack C. Waters.
pages cm
Includes bibliographical references and index.
ISBN 978-0-8173-1822-2 (trade cloth : alk. paper) — ISBN 978-0-8173-8745-7
(e book) 1. Cash, James Bailey, Jr. 2. McCall, Franklin Pierce. 3. Murder—Florida—
History. 4. Kidnapping—Florida—History. 5. Murder—Investigation—Florida. I.
Waters, Zack C., 1946– II. Title.
HV6533.F6W377 2014
364.152'3092—dc23

2013035330

Truly the hearts of the sons of men are full of evil; madness is in their hearts while they live, and after that they go to the dead. But for him who is joined to all the living there is hope, for a living dog is better than a dead lion. For the living know that they will die; But the dead know nothing, And they have no more reward, For the memory of them is forgotten. Also their love, their hatred, and their envy have now perished; Nevermore will they have a share in anything done under the sun.

Ecclesiastes 9:3–6
New King James Version

# Contents

# Preface

In 1939, "Murderer's Row" at Florida Prison Farm consisted of six steel cages. Called death cells, they stood in a compound separate from the main housing unit. The prison, located near a backwater town called Raiford, had been designated the state's execution facility since Florida's legislature abolished hanging in 1922.[1]

Inside a chamber barely ten feet away from the death cells, "Old Sparky," the electric chair, crouched like a foreboding, fire-breathing monster. Its leather straps, metal clamps, and hard-edged oak slats no doubt haunted the nightmares of many inmates waiting to be consumed by it.[2]

Franklin Pierce McCall, twenty-one, was one of those condemned souls. On February 24, 1939, at eleven o'clock in the morning, surrounded by guards and other prison staff, he began the walk from Cell Number One into the death chamber.[3]

Less than a year before, McCall had kidnapped and murdered five-year-old James Bailey Cash Jr., nicknamed "Skeegie." There was no doubt as to his guilt. He'd confessed and led FBI agents to two different sites where he'd hidden portions of the ransom money. He'd guided none other than media star J. Edgar Hoover through a maze of swamps to the boy's body in the Everglades. He'd pled guilty at his trial, providing details that could have been known only to the killer.[4] Finally, in a letter written to his mother, McCall admitted the crime and claimed to have made peace with God.[5]

A few weeks before his execution date, however, he'd begun proclaiming his innocence. Led to the chair by guards and followed by a chaplain intoning the Lord's Prayer, McCall sat down and began reading a final statement.[6]

"Judas Iscariot betrayed Jesus for thirty pieces of silver," he read, his nasal Cracker accent echoing through the room. "It would be interesting to know just how much some received who were instrumental in this present-day cruelty. I hope that I may be excused from drawing a parallel between the Master's death and my own, [but] the Master died for a cause while I am dying for nothing."[7]

McCall knew his scripture. His father and brother were gospel preachers, and other members of his family were reputable, church-going people. He alone had strayed from the faith.

Leonard C. Chapman, superintendent of prisons, stood next to McCall, listening patiently. About fifty spectators sat in high-backed chairs against the far wall. A wooden partition separated them from the prisoner. Witnesses included newspaper reporters, lawmen who'd investigated the case, and a couple of Skeegie's relatives. Conspicuously missing were the murdered boy's still-grieving parents and family members of the condemned.[8]

By now, McCall was on a roll. "One of the most horrible aspects of this case," he continued, "is the precedent it has established. For in this regard, matters of far more importance than my life were at stake. To be explicit, that infinite something called justice."[9]

The convicted killer added that he opposed the death penalty because "it does not deter crime." However, he said he'd rather die than spend another year in prison "unjustly."[10]

McCall ended by unequivocally stating that he was innocent of the murder and hinting that dark forces had framed him.[11]

When he finished reading, he handed his notes to Chaplain Leslie Shepherd.[12]

Grim-faced, the superintendent nodded to prison staff and moved away. Two guards began strapping McCall's arms and legs to the chair, cinching the buckles tight. An assistant rolled up the prisoner's left trouser leg and attached an electrode to his thigh.[13]

One of the guards removed McCall's hat, placing a bowl-shaped helmet over his freshly shaved head. Inside the helmet, a copper cylinder fit snugly against the prisoner's skull. This device was designed to direct a surge of electricity into his body. If all went as planned, the current would instantly fry the condemned man's brain and cause massive organ failure.[14]

Power for the conductor came through a gray electric cord that snaked along the floor and connected to three ceiling-high plywood cabinets standing against the back wall. These units contained a wild jumble of wires, outlets, plugs, sockets, and other apparatus that somehow, time and again, completed their gruesome task.[15]

McCall said nothing as prison staff pulled the helmet's leather strap tightly against his chin. A guard then placed a black hood over his head and moved away.

Dade County sheriff D. C. Coleman, who had solved the case (although J. Edgar Hoover and the FBI snatched the credit from him), waited a few extra moments before pulling the switch. Coleman, whose views on the death penalty differed from those of many Florida sheriffs, hated this part of his job.[16]

After stalling for as long as possible, he slammed the lever down. A loud bang sounded, followed by the crackle of electric static. Twenty-four hundred volts roared through McCall's body. The smell of burning flesh flooded the room and a smoky haze drifted toward the ceiling. No sound came from the prisoner, but the audience gasped as they watched him straining against the straps.[17]

Finally, the killer slumped back into the chair.

At 11:16 A.M., barely eight minutes after Coleman threw the switch, Dr. Walter Murphree, the prison physician, pronounced Franklin Pierce McCall dead.[18]

Thus ended the tragedy that newspapers had called Florida's "Lindbergh case."[19]

World War II soon dominated the headlines, and the kidnapping and murder of little Skeegie Cash faded from the national spotlight.

But the tragedy that played out among the swamps and palmettos and pines in Dade County, though largely forgotten today, provided the backdrop for a political struggle that would involve J. Edgar Hoover, the United States Congress, and even President Franklin D. Roosevelt.

This book tells that long-forgotten story.

# Acknowledgments

The authors owe a debt of gratitude to a number of individuals and institutions that helped in the preparation of this book.

Since the very foundation of our research consisted of the documents prepared by the Federal Bureau of Investigation in 1938, totaling over four thousand pages, we must first thank the two people who copied the mountains of reports, memos, and letters for us. Mr. Edward A. Singer and Orah Hurst, of Paper Trails Historical Research, LLC, replicated the files and transferred them to computer disks. We thank Edward and Orah for their professionalism and positive attitudes.

The Florida State Archives in Tallahassee provided the authors with transcripts of Franklin Pierce McCall's trial and various appeals, as well as rare photographs from their archives. The staff was prompt, professional, and gracious in their dealings with the authors. We give a special thanks to Dr. Ridgeway Boyd Murfree, a fine young Florida historian, for his help.

Dade County sheriff D. C. Coleman actually fingered Skeegie's killer, though FBI director J. Edgar Hoover claimed complete credit for the bust. Luckily, Sheriff Coleman's family and colleagues kept dozens of scrapbooks detailing the Cash abduction, as well as other high points in his career as sheriff and state legislator. Mr. Brien Coleman, the sheriff's grandson, and Ms. Ann Coleman Hicks, his granddaughter, allowed us access to those valuable keepsakes and permitted us to copy important records and accounts. Dr. Gary Mormino, professor of history at the University of South Florida, first made us aware of the Coleman scrapbooks, and we also appreciate his help.

Another historian, Dr. James M. Denham, director of the Lawton M. Chiles Center of Florida History in Lakeland, Florida, also sent us pages from a hard-to-find book and provided valuable assistance. He has our gratitude and thanks.

Zack's acknowledgments: Our grandparents, Zack and Henrietta Crumpton and George Augustus "Gus" and Mary Waters, lived through the Great Depression without losing their faith in God or humanity during a time of trial. Their stories made the difficulties they experienced come alive. If I close my eyes I can still hear Grandfather Crumpton singing the songs of Jimmie Rodgers, gospel hymns, and other songs of the era, and see Grandfather Waters working (always behind the scenes) to establish a school for orphans in central Florida. The influence these four people had on my life can never be quantified.

A special thanks to the staff of the University of Alabama Press for their confidence in this project and the quality work they do in turning a manuscript into a book. They are any writer's "dream team."

My thanks to Vonda, the love of my life, who encouraged me to tell the stories of history that intrigue me, made my life a true joy, and ignored the laptop that seemed at times, I'm sure, almost like a permanent appendage to my hands. To my children, Luke and Lauren Rose, know that I'm proud of you and love you very much. Finally, to my brother Bob, I thank you for inviting me to be a part of this project. I've enjoyed our collaboration immensely and hope I've contributed a bit to telling the story of a father and mother's love, of an innocent child murdered, of ambition and power run amok, and of evil that destroyed many lives and the innocence of a whole community.

Robert's acknowledgments: This book has been in the works for nearly a decade. As I began wading through the mountains of documents about this case that I'd collected over those years, I found it was too daunting a task to complete alone. So I asked my brother Zack, Florida historian extraordinaire, to be my coauthor. I'm gratified he accepted, and I can't thank him enough for postponing his work on another Civil War project to help me follow through on this little-known story. I also am thankful to my brother John for his continued encouragement, even as his health declined. I wish to thank three longtime friends who have always encouraged me: Fran, Dot, and Glenn Moore. I am so thankful for the spiritual encouragement of my friends and fellow Christians at Central Church of Christ in Ocala, Florida.

A special thanks, as always, must go to my children, Sim Waters and LeAnn Deliberto. They keep life interesting, to say the least. Finally, I thank God every day that I had the good sense to marry my life partner, Marilyn. We've shared much joy and some sorrow, but have always stood together in love. Thanks for the ride.

# The Kidnapping and Murder
## of Little Skeegie Cash

# I

# The Lost Boy

## Saturday, May 28, 1938

At about nine o'clock in the evening, Vera Cash gave five-year-old Skeegie a bath, then dressed him in white-and-rose-colored one-piece pajamas. Placing her child in his crib, she read to him from the *Miami Herald*. Stories about Adolph Hitler's occupation of Austria and Josef Stalin's latest Five-Year Plan might portray human suffering on a grand scale, but Skeegie normally went to sleep quickly when his mother began reading.[1]

On that night, however, he tossed and twisted about in his crib. Only when Vera got to the "funny papers" did the youngster finally fall asleep.[2]

Skeegie had striking milk-blond hair. Tow-headed, he stood three feet, seven inches tall, and weighed forty-three pounds. Mischievous blue eyes sparkled with wonder at the new world that greeted him every morning. Skeegie had attended kindergarten the previous school year, and his teachers considered him to be very bright. He was also playful. He'd just gotten a new tricycle and loved to race it through the house. Friendly and outgoing, most people quickly became attached to the boy.[3]

Vera Cash and her husband, Bailey, lived with their son in Princeton, an agricultural hamlet twenty-two miles south of Miami, Florida. They owned a general store and Standard Oil service station. Next to their businesses, they resided in a two-story home beside US Highway 1-A, alternately called the Dixie Highway or, locally, the Miami to Key West Highway.[4]

After putting her son to sleep, Vera walked next door to the general store. There she spent forty-five minutes helping Bailey count the day's receipts.[5]

At 10:10 P.M., Bailey and Vera locked up and started home. The night air hung low and wet in that peculiar subtropical way as they crossed the ten-foot path to their front door. Nothing seemed to be stirring, and they saw nothing unusual.[6]

As Bailey and Vera entered their home, they found it quiet. Luther Williams and his wife, paying boarders, lived upstairs. But evidently they'd gone to bed.

Vera made her way into the darkened master bedroom and switched on a light.

Skeegie's crib stood a few feet from the bed—close enough so his parents could listen for him, but far enough away so he wouldn't be disturbed. As she did every night, Vera crossed the room to check on her son and to make sure he was resting comfortably.

But on this night, she found only an empty crib.[7]

One mile south of the Cash residence sat a two-room clapboard house (called a "negro shack" in the FBI reports). It had been built many years before, and the only unique thing about the dwelling was a large tin Nehi Cola sign that had been tacked to the bottom of the front door to keep the slats from splitting apart.[8]

John Emanuel and his common-law wife, Geraldine Barnes, had labored many seasons in the area and currently worked as tomato pickers for John Campbell. The couple had lived together for four years, most of that time in the home they now shared.[9]

By eleven o'clock, Emanuel and Barnes lay in bed. Exhausted from a week in the fields, they looked forward to Sunday, their day off. On Monday, Americans would celebrate Memorial Day, and they had that day free as well. But as the couple drifted off to sleep, a loud crash outside jerked them awake.[10]

Suddenly, someone began pounding on the back door. The noise echoed inside their small home like shotgun blasts.

Emanuel was a simple man. He worked hard, minded his own business, and had done nothing to provoke anyone. The loud, persistent banging perplexed him.[11] Emanuel and Barnes cowered silently beneath the sheets, hoping the intruder would leave. (About a year before, Emanuel had been shot in the shoulder when he stepped outside his house to try to break up a fight between strangers.)

The person pounding on the door didn't let up.

"Hey Big Boy," he called out. The man spoke in an uncommonly low tone, and Emanuel could tell he was trying to disguise his voice. The stranger also feigned a foreign accent. Instead of "Big Boy," he called Emanuel "Beeg Boy."[12]

When he got no response, the man tried again. "Talk to me, Beeg Boy," he demanded.

Somewhere far away, a dog started barking. It must have awakened others because soon a whole pack took up howling.

The man on the porch called again. "Come on, Beeg Boy," he said. "I got a way you can make some money."

"You got the wrong negro," Emanuel shouted. "Go away."

"Get up, Beeg Boy. Don't you want to make some dough?"

"Go away," Emanuel repeated.

"I have a note I want you to take to J. B. Cash," the stranger said. "Mistah Cash owns the Standard Oil station. He'll pay you five dollars when you give this letter to him."

"I don't know no Mr. Cash. I never worked for that man." Sweat poured down the face of the beleaguered farmworker. He later said he thought someone was trying to "set him up," to make him a responsible party to a crime.[13]

After a pause, the darkness grew quiet except for the barking dogs. Then, all of a sudden, the stranger outside began kicking the front door. He continued until the little house rattled and shook. "Listen here, you son of a bitch," he shouted. "You better get your black ass up and go do what I'm telling you." In his rage, he'd forgotten the phony foreign accent.

"You got the wrong man. Leave me alone!"

"If you don't do what I say, I'm gonna take this shotgun and blow your damn door off. You better believe me when I say I'm gonna come through that door and kill you."[14]

Then, as suddenly as it had started, everything got quiet. Even the dogs stopped yelping.

The couple, fearing they might be lynched, breathed a sigh of relief when they heard a car engine rev to life.

After waiting in the darkened house a few more minutes, they climbed out of bed and pulled on their clothes. Peering out the window, Emanuel looked for the stranger. Seeing nothing except darkness, he grabbed Barnes by the hand and they darted out the back door.

Emanuel and Barnes ran down a dirt trail, tramped through dark, overgrown fields, and fled into the Everglades.

There they waited, swiping at mosquitoes and terrified of the "painters" (panthers) that roamed the area. Soon they sought refuge at a friend's house and hid out until the FBI located and interviewed them.[15]

With a mother's intuition, Vera knew immediately that Skeegie had been taken. Her husband, however, didn't seem worried. "He probably just got up to get some water," Cash said.

"He's never done that before," Vera stammered.

"Let's check the house."

Bailey headed toward the kitchen. Vera followed, her knees weak. They quickly filed through all the rooms on the first floor, checking closets and niches where their son could be lost or hiding. After failing to find any trace of the boy, the now-concerned father raced upstairs and knocked on the door of his boarders.[16]

Luther Williams, a farmworker, answered immediately. He denied knowing Skeegie's whereabouts but stated that sometime just before he went to bed he heard the back door open. He recalled hearing heavy boots clomp into the house, but Williams thought nothing of it. "People come and go all the time," he said. Williams asked his wife, who was still in bed, if she had any information, but she could shed no light on the boy's disappearance. The renter quickly threw on some clothes and offered to help search for Skeegie.[17]

As Cash walked back downstairs, something caught his eye. He noticed that the back door gaped wide open and the outside screen door had been cut. An *L*-shaped slash was directly adjacent to the handle—the shiny copper from the cut contrasted with the black mesh of the screen. Cash rushed to the door and inspected it. He saw that the gash in the screen could have allowed an intruder to reach inside and remove the latch. Then he could open both the screen door and the unlocked wooden back door.[18]

A wave of fear washed away the father's previous confidence. Cash recalled another missing child he'd read about in the Miami newspapers. Just a month before, twelve-year-old Peter Levine had vanished while walking home from school in New Rochelle, New York. According to the latest news reports, the boy still hadn't been found.[19]

Since the abduction and murder of Charles Lindbergh's son in 1932, kidnapping had become a nationwide "epidemic." Even new laws making some kidnappings a federal crime hadn't stemmed the tide. In 1933 the *New York Times* began running a front-page "box score," listing the victims, the amount of ransoms paid, and the names of those caught and tried for the crimes. The newspaper cited dozens of cases.[20]

In 1935, nine-year-old George Weyerhaeuser had been returned home after his wealthy parents paid a hefty ransom.[21] A year before that, Dorothy Ann Distelhurst had been abducted as she walked home from kindergarten in Nashville, Tennessee. A month later, workers tending a garden at the Davidson County Tuberculosis Society found the child's body. By 1938, the case had gone stone-cold.[22]

Skeegie Cash seemed to be an unlikely victim. Levine's father, an attorney, could afford to pay thousands of dollars for his son's return. Bailey Cash, on the other hand, had been born in Perry, Florida, the son of an impoverished dirt farmer. The family moved to Princeton in 1923, but their living conditions hadn't improved. Throughout his life, Cash would be haunted by those days when he and his family could barely scrape up enough to eat. The emotional scars never healed, and when he became an adult, he determined that he would never be poor again.[23]

In 1902, Gaston Drake had founded a small logging community and named it Princeton, after his college alma mater. He cut the massive stands of slash pine surrounding the town, then moved on.

Residents noticed the unique rust-colored soil in Drake's stripped-out fields and began calling the area the Redlands. The half-clay, half-muck sod combined with subtropical weather proved to be a perfect blend for growing a variety of produce, including squash, peppers, and beans. Tomatoes, however, became the region's major cash crop since Redlands was the only place in the United States where they could be grown in the winter. Exotic fruits such as avocados, guavas, and mangos also contributed to the local economy.[24]

By 1938, Princeton had a population of six hundred. African Americans comprised more than half of the hamlet's population, many living in the "quarters" on John Campbell's truck farm.[25]

Six days a week, Bailey Cash opened his businesses before daylight to accommodate the farmers, fishermen, and laborers who made up his clientele. In addition to the general store and filling station next to their home, Bailey, thirty-eight, and Vera, thirty-six, also owned a filling station and wholesale gasoline company in Homestead, six miles to the south. To make extra money, the family rented their second-story rooms to boarders.[26]

Vera cooked, cleaned, managed the renters, and took care of little Skeegie. In addition, she assisted her husband with bookkeeping.

By a combination of ambition, intelligence, and hard work, the Cash family had become prosperous enough for local residents to consider them wealthy. Even so, at the time of Skeegie's disappearance, the family's bank accounts consisted of less than $7,000.[27]

Several of Cash's relatives lived in the area. His brother, Wilson Cash, resided just three doors down. As Cash and Luther Williams headed that way, they noticed several men loitering in the streets.[28]

Marshall Frampton Braxton, nicknamed "Frampy," stood with the group. Earlier that evening, he'd been loafing at Cash's store, drinking beer and chatting up customers. A self-employed carpenter, Frampy always seemed to have plenty of time on his hands.[29]

Franklin Pierce McCall was in the crowd. Bailey considered him a drunk, a loudmouth, and a braggart. His father, a minister who'd recently passed away, had a sterling reputation. In fact, area residents respected the entire McCall family, except for Franklin.[30]

About six months before, the twenty-one-year-old had married a local girl, Claudine Hilliard, and moved to Princeton from his north Florida hometown of Jasper. Since then, he'd worked sporadically and unenthusiastically, packing limes and avocadoes, grading tomatoes, and driving a truck. He'd obtained a job with the state road department but quit after a few weeks. When they first moved to Princeton, McCall and his wife had rented a room from Bailey and Vera Cash. Now they lived in a dilapidated, rat-infested house about two blocks west of the Cash residence.[31]

Braxton and McCall joined the searchers. Bailey asked the carpenter if he'd brought his pistol, and Braxton assured him that he had it in his pocket.[32]

Even before Bailey and Williams walked outside, the news about Skeegie's disappearance had gotten around. (After the unsuccessful search inside the house, Vera rushed to the homes of several neighbors to inquire about her son.) Wilson quickly joined Bailey and his boarder. Jim Mizell, who managed Bailey's Standard Oil station, also fell in with the search party. The group headed down the road, some on foot, others in cars, picking up neighbors as they went. Stopping at every house along the way, they found no trace of the boy.[33]

Eventually they made their way into what the FBI reports termed the "negro quarters."

Cash was well liked by most of the black workers. Unlike some storeowners who overcharged the illiterate or the ill informed (black *and* white), the merchant was meticulously fair with everyone. He also willingly extended credit to members of both races. Now, as the panicked father implored their help, many of the residents in the quarters allowed Cash and the other searchers to come in to their homes and look around. Bailey and his friends quickly determined that Skeegie had not been hidden in the quarters (although that would remain one of the FBI's favorite theories for many days).[34]

Beatrice Cash, the wife of another Cash brother, Asbury, learned about Skeegie's disappearance shortly before eleven o'clock. Beatrice sat in her car outside the Seminole Theatre in Homestead while her sixteen-year-old daughter, Josephine, watched *Rebecca of Sunnybrook Farm*, the new Shirley Temple movie. As Beatrice sat chatting with other mothers, a stranger came by and told her about the suspected kidnapping of Skeegie Cash.

A few minutes later, the film ended. Beatrice hustled Josephine into the car and drove straight to her brother-in-law's residence. After assuring Vera that she would return, Beatrice transported her daughter the half-mile back to her own home.[35]

As she opened the front door, Bailey's sister-in-law noticed a piece of paper wrapped around the handle. She removed the rubber band attaching the message to the door handle, stepped inside, and opened it. The note looked as if it had been torn from a grocery bag. Beatrice saw that a message had been scrawled in pencil.[36]

She turned on the living room light to read it. "If you have no note yet go to first nigger house on left on first oil road south of Princeton and get note there."[37]

She turned the note over and saw that it was addressed to "J. B. Cash."

Richard Asbury Cash and twenty-one-year-old Ishmael owned a one-truck produce transportation company called Cash & Son. They were sound asleep when Beatrice rushed into the house like a storm, shaking them awake. She blurted out the news about Skeegie's disappearance and the note she'd found. While Asbury and Shorty prepared to go help with the search, Beatrice climbed into her car and raced back to the Cash home.

There she handed the note to Bailey's brother, Wilson.[38]

It was nearing midnight. By now, the frustrated searchers had returned.

Nearly fifty men and women milled around the Cash residence and filling station. Many were angry. They'd all heard of kidnappings in big cities like New York and Chicago, but someone, it seemed, had snatched one of their own. Everyone knew the boy—he hung around his daddy's store wearing a big grin and joking with the customers. He even had nicknames for many of them. For instance, he called Franklin Pierce McCall "Preacher Boy" because McCall's father was a pastor.[39]

Anger quickly boiled into threats of lynching. The shocking abduction had turned the hardy country folk into a dangerous mob.

Bailey Cash and Wilson, however, just wanted to get Skeegie back. Justice could come later. Shortly before midnight, as they left to go to the house mentioned in the note, Wilson Cash called the Dade County Sheriff's Department and informed Deputy R. B. Eavanson that his brother's son had likely been abducted.[40]

# 2

# "We Have the Child"

## Sunday, May 29, 1938

At about one o'clock in the morning, a caravan rolled up to John Emanuel's house. Bailey Cash drove his 1936 Plymouth sedan while several relatives, employees, and neighbors followed. Cash had previously requested that the group circle the house, and they did so, their headlights illuminating the exterior of the shack.[1]

Bailey and his brother, Asbury, quickly walked toward the front door. The rickety porch looked like it might collapse under the weight of the men. The wind howled in wild gusts, and loose tarpaper flapped a drumbeat against the window. Cash hailed the homeowner but received no answer. The brothers then walked around the building as they searched for the second ransom note.

Skeegie had been missing for four hours now. They were racing against time and Cash knew it.

He and Asbury returned to the front porch. If they couldn't find the note outside, they planned to break in to the house. As they stepped onto the porch, the glare of headlights washed off the white Nehi sign.

And there it lay. Stuck beneath the door, Bailey observed a folded piece of paper.[2]

He seized it and stepped into the circle of headlights.

Holding the crumpled note tightly so the wind wouldn't rip it from his hands, Cash opened it and read the message aloud to Asbury.

*First side of first sheet*: We have the child. You will follow these instructions. Notify any officer, give serial number of any bill, fail to burn this note and you won't see him again. Place 500 $5 100 $20 500 $10 & 10 $50 total $10,000 in a shoe box and take this route

*Second side of first sheet:* [Hand-drawn map] Myra St Homestead Moody Dr. 1st oil road follw arrers use old unmarked bills with serial numbers not running in order. Leave Princeton at exactly mid-

*First side of second sheet:* night Monday nt. Take first oil road to left, continue to Moody Dr. turn left go to Allapattah Dr. turn right to Myra St. then to Homestead go 20 M.P.H. full route at some point in route light will flash two times. STOP. Place box on right side of road then proceed full route

*Second side of second sheet:* The child will be released in a few hours if all instructions are followed and *NO ONE* notifyd give bearer of this note $5 then step in *FRONT OF PLACE AND BURN IT AVYE ANY-SLIP-UP AND YOU WON'T SEE HIM AGAIN!*[3]

The distraught father's hand shook as he placed the note into his shirt pocket.

"What're you gonna do, Bailey?" Asbury asked.

Cash didn't hesitate. "Everything they ask," he said.

The haggard-looking men climbed back into the car, signaled to the others, and soon the small procession headed back down the Dixie Highway toward home.

By two o'clock that morning, close to one hundred neighbors still milled around in front of Bailey Cash's service station. Others drove back roads searching for anything out of the ordinary. Periodic reports of suspicious activities would get the crowd excited. But once the rumors proved unfounded, the air of hope would leak out of the group like air seeping from a tubed tire.[4]

A single incandescent bulb attached halfway up a pole next to the Standard Oil station cast a dim light over the crowd. The streets, still slick from the previous day's heavy rain, glistened eerily in the shadows.

Suddenly, everyone quieted. Bailey Cash emerged from the darkness. No one had seen him since he'd returned home after finding the ransom note. Now he strode toward the group, still wearing the blue suit, white shirt, and dark tie he'd had on when he locked up his store.

Cash stepped to the front of the crowd.

"I want to thank everyone for helping me search for my boy," he said, his voice echoing through the silence. "I plan to follow every instruction I've received from the person who snatched Skeegie. I was asked by the kidnapper to burn this note in public. I will do so now. I also wish to let whoever it was that took Skeegie know that I plan to pay the ransom. All I want is to get my son back."[5]

Ever since he'd found the ransom note, rumors had swirled about its contents. Everyone in town seemed to be speculating on whether locals or outsiders had carried out the abduction.

Cash pulled a small, torn piece of paper from his shirt pocket.

"This is the second note I received," he said.

He pulled a matchbox from his pants. As the crowd gasped, Cash struck a match and held it up to the note. The paper caught fire, and he quickly dropped it. Like a leaf, it fluttered to the asphalt where it continued to burn. After the note flamed out, Cash made a show of stomping on it until nothing remained.[6]

The crowd, mesmerized by the strange scene, stood silent.

Cash spoke again. "If the kidnapper is here," he said, "please take care of Skeegie. Now I'm asking y'all to go back home and get some rest."

One at a time, the townspeople began to leave. Most faded away into the darkness, but a few stopped to whisper words of encouragement.

There was a paradox here, and Cash knew it. Everyone in town knew of the abduction, yet his boy's kidnapper had ordered him to tell no one.[7]

When the last person left, Cash turned to go back home. He could see a candle flickering in the front window of his house. Vera had placed it there. A beacon, she said. For her lost son.

Arthur Rutzen, special agent in charge of the Miami FBI office, was sound asleep when the jangling of the telephone jerked him awake. He glanced at his watch and saw that it was three o'clock in the morning.[8] A graduate of Fordham Law School, Rutzen had been with the bureau for only three years, but had impressed director J. Edgar Hoover with his efficiency and attention to detail.[9]

The caller identified himself as a Dade County sheriff's deputy. "I just got back from Princeton," R. B. Eavanson said. "Looks like there's been a ransom kidnapping there."

At first, Rutzen's sleep-fogged mind wondered why someone would be calling him about a crime in Princeton, New Jersey. Then he remembered a small town by that name a few miles to the south of Miami.

"I spoke with the father of the victim," Eavanson continued. "He's a businessman named James Bailey Cash—friends call him Bailey. Said him and his wife discovered their five-year-old son missing from his bed sometime around ten thirty Saturday night. Kid's name is James Bailey Cash, Junior, but they all call him 'Skeegie.'"[10]

The deputy paused. "This ain't just a missing person," he said. "Looks like another Lindbergh to me."

Fully awake now, questions began swirling through Rutzen's mind. Why Princeton, a small town nobody's ever heard of? Is it truly a ransom kidnapping, or did someone want a child to raise as his own? Were his parents or other family members involved?

"Can you meet me at the Roberts Hotel?" Rutzen asked, referring to a well-known Miami Beach establishment.

"Sure."

When the agent arrived, he found Eavanson already waiting for him in the all-night diner. Local residents considered the luxurious hotel, with its large rooms and gold-plated faucet handles, one of south Florida's choicest hostelries. It was also controversial—the hotel openly advertised that it catered only to "gentile customers," excluding Jews.

Over coffee, the deputy explained the events surrounding the disappearance. "The searchers came up empty when they went to look for the boy," Eavanson said. "But they did find two notes from the kidnapper."[11]

"Where are they?"

"Mr. Cash still has them," the deputy said. "He pretended to burn the second note, as requested, but kept the original."[12]

Within an hour, Rutzen and special agent Samuel K. McKee had arrived in Princeton. McKee, a lean, wiry former Texas sheriff, craved action. A veteran of the shootouts that had brought down such infamous outlaws as George "Pretty Boy" Floyd, the notorious Brady Gang, and Fred and Kate Barker, he couldn't get overly excited about this case, sensing that it would be a whodunit, not an adrenalin-pumping gun battle.[13]

(While FBI director J. Edgar Director Hoover publicly maintained that he hired only lawyers and accountants to be special agents, he'd quickly learned that the bureau needed "shootists" as well. So he quietly began recruiting lawmen from the Southwest. These men, almost all from Texas and Oklahoma, had been the backbone of the group of agents that eliminated many Prohibition-era gangsters.[14])

Rutzen and McKee drove directly to the Cash home.

A May 29 interoffice memorandum from Percy E. Foxworth, administrative assistant to Edward A. Tamm, assistant director, described the residence. "Mr. McKee told me that the house is a two-story affair," it read, "with a filling station and a little store in front. There is an office on one side (of the home) and there are living quarters on the first floor. The second floor is broken up into a half dozen very, very small apartments [with] only one family living there at the present time."[15]

Since the home had no telephone, Rutzen and McKee would arrange for one to be installed by Southern Bell Telephone Company. In addition to the phone, recording equipment would be shipped from FBI headquarters in Washington, DC.[16]

Vera, a brunette, lay prostrate on a couch in the living room. Several women from the community, including her sister-in-law, Beatrice, and Jim Mizell's wife, attempted to console the frantic mother, but her agonized sobs could be heard up and down the street outside. One of the women informed Rutzen that a doctor would soon arrive to give Vera a sedative.[17]

The agent immediately noticed that Bailey Cash maintained a steely calm exterior. His demeanor raised the agents' suspicions. Cash handed Rutzen the first note Beatrice had found. As the agent read it, he concluded that the writer was from the area.[18]

Then Cash informed the agents that he and his brother, Asbury, had located a second note at the home of John Emanuel, a "negro" who worked as a tomato picker for John Campbell's farm. But they weren't able to question him. Before they reached his house, Cash said, Emanuel seemed to have fled.

The second note contained much more detail than the first. Hand printed in lead pencil, the writer had folded the soiled paper in half and written his message on each of the four sides.

Rutzen held it up to the light. "Looks like it was torn from an ordinary brown paper bag," he said.

The misspellings and wild penmanship made Rutzen suspect that the perpetrator might be attempting to throw investigators off. On the other hand, many Florida natives, who called themselves Crackers, commonly pronounced "arrow" as "arrer." The "oil road" referred to in the note also struck Rutzen as odd. Bailey explained that local residents referred to gravel roads that had been sprayed with petroleum to keep them firm as "oil roads."[19]

"It has to be somebody from around here," Cash said, as if reading the agent's mind. "You'd have to know the area to write a detailed note like that."

While they discussed the notes, a physician arrived and handed a bottle of pills to Vera. On the way out, he shook Bailey's hand.

Cash was all business. Looking Rutzen straight in the eye, he said, "I want the FBI to stay out of this until I make the payoff."[20]

The agent nodded. Bureau policy allowed parents to make their own decisions on matters such as whether to pay a ransom.

"We'd like to do some investigation behind the scenes," Rutzen said. "But we'll remain in the background."

That was okay with Cash. "As long as the kidnapper doesn't find out," he said.[21]

Six years earlier, the kidnapping of Charles Augustus Lindbergh Jr. had stunned America. After flying solo across the Atlantic, the elder Lindbergh had returned to parades, awards, and all the accolades of a sports star. Basically shy and conservative, he married his sweetheart, Anne Morrow, and retired to Hopewell, New Jersey. There they had their first child, a son, Charles Jr. Since Lindbergh had once flown a plane called the *Lone Eagle*, newspapers, in the inane style of the day, nicknamed the child "Little Eaglet."

On the night of March 1, 1932, Lindbergh's nanny found the child's crib empty. A muddy homemade ladder, leaning against an open second-story window, provided graphic evidence as to how the abductor had entered and exited the child's room.[22]

The kidnapping was, as H. L. Mencken wrote, "the biggest story since the Resurrection." While there had been child abductions before, the country had never seen anything like this. The media relentlessly pursued the story, and when Lindbergh received a ransom note for $50,000, it made front-page news everywhere.

After many twists and turns, an eccentric go-between nicknamed "JAFSIE" (Dr. John A. Condon) delivered the ransom money to a man who called himself "John." Before the kidnapper fled with the cash, he informed JAFSIE that the child could be found alive in a boat off the coast of Massachusetts, near Elizabeth Island. A widespread search by state authorities and the United States Coast Guard, however, proved fruitless.

Two and a half months later, on May 12, 1932, a motorist located the child's body in a wooded area just a few miles from Hopewell. The discovery of the badly decomposed remains devastated the Lindbergh family and the nation.[23]

Scholars later contended that the discovery of the child's body robbed the nation of its innocence.[24]

The Secret Service had copied the serial numbers of each ransom bill, and soon the money began showing up, mostly in New Jersey and New York. But the man who passed the bills always managed to stay one step ahead of the lawmen. Before store clerks and police realized he had passed a note from the ransom payoff, the suspect would be long gone.

Finally, on September 18, 1934, someone spent a ten-dollar gold certificate at a Manhattan gas station. (Because such notes had been withdrawn from circulation, the service station attendant wrote down the customer's license tag number.) The discovery that the bill had been one of the ransom notes brought authorities dashing to the scene.

Bruno Hauptmann, an illegal immigrant with a police record in his native Germany, owned the car. When lawmen searched his home they uncovered more than $14,000 hidden in his garage. Checking the serial numbers, it turned out that all the bills were from the Lindbergh ransom.

Even though police tortured Hauptmann unmercifully, he refused to admit to being the kidnapper. He claimed that a friend from Germany had left the cash in a shoebox in his (Hauptmann's) closet, then returned to his home country and died. Hauptmann contended that his friend had owed him money, so he kept it.

The story strained credulity, and prosecutors charged the German with kidnapping and murder. In America's first "trial of the century," a jury convicted Hauptmann, and two years later, he died in the electric chair.[25]

At the time of the Lindbergh abduction, the Federal Bureau of Investigation was in its infancy. In fact, the New Jersey State Police and the Secret Service conducted most of the investigation. When Hoover attempted to insert the FBI into the case, local lawmen and the Secret Service proved extremely uncooperative.[26]

After the abduction, Congress hastily wrote and enacted an antikidnapping bill. Called the Lindbergh law, it authorized imprisonment for life to anyone convicted of abducting a person for ransom. More importantly for the FBI, the law presumed that kidnappers would cross state lines, making Hoover and his FBI the primary law enforcement agency of record. (Several states, including Florida, passed similar statutes, called Little Lindbergh laws. In Florida, the edict called for the death penalty in any kidnapping for ransom.)[27]

Over the next six years, the FBI investigated most kidnappings in America. For instance, in 1933, an unknown kidnapper snatched a Minnesota banker named William A. Hamm. After his family paid $100,000, the kidnappers released the victim. FBI agents soon arrested gangster Alvin "Creepy" Karpis for the crime, and he received a life sentence.[28] In another case, George "Machine Gun" Kelly's gang kidnapped Charles Urschel, in Oklahoma. Kelly released the victim after his family paid a $200,000 ransom. The bureau did a masterful job in this case. Agents soon captured Kelly and his gang, and the kidnappers received long prison terms.[29]

By the time of the Skeegie Cash abduction, the G-men had investigated hundreds of kidnappings. Along with local authorities, they solved most of them. However, they alienated many local cops by always taking full credit for any successful case and blaming local police for any failures.

Hoover, knowing the value of good publicity, had cultivated many well-known journalists, including Walter Winchell and Drew Pearson. Realizing the popularity and influence of radio, the director also ingratiated himself to popular broadcasters, such as radio commentator Gabriel Heatter. Hoover regularly leaked case information to these and other media heavyweights.[30]

Even the popular term "G-men" likely originated in the mind of J. Edgar Hoover. When FBI agents burst into a Memphis bedroom to take down Machine Gun Kelly, the thug reportedly shouted, "Don't shoot, G-men!" It made a great story, and the media lapped it up, but many historians contend that Hoover fabricated the fiction to generate positive publicity for the bureau. It worked. Forever after, FBI agents would be known as G-men, short for government men.[31]

Inside the Cash home, Rutzen and McKee interviewed Luther Williams, the upstairs boarder. The farmworker stated that his apartment was directly above the back door. Sometime between 9:30 and 10:00, he said, he "heard someone enter through the back door and walk heavily through the lower hall and shortly thereafter go out the back door." Williams recalled that "the second time the door opened and closed, it slammed with a rather loud bang." Williams's wife confirmed his account. In a significant observation, neither had heard an automobile crank up after the visitor left.[32]

The agents next interviewed Bailey Cash. He'd worked all day at the store, he said. Even though it had stormed for much of the day, many customers came and went. At around five o'clock, he remembered seeing Marshall

Frampton "Frampy" Braxton and Franklin McCall come in. They "hung around" for several hours. Braxton would occasionally buy a soft drink or beer, but McCall never purchased anything. Cash said he knew his former renter had no job and was broke. McCall always spun a series of hard-luck yarns to customers, and once in a while he would talk someone into buying him a soda or beer or a box of crackers.[33]

Cash stated that as he prepared to close the store, at about nine thirty, Vera walked in. McCall asked her what time it was, then left.[34]

Braxton, Cash recalled, had departed a few minutes earlier.

As he recounted the events of the day, his mind seemed to be racing ahead.

"I've got about eight thousand dollars in the bank," he said. "But I'm sure I can raise the rest."[35]

Vera, who at times appeared close to being catatonic, seemed incapable of providing any useful information. It didn't help when friends and family assured her that Skeegie would be found soon, and that he would be alive and well.[36]

As the agents continued to probe Bailey Cash for information, he informed them that he and Vera had been married for ten years. Neither had been previously married, he said, and both were longtime residents of Princeton.[37]

Vera Howard was born in Folkston, Georgia, and still had family there. One of her uncles had been a well-known politician in the Peach State. At fifteen years of age, she'd moved to Princeton with her parents. Vera was twenty-five when she and Bailey married. Although the Depression hit her family hard, Vera hadn't grown up in the grinding poverty that had afflicted many, like her husband. She had a reputation around town as a fine cook and a formidable businesswoman.[38]

Rutzen asked Cash if he knew of anyone who might wish to harm him or his family. While conceding that he had a few business rivals and disgruntled former employees, Cash said he could think of no one angry enough to abduct his son.

"It's my opinion," Cash said, "that this was done for money, not revenge. The kidnapper knows how much money I have and how much I can raise. He has to be someone who lives close by and is familiar with me and my habits. How else could he have known that my wife would come to the store at 9:30 and leave Skeegie alone in our house?"[39]

Rutzen asked Cash to lead him to the back door of the home. Dawn had begun to herald sunrise over the little community.

Crushed rock covered the ground around the back door, the G-men observed, eliminating any hope of finding usable footprints.

"Did anyone come through here after your son went missing?" Rutzen asked.

Cash nodded. "Sure," he said. "Maybe fifty, a hundred people. I don't really know how many, but this is the door most people use when they visit."[40]

Rutzen grimaced. The amount of traffic coming and going ruined any opportunity to obtain fingerprints from the door.

The agents noticed the copper wire where the screen had been slashed. Agent McKee asked Cash if he had a pocketknife. The father produced an old, rusty junker. McKee checked the blades and determined that the knife hadn't been used to cut the screen—no flakes of copper adhered to it.

By now, Rutzen and McKee knew they needed help. At 10:15 A.M., Sunday morning, Rutzen called headquarters in Washington, DC, and requested additional agents. He spoke to assistant director Percy Foxworth.[41] A few minutes later, the agent in charge of the Miami office received a call from J. Edgar Hoover, who was in New York. The director, all business, informed Rutzen that he would receive the necessary assistance.[42]

Later that morning, special agent in charge Earl J. Connelley flew from Washington, DC, to Miami to take charge of the investigation. Three years earlier, Connelley, a veteran agent, had helped orchestrate the shootout in Ocklawaha, Florida, that ended the murderous careers of Fred and "Ma" Barker. In the last decade, he'd worked many kidnapping cases, and Hoover depended on his experience in child abductions.[43]

In most small towns across America, Sunday is a day of worship. But on this day in Princeton, everyone's thoughts turned to a plague that had shaken America to its core: kidnapping for ransom.

Cash and his wife, both avid readers of the Miami newspapers, had familiarized themselves with dozens of such cases. In fact, Bailey Cash decided to pay the ransom while keeping the FBI at arm's length partly because of a still-unsolved abduction he'd read about a year and a half earlier.

On December 27, 1936, ten-year-old Charles Mattson, son of a wealthy physician in Tacoma, Washington, had been kidnapped from his home. While the child's parents were away, a masked gunman entered the room where

Charles played with his brother, sister, and a friend. At first, the intruder demanded money. But after being told there was no money in the house, the stranger said, "All right, then I'll take the kid."

With that, he seized Charles and dragged him away. On the way out, he dropped a prewritten note on the floor demanding $28,000 for the safe return of the child.[44]

A few weeks before, after capturing two men suspected in the abduction of little George Weyerhaeuser, J. Edgar Hoover had confidently bragged to reporters that this would be the "last child" abducted in America.[45]

When the Mattson kidnapping occurred in the same neighborhood as the abduction of the Weyerhaeuser child, an embarrassed Hoover flooded the area with nearly fifty agents. The massive publicity surrounding the whole event scared off the kidnapper, and he stopped corresponding with Charles Mattson's parents. Then, as the worried father attempted to reestablish communication through newspaper ads, a hunter found his son's frozen body in a snow-covered field. The boy had been beaten unmercifully, presumably in a fit of rage because the ransom negotiations had broken off.[46]

The Mattson kidnapping and murder, still unsolved when Skeegie Cash was snatched, profoundly troubled Bailey Cash. Because of that case and others, he demanded secrecy from both the media and law enforcement officials.[47]

Unfortunately, the parents and authorities wouldn't be able to keep this sensational story under wraps for long. Everybody in Princeton knew about it, and agents had heard that Ellis C. Hollums, managing editor of the *Miami Herald*, already knew the contents of the second ransom note. Dan Mahoney, editor of the competing *Miami Daily News*, was also privy to many facts about the case. Both newspapers had several reporters in town.[48]

Early that afternoon, Rutzen met with the two editors and, in his words, "solicited their cooperation in suppressing news as to the kidnapping in order that [the] investigation might not be hindered." Hollums and Mahoney reluctantly agreed to wait until the payoff had been made before publishing any stories about the case.[49]

While the Miami office of the FBI and the Dade County sheriff's office continued their investigations, agents from Birmingham, Atlanta, New Orleans, Memphis, and Louisville began booking flights to Miami. Many of these G-men had previous experience with kidnappings. By the time the Cash case reached its shocking conclusion, nearly one hundred agents, as well as Director Hoover himself, would come to south Florida to assist in the search for the missing boy.[50]

Late Sunday afternoon, Rutzen and McKee sent a report to the Washington bureau describing Skeegie: "He is between five and six years of age; three feet, seven inches tall; weighs forty three pounds; of medium build; hair that is almost platinum color; he has full teeth with the exception of one tooth in the front lower jaw, where the permanent tooth is now making an appearance; there is a burn scar on the back of his head which is covered by hair." Just a few days before the kidnapping, Skeegie's adoring parents had weighed him, measured his height, and taken a photograph of their son. This photograph would later be distributed to newspapers and law enforcement agencies across the country.[51]

G-men collected some of the child's toys and sent them to the Washington bureau in an unsuccessful effort to obtain Skeegie's fingerprints.

As the day wore to a close, Rutzen and McKee finally got an opportunity to speak with Vera Cash. She confirmed Bailey's account of their discovery that Skeegie was missing. She stated that at nine o'clock she "washed" the baby and dressed him in a "one-piece pyjama suit bearing white and rose colored stripes running in a lengthwise direction." He wore no slippers or any other item of clothing, she said. At about nine thirty, Skeegie went to sleep and Vera closed the bedroom door, leaving it cracked open so her son could see a sliver of light from the kitchen. She stated that she then walked over to the general store to help her husband count the final figures of the day's sales.[52]

Vera said she worked with her husband until 10:10 P.M., then they left to come home. They entered the house a minute or two after that. She discovered her son missing soon after she returned home, she said.[53]

Vera told the agents she had no idea who would kidnap Skeegie. The family had no enemies, she said, and she understood that they were well liked in the community.

Rutzen and McKee also interviewed Beatrice Cash, her husband Asbury, and son, Ishmael. Beatrice repeated her story about finding the first note on the door handle. She added that Ishmael had noticed several cars drive by their house between midnight and 2:00 A.M. One of the automobiles, Beatrice said, had its lights off and circled the block several times. Her son confirmed the story. Finally, according to Ishmael, the vehicle departed and all was quiet.[54] Rutzen and McKee listened intently but seemed baffled as to what to make of the story.

As agents continued interviewing family members, special agent Harold P. Turner drove to the home of Max Losner, president of the First National Bank in Homestead. In 1932, as banks across the nation were locking their doors, Losner convinced a group of investors to open First National. His bank beat the odds, becoming one of the strongest, most successful in the area.[55]

After securing a promise of secrecy, Turner informed Losner of the kidnapping and demand for a $10,000 ransom.

"How much money does Mr. Cash have in your bank?" Turner asked.

After thinking for a minute, Losner guessed four or five thousand dollars.

"I doubt that he'd be able to raise the full amount from his personal resources," Losner said. "However, he has several brothers who are in business and they may be able to help him."

As an afterthought, he stated that two weeks before, Mrs. Cash had transferred $1,500 from a postal savings account to checking. (In 1938, the United States Postal Savings System was operated by the United States Postal Service. Although primarily designed to encourage poor people to save, offering a high interest rate of 2 percent, businesses also used the system because the funds were insured by the government.)[56]

"This contact with Mr. Losner," Foxworth later wrote, "resulted in an arrangement whereby the Florida National Bank & Trust Company of Miami, Fla. were to make available on the early morning of May 30, 1938 bills in the total sum of $10,000 as designated in the second ransom note."[57]

The night passed slowly in the Cash home. Two agents had moved into upstairs rooms and would stay until the outcome of the case was decided. Vera, attended by a nurse, had trouble sleeping, even with the sedatives given to her.

Bailey Cash, unlike his wife, confidently believed that Skeegie would be returned alive. It would be as simple as driving the route designated by the kidnapper and dropping the money off when signaled.[58]

In his mind, Cash could already see his son's smiling face approaching him in the darkness.

# 3

# "An Obscure Country Merchant"

## Monday, May 30, 1938

The morning news must have rattled Bailey Cash.

Headlines of an Associated Press story read, "Find Body of Peter Levine Near His Home."[1]

The article itself spared none of the gory details: "One hundred local police and G-men searched nearby shores today for the remnants of the body of kidnaped 12-year-old Peter Levine, whose wire-trussed, headless torso was yielded up last night by the waters of Long Island Sound after three tragic months. Scores of irate residents joined the search. Dozens of small volunteer boats patrolled the coast, seeking evidence that might point somehow to the killer."[2]

As he read the article, Bailey may have asked those in the home to keep the news from Vera. Still under a doctor's care, his wife could barely function. In addition to Beatrice Cash, Vera's sister, Zoe Henderson, had arrived to help.[3]

Two agents, Clarence E. Weeks and L. A. Newsom, had been stationed inside the Cash residence almost from the beginning. The agents followed through with their plan to have Southern Bell install a telephone in the Bailey Cash home. With the phone in place, G-men attached a modern "Presto" tape recorder to the receiver. For days, they would record every conversation that came in. The two feds kept in close contact with Skeegie's parents and reported regularly to headquarters.[4] The agents interviewed Vera twice, but for much of the last forty-eight hours, she'd been too distraught to provide any usable information. Somehow, with a mother's intuition, Vera sensed that she would never see her son again.

The article about Levine may have shaken Cash's confidence in the G-men. If agents had been unable to bring the boy back home alive, would Skeegie suffer the same fate?

The investigation into that case dominated national headlines until Skeegie went missing. Then the two cases ran parallel to each other, as agents scrambled to solve them both.

On the afternoon of February 24, in New Rochelle, New York, twelve-year-old Peter Levine walked home from school with a classmate. They separated when Peter told his friend that he wanted to go into a nearby store. He never made it inside.[5]

Newspapers described Murray Levine, Peter's father, as a lawyer of "modest means." After the kidnapping, it took several days before the abductors contacted Levine. They demanded a ransom of $60,000. Levine had trouble raising that amount. He finally came up with half, and offered that to the kidnappers.[6]

In the meantime, many "chiselers," as the newspapers called them, contacted Levine, claiming to be the abductor and attempting to collect the money. The FBI caught two of the con artists, and the courts sentenced them to seven years.[7]

On February 28, the desperate father received a poignant note from his son. Written on a scrap of newspaper, it read: "Dear Dad—please pay. I want to come home. I have a cold. Your son—Peter."[8]

Levine, using local newspapers as a platform, pleaded with the kidnapper to spare his son. But soon all communication stopped. The abductor never again contacted Levine or the newspapers.

On May 29, the torso of little Peter Levine washed ashore behind a fashionable home on Long Island Sound. The head, arms, and legs were missing, but the shirt clinging to his dismembered trunk bore a monogram that read "Peter Levine."[9]

In the days before criminal profiling became a standard investigative tool, the FBI published a "pattern of the kidnapper" in newspapers. The report read, in part: "The kidnapper is younger than middle age and of alien (i.e., foreign) ancestry. He is familiar with boats and with marine and automotive machinery. He lived on the shore of the Sound and he knew Peter Levine, by name and by sight." According to the report Cash read that morning, copper wire had been used to tie Peter's body to a heavy weight.[10]

The coroner who examined the child's remains theorized that the electrical cord had been tied to a heavy object in order to hold the boy's corpse beneath the surface of the water. Once the wire broke, the body surfaced. The coroner, however, couldn't tell if Peter had been alive or dead when the kidnapper dumped his corpse in the water.[11]

In the following days, G-men sent out more than a million "circulars," or flyers, to public officials throughout the United States asking for their aid in helping to identify the killer. More than three hundred agents eventually worked the case.

Finally, two years later, in desperation, the FBI tried applying psychological pressure to make the killer crack. Using media contacts, G-men publicized the fact that they were zeroing in on a "super-suspect," that they knew his name, and that they would be arresting him in less than six months. According to media reports, the FBI had all the pieces of the puzzle except one.[12]

The ploy, designed to panic the kidnapper and cause him to make a mistake, didn't work.

While the Cash case would be solved within days, the Levine investigation dragged on for years until all involved abandoned any hope of ever finding the boy's killer.[13]

Outwardly, Bailey Cash presented a more optimistic attitude. Normally reticent, now he seemed to want to talk. "In most cases," he informed the agents, ignoring the morning's headlines, "the ransom is paid and the child is returned safe and sound. At least that's what I read in the news."

While a few agents still suspected that Cash might have had something to do with the disappearance of his son, Weeks and Newsom knew better. Beneath his calm exterior, they saw desperation. So far, Cash had held his emotions at bay, but if Skeegie wasn't returned, they knew he could easily give in to the hovering darkness of despair.

"They're just after the money," Cash said, returning to an old theme. "They don't really want Skeegie, just the cash. If they wanted a boy to raise, they wouldn't have asked for a ransom."[14]

It seemed to the agents that everyone in the home was in denial except Vera. Having worked many child abductions, the G-men knew they rarely had happy endings. Agents took it as a bad sign that no one had heard from Skeegie in two days. Peter Levine's tortured body provided sufficient proof of what kidnappers can do to a victim.

Since May 30 was a holiday, most businesses in town were closed. Traditionally, small-town Memorial Day celebrations featured parades, patriotic music, speeches, and fireworks. But on this day in Princeton the remembrance of the war dead had been quietly canceled.[15]

G-men continued to pour into south Florida from other parts of the country, including many of the furloughed agents. Hoover hoped he could later use the presence of these agents as the reason he had been able to capture another brutal kidnapper when he went before Congress to justify his budget.

In 1938, the Depression still festered, like a sore that wouldn't heal.

Even so, America had begun to modernize. Most homes had electricity and more than a million new automobiles were sold each year.

All but the poorest households boasted a radio. In most parts of the country, Bing Crosby and Ella Fitzgerald ruled the airwaves, but in much of the South, "hillbilly" music held sway. Roy Acuff's "Great Speckled Bird" remained at the top of the country charts for two years, and the Carter Family had begun popularizing the music of Appalachia.[16]

All cities and most towns had at least one movie theater. Errol Flynn, Lionel Barrymore, Olivia de Havilland, Spencer Tracy, and Bette Davis dominated the box office. Popular films of the day included *Alexander's Rag-Time Band*, *A Christmas Carol*, and *Red River Range*.[17]

In 1938, the Deep South, including Florida, used Jim Crow laws to enforce racial segregation. Politicians from below the Mason-Dixon Line tended to be more conservative than those from other areas.[18]

To some politicians, the new Federal Bureau of Investigation smacked of a "national police force." It reminded some folks, particularly those in the South, of Germany, Russia, or the Yankee invaders from seventy-five years before.

Senator Kenneth McKellar, the longtime senator from Tennessee, proved to be one of the strongest and most effective opponents of the FBI. A Democrat, the senator took pride in berating J. Edgar Hoover each time he appeared before the Senate to lobby for funding. In one famous exchange, McKellar asked Hoover how many crooks he had personally arrested. When an embarrassed Hoover answered that he'd never made an arrest, McKellar guffawed and insinuated that Hoover lacked the courage to face gangsters head on.[19]

Shortly after this public relations fiasco, agents in New Orleans located Creepy Karpis, the notorious robber, kidnapper, and cold-blooded killer. G-men notified Hoover and he immediately flew south to make the arrest. In his autobiography, Karpis, a three-time loser, claimed that agents Clarence

Hurt and Dwight Brantley took him into custody. Karpis wrote that he spotted the director peeping around the corner of a nearby building, and only after being secured, did Hoover appear.[20] Newspapers all across the country, however, printed photographs of Hoover "making the grab." Because of this and other such publicity stunts, the bureau chief became a national hero.[21]

Hoover received the appointment as director of the Bureau of Investigation (BOI) in 1924. He'd quickly cleaned up the once-corrupt organization and began to streamline it. In 1935, just three years before Skeegie Cash's abduction, the BOI changed its name to the Federal Bureau of Investigation.[22]

In his years as director of the BOI, Hoover learned two lessons he never forgot. Good publicity, he understood, was one of the keys to surviving the backstabbers and sycophants that seemed concentrated in Washington, DC. And, as the Karpis case proved, perception mattered more than truth.[23]

Hoover also discovered that many, if not most, powerful people led secret lives and would go to almost any length to keep their dirty laundry hidden. By ferreting out those secrets, the director recognized that he could maintain power for decades to come. Throughout his years as chief of the FBI, Hoover went to extraordinary lengths to dig up dirt on senators, congressmen, presidents, and others who could make or break him and his organization.[24]

In 1938, to the amazement of many, the FBI had almost run out of money. In recapping the Skeegie Cash case later that year, *Time Magazine* reported: "During May, for lack of funds, John Edgar Hoover furloughed half the 670 operatives of his Federal Bureau of Investigation and closed five regional offices."[25] Hoover claimed that the shortage of funds had been precipitated by two factors: first, Congress hadn't appropriated enough funds for his agency in its annual budget; and second, a series of unexpected kidnappings had drained the FBI's coffers.[26] At the time, Hoover desperately needed a sensational (and successful) case he could use to prod Congress to approve additional resources for his struggling agency.[27]

The kidnapping of Skeegie Cash couldn't have come at a better time. At almost that exact hour, the Deficiency Committee of the House and Senate was debating whether to increase funding for certain programs.[28] Since the middle of May, this committee had been considering President Roosevelt's so-called Recovery Bill. (Legislators, desperate to return home and rally their constituents before the upcoming November elections, had set a deadline for the final vote on June 5. Because of this, compromises of all sorts were in the works.)[29]

The prize amounted to nearly $4 billion in additional federal funding. Because FDR's New Deal programs depended on the appropriations of these funds, the president and his staff exerted enormous pressure on Congress to pass the legislation. Funding for the Rural Electrification Administration, the National Emergency Council, the Federal Surplus Commodities Corporation, the Works Progress Administration, and money for the US military all hinged on the June vote.[30]

Other New Deal proposals were pure pork. A pump-priming bill, for instance, seemed to many to be nothing more than an attempt to buy votes from politicians in rural states.[31]

As the Deficiency Committee met, a fierce battle over new wage and hour legislation threatened to derail the whole package. (The southern bloc opposed wage and hour hikes because they felt increased wages would stifle the creation of new jobs in their region.)[32]

Publicly shutting down five FBI offices and laying off hundreds of agents elicited just the effect Director Hoover desired. Howls of outrage from citizens, local politicians, and the news media echoed through the halls of Congress. FDR requested $308,000 in a supplemental bill to restore the bureau's original funding. While this amounted to small potatoes when compared to the massive spending proposed in other areas, it would at least allow the agency to reopen the offices it had closed.[33]

As soon as he heard the news about Skeegie Cash's abduction, Hoover sensed that this case possessed everything he needed to appeal to the public and the media: small town America, an "obscure country merchant," and an attractive child victim. The kidnapping also offered one additional benefit—the town of Princeton would have a very small pool of suspects.[34]

Before the third ransom note was even found, Hoover knew he would soon be on a plane to Miami.

For many agents, the Redlands represented a critical example of culture shock. To G-men reared in Boston, New York, or Chicago, the accents they heard seemed almost undecipherable. Farmers in overalls listened to weird music complete with wailing fiddles and nasal twang. Many of the homes amounted to little more than a few planks thrown together to form a room or two. A high percentage of the residents seemed infested with lice or fleas or ticks—their children looked thin and wasted. After the case had been solved and the agents left for home, Walter Winchell wrote: "G-Men say that after seeing how many of the people live in that section of Florida, contributions should be given to help them instead of missionaries who gather funds to help Orientals and others in in Asia or elsewhere. . . . The Chinese and others couldn't possibly live in such squalor as in some parts of Florida."[35]

If that wasn't enough, it rained almost every day. The clouds would accumulate in the sky and suddenly drench the land, sometimes for hours. And over it all, the frightful shadows of the Everglades seemed to lurk like a malevolent spirit waiting to entrap the innocent or strike the unprepared like a coiled diamondback rattler.

At eight o'clock that morning, several men, each dressed in distinctive dark suits and ties, arrived at the Florida National Bank and Trust Company in Miami. Dean S. Campbell, the bank's president, ushered the agents into a meeting room. He'd been contacted earlier in the day and asked to set aside the currency needed for the ransom.[36]

Connelley had placed special agent Harold P. Turner in charge of recording the serial numbers of the bills and securing them so Bailey Cash could pick them up later that day. Bank officials provided Turner and three agents with a table in the meeting room. As they worked, bank employees hovered nearby, keeping an eye on the proceedings.[37]

It took several hours to complete the task. After writing every denomination and its corresponding serial number on a pad, agents then photographed each bill. Experience had taught the G-men that it's not possible be too careful with potential evidence.

The notes corresponded exactly to the demands of the kidnapper. Agents stuffed 500 five dollar bills into the box, then followed with 100 twenties, 500 tens, and 10 fifties. It amazed them how snugly the currency fit into the container—the perpetrator had clearly done his homework.[38]

After the agents completed their task, the bills were double-checked by both FBI agents and bank officials.

Turner had requested that the bank supply as many notes as possible from the Federal Reserve Bank of Atlanta. This would make them easier for merchants to identify. All the tens and twenties had indeed come from the Atlanta bank, but some of the other silver certificates came from regions outside Georgia.

An FBI report described the process of getting the bills ready for delivery to Cash: "Following the check the original lists were initialed by the Agents concerned in this work and the currency was placed in a manila envelope, sealed with sealing wax, and initialed by the three Agents and Dean S. Campbell. The money was then placed in the bank vault."[39]

The Feds immediately transferred copies of all bills to a chartered plane, flew them to bureau headquarters in Washington, DC, and filed them for safekeeping. As soon as Cash paid the ransom, businesses in Florida and across the nation would receive copies of the serial numbers. It was a tried-and-true method of catching kidnappers.[40]

Attempting to remain low key, agents worked behind the scenes on the case. Several items had been collected from the Cash home and transported to the Miami FBI offices for further examination. These items included toys from Skeegie's room and the two original notes addressed to Bailey Cash.

FBI technicians spent long hours poring over the ransom notes in an attempt to find evidence, including prints. The search proved unsuccessful and the notes were eventually photographed, placed in plastic bags, and securely locked in a vault.[41]

Connelley directed an agent to remain at the local telephone company to monitor all calls coming in to Princeton. G-men asked telephone operators to eavesdrop on incoming calls and pass any pertinent information along to the agent.[42]

Even as the case moved forward, Director Hoover couldn't keep from meddling. A memo from assistant director Edward A. Tamm to Agent Connelley reads: "The Director wants Agent Chapman removed from the [Cash] home and a more experienced man substituted."[43]

While Bailey Cash waited impatiently for his midnight date with destiny, agents fanned out all over town in an attempt to surreptitiously collect information.[44]

One of the prevalent theories among agents, and shared by Hoover, posited that little blond-haired Skeegie Cash had been hidden in the "quarters" by one or more of the kidnapper's black accomplices. According to this hypothesis, white perpetrators abducted the boy and hired one or more black coconspirators to keep him captive. After Cash paid the ransom, the child would be left at some location in the quarters where he could be found.[45]

Even though Bailey Cash and his entourage had searched almost every house in the black sections of town on Saturday night, G-men continued to check and recheck the "negro shacks" in the area.[46]

Some agents dismissed that theory and thought the kidnapper had abducted Skeegie because he had a grudge against Cash. (Bailey Cash had a reputation as a tough businessman. In addition to his businesses, he purchased homes that the county sold at auction when owners could no longer pay their taxes. These he rented out or sold for a profit. The G-men wondered if someone who'd lost his home decided to take revenge on the businessman by kidnapping his son.) Agents questioned Cash time and again in an attempt to compile an "enemies list."

While he dismissed this theory, the grieving father reluctantly supplied a few names of those with whom he'd had minor disputes. The Feds hounded those unfortunate people until they finally found the real culprit.[47]

During the intense questioning of Cash, he mentioned a confrontation he'd had with his brother. An FBI report described the encounter: "Mr. Cash stated there had never been any family disputes in his family which would justify any suspicion that any member of the family might be responsible for this kidnapping. He said about two years ago he had had an argument with his brother, [Wilson] P. Cash, over the location of a telegraph pole, which had originally been situated on the property of W. P., next to his own property. W. P. Cash had found the pole to be in his way and without consulting J. B. Cash, had had it moved over on J. B.'s property. J. B. Cash said he would not stand for this and had the company move the pole back. He said there had been no hard feelings about this as he and W. P. Cash had gone fishing together despite this and had continued to do so since."[48]

G-men interrogated Wilson Cash, who claimed he barely remembered the incident.

Agents also questioned Vera about possible enemies. She revealed that a boarder, an eighteen-year-old girl, had once "squabbled" with Skeegie. Vera stated that she'd seen the girl throw water on the boy, and he threw water back at her. The girl quickly left the Cash home and Vera never heard from her again. FBI agents unsuccessfully attempted to locate the former renter, finally dismissing her as a suspect.[49]

The G-men obtained telephone books and local business directories in an effort to locate the names of as many area residents as possible. They interviewed hundreds of these people, none of whom had any involvement in the case.

Even though the FBI attempted to maintain its public hands-off stance on the case, tips began to trickle in. Some appeared viable and were checked out, while others obviously came from publicity seekers or disturbed individuals.

A local farmworker told agents about a former Cash employee who once called Skeegie a "pain in the ass." The FBI located the man and eliminated him as a suspect.

A Florida state employee working on the East-West Highway (what would later be called "Alligator Alley") reported seeing a green sedan traveling at breakneck speed. Because the road crew was working in the middle of the highway, the car slowed down to avoid an accident. The informant told agents he noticed several men in the vehicle—one held a small boy who was crying loudly. The FBI spent many hours following up this lead but never located the auto or its passengers.[50]

Darkness crept in to the little community of Princeton like an Everglades panther stalking its prey.

Earlier that afternoon, Bailey had driven to Miami and picked up the shoebox full of currency. He quickly counted the bills and signed for the package. As he left, banking officials and FBI agents wished him luck on his midnight ride. Some even had tears in their eyes.

On his way home, Bailey surveyed the town he'd grown up in. But now each home and business he passed had a sinister "feel" to it. The kidnapper could be in any of these places—worse yet, Skeegie could be secreted away in one of the buildings. If so, Cash prayed he was being treated well.

Back home, he informed the agents that he had the package and was ready to make the trip. He said he planned to try to relax until about eleven thirty, at which time he would prepare for the midnight rendezvous that would bring his son home.[51]

For the last forty-eight hours, the Cash residence had been the scene of chaotic activity. FBI agents seemed to be everywhere. Friends dropped by at all hours and offered to help. Several relatives stayed in upstairs rooms and worked in shifts to cook, clean, and provide assistance to Vera.

Cash had memorized the second ransom note and knew each road to take. He'd driven them all at one time or another, so he was familiar with the route. He gave silent thanks that the rainy weather had finally cleared. Now it was fair and cool, the perfect backdrop, Cash thought, for the payoff.

He and the FBI agents figured the trip would take exactly one hour. Soon after he dropped off the ransom, Cash hoped Skeegie would be released in an area where he could find his way back home.[52]

In order to inform Bailey and Vera of various locations where kidnapped children had been released, agents advised them of the Billy Whitla case, in Pennsylvania. The young boy, about the age of Skeegie, had been abducted from his school. His father, a wealthy attorney, had paid a ransom of $10,000.

Later that day, the kidnappers placed Billy on a train, where he was found and reunited with his parents. (The abductors, a man and woman, were caught, convicted, and sentenced to long prison terms.)[53]

In Princeton, several figures darted among the darkened homes and stores. They were "spies," a few trusted local citizens who had been assigned to watch the homes of "suspicious" characters. Others, FBI agents and townspeople, jotted down license plate numbers of any car seen on the roads in and around Princeton.[54]

The FBI files do not make it clear whether James Bailey Cash or the G-men themselves arranged the midnight surveillance, but the records make it clear that the FBI often used that method to obtain information. (From the start, Bailey Cash had insisted that the return of his son was more important than an immediate arrest.) But with dozens of agents in the area pursuing leads, this was just one of several means they used to attempt to track down suspects.

Whoever arranged for the "watchers" to spend that long night searching the shadows did Bailey Cash no favors.

In fact, the kidnapper was spying on the spies.

There would be no drop-off at midnight.[55]

# 4

# "Call in All the Spies"

## Tuesday, May 31, 1938

At exactly midnight, James Bailey Cash walked to his car. A crowd of about five hundred people had gathered in the street outside his house and store. As Cash placed the shoebox on the seat beside him, reporters, radio broadcasting crews, and photographers crowded close, hoping to get a scoop.[1]

Before pulling away, Cash asked those in the crowd not to follow. "Skeegie's life depends on it," he said.[2]

The route measured exactly twenty miles, and he estimated that it should take an hour to traverse. The kidnapper seemed highly organized and familiar with his surroundings. That made him dangerous, Cash thought. A well-placed bullet could easily eliminate the only witness to the ransom drop.

Driving exactly twenty miles per hour, Cash drove up Myra Street as directed. Once he left Princeton's tiny business district, he saw only darkness ahead. The area looked deserted, but he suspected teams of FBI agents and private citizens watched him from the shadows. A few miles to the south, as he entered Homestead, traffic increased. Following the kidnapper's instructions, Cash drove the back roads, many of them "oil roads" referred to in the note. He carefully scanned the sides of the road, waiting for a signal.[3]

As Cash drove, he thought about his wife and child. Vera had been thirty years old when Skeegie was born. He wanted his child to have all the advantages he lacked as a child, so they had purposely waited several years before starting a family. After serving sixteen months in the navy during World War I, Cash obtained an honorable discharge and used his separation pay to help purchase the home and general store. Because of his fair dealings and frugal nature, his business soon showed a profit. Cash used the extra money to buy two gasoline stations, the one in Princeton and a second in Homestead. In addition to these enterprises, he'd recently opened a grocery store in Miami.[4]

He continued driving, peering into the darkness ahead. His virtues—honesty, self-control, perseverance, and frugality—seemed to have enmeshed him in this nightmare. Because he'd worked hard to achieve success, his beloved Skeegie had been abducted.

Cash drove through Homestead, then turned onto Allapatta Drive. The route coiled here and there, with a deceptive randomness, through the south Florida darkness. There seemed to be plenty of isolated areas along the back roads where a drop-off could be made, but the kidnapper's light never appeared.

More than an hour after he first started, Bailey Cash, perplexed and despondent, headed for home.[5]

At midnight, as Bailey Cash drove off in his futile attempt to deliver the ransom, Franklin Pierce McCall and Harry Wright, an attendant at the Sinclair filling station managed by Wilson Cash (but owned by Hal McLaughlin), sat on the front steps of Bailey's store, discussing the events of the day. The two had been friends since McCall moved to Princeton. The FBI later discovered that McCall and Wright "habitually" played poker in a railroad boxcar near the packinghouse. Wright had a familial connection to the Cash clan—he was the son-in-law of Wilson Cash, Bailey's brother.

While discussing the case, Wright expressed his belief that the FBI would quickly catch the kidnappers. "I don't think they'll ever get caught," McCall replied. "These birds are smart."[6]

Because of the crowds and the spies, Preacher Boy couldn't risk attempting to collect the ransom at midnight. But, ever resourceful, he came up with a new plan.

McCall later wrote a detailed confession, outlining to investigators his movements that night. "I saw that the crowd that was in Princeton at the time had no intention of leaving," he wrote, "so I went to Hal McLaughlin's house and copied the third note . . . onto a brown paper I had with me."[7]

McCall walked to the nearby home of Joseph Hilliard, his father-in-law, and returned driving Hilliard's pickup truck. He asked Wright if he had his key to the filling station. "I need to buy three gallons of gas," Preacher Boy said.[8]

The Sinclair station was located only about fifty yards from Bailey's general store, so Wright perched on the vehicle's running board while McCall drove.[9]

They approached the station with the lights off.[10]

Again, they discussed the case. McCall reminded his friend that he'd lived with the Cash family for six months. "You know, I loved that kid," he said.

Pulling the truck up to the pump, the two friends got out.

Suddenly McCall shouted: "There's that man again."[11]

The cry startled Wright. He'd been facing away from the station and hadn't seen anyone. "What are you talking about?" he asked.

"I saw someone over there," McCall replied, pointing to the door.[12]

At night, the south Florida landscape possessed a sort of eerie, netherworldly quality. Breezes from the ocean shook the pines and palms and palmetto bushes, making the darkness seem almost alive. Wright later said he thought the night was playing tricks with his friend's senses.

"You just mistook those shadows for a person," he said.

"No I didn't," McCall said. Again he pointed toward the side of the filling station. "I saw somebody going back that way."[13]

In McCall's confession, he wrote: "Harry went in front of the pickup and I went to the back of the station towards the men's rest room, supposedly trying to see where this man that I had said that I had seen had gone."[14]

Wright then pulled out a ring of keys and unlocked the front door. An FBI report describes what happened: "Attempting to open [the door, Wright] noticed that it was bound to some extent, so that it required an unusual push to open it; that he turned on the light inside the filling station, walked behind the partition and . . . turned on the pumps. McCall had entered the station just behind him, and after [Wright] turned on the pumps, put three gallons of gas into the truck as requested, then went back in the door of the station, walked behind the partition and turned the pumps off; that as he walked from behind the partition, [Wright] saw McCall lean over and pick up a piece of brown paper; that McCall immediately opened the paper, put it on the counter and started to read, making a remark such as, 'Look what we have here.'"[15]

"I bet it was stuck in the jamb," Preacher Boy said.

The two men noticed that the paper had likely come from a brown paper bag.[16]

"Oh my God," McCall shouted, "this is another ransom note!"

They spread it on the counter and read it.

"To many people. Take the same route at 4 A.M. but first call in all the spies. Put all notes in box with money. Light will blink twice."[17]

"What should we do?" Wright asked.

"Let's call 'Shorty' and ask him what to do," McCall suggested.[18]

Ormond "Shorty" Cash was the son of Asbury Cash. On this night, the FBI had stationed Shorty in Homestead so he could attempt to identify any suspects the G-men located in that area.[19]

McCall's confession described what happened next. "Shorty, Donald Cooper, Bill Bethea, Harry Wright and myself got into George Cooper's car, drove east on Cocoanut Palm Drive to the little Rock Road just west of the broom factory. We turned on the dome light in Donald's car, and all of us read the note. Cooper and Bethea said the thing to do was to get it to Bailey Cash as quick as we could. We went on down to this rock road to where it runs into 4-A. Donald Cooper, I believe, was the one who recognized Bailey's car and we turned around and chased it. Cooper blinked the car lights at Bailey, [and] I don't know whether he saw the signal or not, but he turned in off 4-A on the oil road by Underwood's filling station and that is where we caught him."[20]

Shorty Cash handed the note to his uncle.[21]

After receiving the message, Bailey Cash drove home and turned the third ransom note over to the FBI agents stationed at his house.[22]

Special agent Clarence E. Weeks, who had been manning the phones at the Cash home, read the note and immediately called special agent in charge (SAC) Connelley. Arriving at Cash's home, the agent in charge called in Harry Wright and Franklin McCall for an on-the-spot interview. Shorty, Bethea, and Cooper were also asked about their knowledge of where the note came from.[23]

To be closer to the action, several agents, including Rutzen and McKee, had taken rooms at the Redlands Hotel in Homestead. They quickly arrived at Cash's home to begin this new phase of the investigation.[24]

While Rutzen and several agents rushed to the Sinclair service station, Agent McKee took the note to the Miami office. There forensics personnel tested it for fingerprints, photographed it, and compared the paper to the previous notes. They checked the handwriting and scoured the note for any possible clue. Since the kidnapper had demanded that Cash include the three original notes in the shoebox with the ransom money, McKee had to work fast. The Texan, however, made it back with thirty minutes to spare.[25]

As soon as Preacher Boy found the third ransom note, he automatically became a person of interest.

In their initial interviews with Bailey Cash regarding possible suspects, it quickly became apparent that Bailey didn't have a high opinion of Franklin McCall. Skeegie may have liked the young man, but Bailey avoided the ne'er-do-well whenever possible. He considered Preacher Boy a "sort of radical and blowhard that had no respect for the opinions of others." This assessment, however, apparently didn't raise a red flag with the G-men.[26]

Agents questioned McCall regarding the man he said he had seen near Wilson Cash's filling station. McCall stated that he'd seen "a large fellow" standing in the shadows between the grease rack and the northern side of the building. As soon as he and Wright drove up, he said, the man took off running.[27]

Preacher Boy gave a fairly detailed description of the man he claimed to have seen for just a split second on a dark night. The suspect seemed, he reported, to be bareheaded. He hadn't been wearing a coat. Instead, Preacher Boy believed he had on dark slacks, and "a polo shirt or tight-fitting dress shirt." McCall stated that in the darkness he couldn't make out any facial features, or even tell if he had been white or black.[28]

After thinking about it a while, though, McCall stated the man may have resembled Frampy Braxton. But he begged agents not to spread it around that he'd ratted out his friend.[29]

McCall's testimony satisfied the G-men. In two separate reports, the agents noted: "It was ascertained that the friend who came to buy gasoline (Franklin McCall) is all right."[30]

Franklin Pierce McCall was born in Jasper, Florida, on March 31, 1917. Located just six miles south of the Georgia state line, Jasper was a farming community. McCall's father had been a longtime minister in the local Methodist Church, and his mother, Linnie, called "Lillie," was a housewife.[31]

Young Franklin attended local schools and had little trouble making good grades. He grew into a strapping young man, standing six feet tall and weighing two hundred pounds. McCall played basketball and football for the Hamilton County High School Trojans. A star player, he received the offer of a football scholarship from a major university, possibly the University of Florida.[32]

At the time of the kidnapping, McCall had never been in trouble with the law, but many friends and acquaintances described the young man as arrogant, self-centered, and willing to skirt the edges on moral issues.[33]

After graduating from high school, he married a petite raven-haired beauty from Princeton named Claudine Hilliard. Joseph Hilliard, his wife, and their teenaged daughter, Joyce, lived on Sunset Drive and had a good reputation in the community. Joseph operated a small produce delivery company, making him a direct competitor of Asbury Cash.[34]

McCall decided to forego college and moved to Princeton with Claudine. On October 30, 1937, he and his new bride rented a room from Bailey and Vera Cash.[35]

They lived there for nearly six months, until April 11, 1938, when they rented a home at the corner of Tallahassee Road and Sunset Drive. The tiny bungalow, a dirty, vermin-infested house, sat about two blocks from the Cash residence.[36]

It must have been a shock for the pretty bride to suddenly be thrown into such squalor. Her husband seemed incapable of keeping a job and spent much of his time mooching off friends and her parents. He spent what little money he made on beer or lost it gambling with his cronies.[37]

Exactly two months before the kidnapping, on February 28, 1938, McCall's father died. He and Claudine drove north to Jasper and attended the funeral. It would the last time his mother would see him before the FBI accused him of abducting and murdering little Skeegie Cash.[38]

In Princeton, McCall felt superior to the farmhands he worked with. After all, because of his status as the star football player and "big-man-around-town" in Jasper, he had become accustomed to receiving special treatment from his hometown neighbors.

In radio scripts later prepared by the FBI, admittedly to publicize and magnify their own role in solving the Cash case, J. Edgar Hoover emphasized that McCall came from a respectable family and had every chance for success. After high school, he could have gone to college and parlayed his good fortune into a comfortable profession. However, he stopped attending church (an important part of his family's life) and gambled and drank with dead-end acquaintances.[39]

In fact, McCall had begun isolating himself from his family. Once he left home, he never wrote or called family members. His wife kept in touch with his mother, providing news about her husband. (Claudine had been visiting McCall's sister in Jacksonville when her husband snatched Skeegie Cash.)[40]

McCall, an avid reader of pulp crime magazines, dreamed of easy money.

*True Detective*, *True Police Cases*, and *Headquarters Detective* were popular at the time, particularly in rural America. Their covers invariably portrayed helpless, half-nude beauties being raped, tortured, and murdered by sinister-looking men. Titles such as "An Ice-Pick Cooled the Roving Divorcee" and "Lust of the Goliath Rapist" took readers far away from the grime and backbreaking labor of the farm or factory. The pulps had given extensive, and lurid, coverage to the recent spate of kidnappings.[41]

The stories, generally written by cops who'd been involved in the cases, provided plenty of detail about police investigations. When FBI agents eventually searched McCall's home, after he became a suspect, they found pulp crime magazines stuffed in rat holes throughout the house. On the back cover of the January 1938 edition of *True Stories*, McCall had written notes describing how to get away with a kidnapping for ransom.[42]

While Preacher Boy may not have gotten the idea of kidnapping a child for ransom from these magazines, he certainly used the stories while formulating his scheme to escape apprehension.

The kidnapping of Skeegie had gone reasonably well.

McCall forced his way into the locked back door of the Cash home shortly after 9:30 on Saturday night. He knew the layout, the routine Vera Cash invariably followed, and exactly where the child slept.[43] Whether he was aware that there were boarders upstairs is debatable. The fact that he wore work boots and made little effort to remain silent when entering the home suggests he may not have known. On the other hand, adrenalin pumping through his veins might have made him reckless.

McCall took the sleeping boy from his bed. While fleeing down the hall and out the back door, he placed two handkerchiefs over Skeegie's nose and mouth. Holding them in place with the palm of his hand, McCall hurried into the darkness.[44]

A wooded lot lay directly behind the Cash house. The kidnapper walked toward it, glancing around to see if anyone had noticed him. Satisfied that he had escaped detection, McCall quickly rushed the hundred yards to his own place.[45]

In his confession more than a week later, the kidnapper claimed that he planned to take the victim to an abandoned house he'd located in the Everglades. There he would conceal Skeegie, leaving him tied and gagged so he couldn't escape or cry out. When he received the ransom, McCall said he planned to release Skeegie.[46]

But when McCall entered his home, he said, he discovered that Skeegie had stopped breathing. He claimed that he attempted to revive the boy by washing his face and performing artificial respiration. Skeegie, however, had already expired.[47]

FBI reports stated that after he determined the boy had expired, McCall then "proceeded with the child to a point east of Bay View Drive, at the edge of [the Everglades], where he deposited the dead body of the child."[48]

Preacher Boy placed the corpse under a clump of palmetto bushes. A single tall, misshapen pine tree, left over from the logging operations decades before, towered over the corpse as it slowly decomposed.[49]

Even though Skeegie had died, McCall was undeterred in his quest for wealth. Still smarting from the debacle at midnight, in which the "spies" scared him off, he knew he would have one final shot at collecting the ransom money.

After his interview with Connelley, he began to put his plans into motion.

Before doing so, he needed to establish an alibi, all the while avoiding the civilian patrols strung out along the roads in and around Princeton. If caught, the mob would lynch him in a heartbeat, and if he somehow made it to a court of law, a conviction would inevitably lead to a date with "Old Sparky." Ten thousand dollars might be a sizable fortune in Depression-era Florida, but it meant nothing if he didn't live to spend it.

At about three in the morning, McCall drove his father-in-law's pickup south toward Homestead, followed closely by poker buddies Donald Cooper and Hal McLaughlin in Cooper's car. Apparently McCall's two friends had places to go because he later testified that they "passed me around the Log Cabin at the Federal Road." That was fine with Preacher Boy. As soon as they vanished from sight, he put on the brakes and turned around.[50]

He had no desire to go to Homestead that night, but he wanted people to think he was there. If questioned by lawmen, he could claim he'd been visiting Homestead, and two friends would vouch that they had seen him on the road.

McCall then drove back to his father-in-law's home. (Joseph Hilliard had chosen to leave the crowd and excitement down at Bailey Cash's store for a night of sleep.) McCall seems to have maintained a good relationship with Hilliard. Franklin awakened the older man and told him about his (McCall's) role in finding the third ransom note. Obviously, he left out the part about planting it, but he now had another person who could confirm his whereabouts on the night of the ransom drop.[51]

The preacher's son asked Hilliard if he'd like to go with him down to Krone Avenue. A group of concerned citizens, he said, had taken their cars to that area to write down the license plate numbers of each car that passed. The ad hoc posse also observed and reported on "suspicious movements" or activity. This example of civic vigilantism apparently did not appeal to Joseph Hilliard, and the older man quickly went back to sleep. It seems that McCall had the old man pegged: the life-long resident of Princeton had little interest in the wild excitement swirling around him.[52]

The brief visit couldn't have worked out better for McCall. If questioned, he could say he was either in Homestead, visiting with his father-in-law, or staked out near Krone Avenue, doing his duty as a good citizen.

It was now about three thirty in the morning. McCall walked outside and sat in his father-in-law's truck. The preacher's son planned on leaving the vehicle there. Moving it might get the truck noticed by some of the spies or watch groups scattered throughout the countryside. But he had come up with a unique scheme to avoid the watchers in the night. Using the element of surprise, he would collect the ransom before Bailey Cash even left the city limits.[53]

At 3:45 A.M., he climbed out of Hilliard's truck and slipped east along Sunset Drive to its intersection with Charles Chambers's lot.[54] Chambers owned or leased a couple of farms in the fertile Redlands.

Chambers's home sat on a lot fronting Sunset Drive. It was bordered on the east by Tallahassee Road and on the west by the Dixie Highway. A rock fence surrounded the structure, and a small orange grove stretched out behind the house.[55]

McCall later testified that he walked slowly east along Sunset Drive until he reached the citrus trees behind Chambers's home. There he went into the grove about fifty feet, to the fourth row of trees. Squatting down to wait, McCall dreamed of becoming a very rich young man. If he thought about the pathetic corpse of Skeegie Cash decomposing in the swamp, he never mentioned it.[56]

At the Cash residence, Bailey assured Vera that their son would soon be home. He'd gone with almost no sleep for three days and nights, but concern for Skeegie drove him on.

At 4 A.M., Cash left his home by a side door.

A writer who later interviewed the distressed father described the second drive as follows: "At the new zero hour Cash again entered his automobile and drove away. It had taken him one hour and thirty-five minutes to cover the route the first time. He peered into the darkness as he turned left at the Nazarene church and rode over the first leg of his journey. Five minutes later he passed the house of Asbury Cash and neared the intersection of Tallahassee Road and Sunset Drive. He was driving exactly twenty miles per hour as instructed in the note. Suddenly two quick flashes of light came from the corner of a small orange grove."[57]

Cash later told FBI agents that he saw "two weak blinks," as if the batteries in the flashlight had lost most of their charge. He stated that he was so "startled by the daring of the kidnappers in selecting a spot three quarters of a mile from the place where the child had been stolen that he had to apply his emergency brake to stop the car."[58]

Cash got out of his car. Standing in the glare of the headlights, his heart throbbing, Skeegie's father lobbed the box of money toward the base of a nearby telephone pole. For a few seconds he stood silhouetted by the car lights, then returned to his vehicle and continued the lonely drive toward Homestead.[59]

Cash had fully complied with the kidnapper's demands. Now he could only hope he'd get his son back. But the worried father had read enough newspaper accounts to know that delivering the payoff did not always guarantee a safe return of the child. As he drove, hope and doubt warred in the soul of Bailey Cash.

The first streaks of daylight painted the sky over the Atlantic as he drove back toward Princeton. Up to this point, Cash had followed the kidnapper's instructions to the letter. But before he could go home, he had to break the rules just once. He turned around and drove back to the corner of Sunset Drive and Tallahassee Road, the place where he'd dropped the shoebox. There he parked on the side of the road, got out, and walked to the utility pole.

The shoebox was gone.[60]

A wave of relief flooded through Cash as he headed toward home. Soon there would be a joyous homecoming. Soon Vera would have something to smile about. Soon things would be back to normal.

An Associated Press story reported that when he returned home "the father appeared jubilant and confident young Cash's release was imminent."[61]

As soon as Bailey Cash's Plymouth pulled away, Franklin McCall left the orange grove and retrieved the ransom money. He later claimed that he had abducted Skeegie Cash to be able to afford fine clothes and luxuries for his wife. As if to excuse himself he added: "No one else ever had money tempt them that much."[62]

"I walked up to where he [Cash] placed the money," he recounted, "picked up the shoebox, turned around and went back into the grove [following] the same route I had used coming into it. About the center of the grove I opened the box, the shoebox, took the money out of the newspaper in which it was wrapped. I took the first stack of bills off the stack, and in doing so the band was broken, and I just put the money in a wad in my pocket. [I] went back through the rear of the grove and came back on Sunset Drive at the same route I had taken going in."[63]

What the unemployed truck driver did next defied any rational explanation. "At the corner of Mr. John Chamber's property the rock fence, there was a rock fence," he said. "I threw the $9,750 into the corner of the weeds."[64]

McCall never explained his reasoning, but in all likelihood, he panicked. A former Bible student, he would have been familiar with the words of King Solomon: "The wicked flee when none pursue." That seemed to have been the mindset of Franklin McCall.

Thoughts of G-men searching his home and discovering the ransom money haunted him. The example of Bruno Hauptmann may have been on his mind. He'd been smart enough to avoid detection thus far but knew that it might be years before he could spend the money since the Feds would start circulating serial numbers for the bills almost immediately.

Gangsters paid fences well to launder their ill-gotten gains, but McCall was an amateur. He knew now that he'd have to maintain the charade of concern and innocence for years before he could make use of his blood money.

He'd assumed that the abduction would remain a local matter, allowing him to slip away in a few weeks and begin living the high life. "I didn't think the FBI would be interested in some little Cracker kid," he later groused. He never realized that several factors, including the very survival of the FBI itself, would bring hordes of G-men into Princeton.[65]

Covering his tracks rapidly became McCall's first priority. He quickly went into the nearby woods and tore the cardboard shoebox into tiny pieces. These he buried under a rock. The three original ransom notes had been included in the moneybox, and being found with them in his possession would damn him to the electric chair as quickly as the ransom money.[66]

Moving deeper into the forest, he set the three notes on fire. After the flames died out, he stomped the ashes until nothing remained.[67]

McCall still had $250 in his trouser pockets, but he knew he couldn't take even that small sum to his rented house. Instead, he walked to the garage his poker buddy Hal McLaughlin owned and placed the remaining money in an oil drum located just outside the service racks. Reporters later speculated that McCall "thought he would be able to get the money easily without arousing suspicion." That made sense, since McCall and McLaughlin were friends, and no one would think twice about him paying his sidekick a visit.[68] The FBI grilled Hal McLaughlin after they discovered the cash on his premises, but concluded that he had no part in the kidnapping.[69]

Franklin McCall, now drained from nearly three days of constant stress and little sleep, stumbled home. He tried to rest as he thought about his next step. Later that morning, he needed to be in the crowd near Bailey Cash's store, preparing to join in the search for little Skeegie.

Early that afternoon, the Associated Press published a story that circulated in every major newspaper in the country. It read: "Agents of the Federal Bureau of Investigation emerged from the home of James Bailey Cash, Sr., today, seized a spectator standing in a nearby crowd and rushed him off in an automobile. The car headed toward Miami before the crowd realized what was taking place. . . . The throng from which the man was taken had been waiting in a school yard for Sheriff [D. C.] Coleman to instruct them in carrying out the hunt [for Skeegie Cash]."[70]

Frampy Braxton, the man arrested, had been the G-men's chief suspect almost since the first day agents arrived. Newspapers described him as a "fleshy, bald, 55-year-old self-employed carpenter."[71]

Lawmen, thus far, had uncovered no evidence against Braxton, but for several days newspapers continued to report his arrest, creating the impression that he may be guilty.[72]

There seemed to be two reasons why the carpenter became a suspect: he allegedly had a poor reputation in the community, and he seemed to be totally consumed by the case. In his defense, however, he could account for almost every minute of his life leading up to and after the abduction.[73]

The G-men were grasping at straws. In one of the many reports written by agents, they described Braxton as "probably the most vicious character in the community and the most logically suspected because of his character and the character of his immediate family, who might be the type to assist in such a crime. . . . He is known to have engaged in moonshining for a number of years and has been of late a constant hanger-on in front of the

Cash family residence and may possibly have been there for the purpose of observing the family's movements so as to act as a front man on the [kidnapping] job."[74]

Braxton's son-in-law, Brent Rayburn, also came under suspicion. "His character," concluded the G-men, "is known to be bad."[75]

Braxton's son, Pedro, also landed on the suspect list. He lived about thirty-five miles south of Princeton at Cape Sable. From the state's earliest days, Cape Sable had been a haven for pirates, wreckers, and fugitives from the law. The G-men suspected Pedro might have done some rum-running during Prohibition. By mining the mountain of small-town innuendo and gossip, G-men learned that young Braxton had once worked for Bailey Cash and had been fired when his accounts came up short by thirty-five dollars. Pedro now eked out a miserable existence by fishing along the coastline. (In his defense, he'd made sporadic attempts to pay off the shortage in his accounts, and Cash didn't seem to hold a grudge against Frampy's son.)[76]

At mid-morning, Bailey Cash met with reporters. "Everything is favorable," he said. "I expect to have my son back by 12:00. I wouldn't be surprised if he's out somewhere already. I'm just waiting for a car to pull up and Skeegie will come hopping out." Reporters noticed he was smiling.[77]

Whether Cash was putting up a brave front will never be known. His brother, Wilson, later said that many in the family, including himself, weren't optimistic that Skeegie would be returned. Vera, still holed up inside her home, had been pessimistic from the beginning.[78]

Outside, throngs congregated along the road from Cash's home to the schoolhouse. Concerned friends and neighbors had vowed to begin searching for Skeegie if he was not quickly returned.[79]

The FBI opposed the search. In Washington, assistant director E. A. Tamm wrote: "I talked to Agent Shivers at Miami at 5:40 P.M. and was advised that Fritz Gordon, a local shyster attorney and Jack Perry, who tried to peddle some Bank of Manhattan bonds about a month ago, have conceived the idea of holding a mass meeting in Princeton tomorrow for the purpose of forming a squad of people to check the territory in an attempt to find the boy. Mr. Connelley is opposed to this and I stated it should be pointed out to the boy's father that he should oppose it."[80]

It's unclear why the Feds were against conducting the search. The reason may have been because Fritz Gordon had once represented "Scarface" Al Capone in a trial in Miami. Gordon handily won the case and received a handsome fee for his services. Hoover, who never let solving a case get in the way of a personal vendetta, may have resented Gordon's legal victory.[81]

As the hours passed, Cash grew more desperate.

But even as he began to lose hope that Skeegie would ever be returned, Cash continued to beg the G-men to hold off starting their investigation. Just one more hour, he pleaded, then another, and another. To their credit, the FBI waited until it became obvious, even to Cash, that the platinum-haired tyke would not be returned.[82]

By late afternoon, newsboys across the nation shouted out the headlines of yet another child snatching. True to their word, both the *Miami Herald* and the *Miami Daily News* had withheld the bombshell story until the ransom was paid. James M. Cox, owner of the *News* and former governor of Ohio, was known for his integrity. When Al Capone had moved to Miami, Cox and his son-in-law editor Daniel J. Mahoney launched a savage media campaign against the gangster. Soon one of Capone's henchmen attempted to purchase the newspaper for the princely sum of $5 million. Cox refused. "If you want to buy the *News*," he said, "you can get it for five cents on any street corner."[83]

Readers nationwide, stunned by one kidnapping after another, obsessively followed the case. The abduction brought out not only the natural sympathy for the handsome, blond child and his parents, but also played on a lingering personal fear. If this could happen to the family of a small-town merchant in the Deep South, it might happen to any of them. No one, it seemed, was truly safe.

"New Kidnapping Horrifies Nation." The headline screamed from the front page of the *Oakland Tribune* while subheadlines read: "Ransom Paid—Where Is Boy?" and "Sleepy Village Startled by Kidnapping of Boy." Photographs showed Skeegie riding his new tricycle as well as a shot of the Cash home and service station.[84]

The *Oshkosh Daily Northwestern* ran the following headline: "Florida Boy Is Abducted, $10,000 Paid." The story, replete with errors, had been written by a reporter from the Associated Press who claimed that Cash had dropped the ransom money after another car blinked its headlights at him. This incorrect information would be repeated throughout the next two weeks as the case dragged on.[85]

In many of the stories, James Bailey Cash was referred to as a "wealthy merchant."

Some articles compared the Cash and Levine cases, while others refreshed readers' memories of old cases. The most poignant of these may have been the brutality committed against six-year-old Shirley Ann Woodburn in Cincinnati.[86]

On the same day Cash delivered the ransom money, a teenage boy was arrested for kidnapping and raping Woodburn. She'd been stabbed twenty-eight times. Being inexperienced in murder, the teen finally completed the grisly crime by stuffing mud in the child's mouth, effectively smothering her. Finally, the "sex maniac," as the newspapers called him, buried Woodburn in a shallow grave.[87]

As the day wound down, the menace of kidnapping gnawed at the souls of many Americans.

That fact was not lost on J. Edgar Hoover. He'd already begun plotting a course that would right the FBI.

# 5

# Searching for Little Skeegie

### Wednesday, June 1, 1938

Dawn came and went. Inside the Cash home, a soul-crushing depression took hold of the occupants. Everyone knew that Skeegie should have been returned long ago.[1]

After returning from the ransom drop-off, Cash rushed to his wife's side and informed her that the money had been delivered. Brimming with confidence, he informed her that he expected their son to be home soon. Although she attempted to act hopeful, Vera knew Skeegie was dead. Over and over, in her mind she replayed that moment of panic when she discovered her son missing. The empty crib haunted her, staring back at her like a silent, hollow coffin.[2]

While Bailey waited anxiously beside the phone, Rutzen and other agents debriefed him. At first he expected a phone call telling him the whereabouts of his child. But as time ticked away and the phone never rang, he grew silent.

As the day dawned, G-men still attempted to maintain a low profile, honoring Bailey Cash's request not to begin the public search for Skeegie. Like Vera, they had long since abandoned hope that the platinum-haired child would ever be found alive. Several of the bureau's younger agents had children at home, and these men empathized with the father's now-dwindling hopes.

Finally, at around noon, Bailey gave the go-ahead.

The G-men hit the ground running.[3]

J. Edgar Hoover seethed with an ill-concealed frustration. Agents had been hamstrung from the beginning because of the father's decision to wait. SAC Earl Connelley, an Ohio native and veteran of World War I, bore the brunt of the director's wrath. Hoover had hired Connelley right out of law school, and the young lawyer hadn't disappointed. But past triumphs meant little, and the FBI's leading expert on kidnapping knew he had to make something happen immediately.[4]

The director didn't have to tell Connelley the importance of this case. Every agent knew that five offices had been closed and 350 employees furloughed, and they realized they could be fighting for their professional lives in Dade County.

Hoover knew that a quick solution to the case would create a tidal wave of public support that would force the penny-pinching Congress to give extra funding to his FBI.

But now the director felt like he was sailing into a headwind.[5]

Franklin McCall wasn't even a blip on the FBI's radar screen during the early stages of the investigation. Although they had few leads, the bureau had developed several theories. Only one looked promising.[6]

Early that morning, when agents arrested Frampy Braxton, they'd rushed him to the Miami headquarters. In order to protect him from a possible lynch mob, lawmen had used their bodies to shield the suspect from the angry crowd.[7]

In a small room, Braxton withstood a grueling, three-day interrogation. From his perspective, agents seemed hell-bent on pinning the kidnapping on him. That perplexed the carpenter—why would anyone consider him to be the boy's abductor? Braxton cooperated fully with the agents in an attempt to convince them that he had nothing to do with the crime. He later told reporters that agents subjected him to a battery of "lie detector" tests and intimidation tactics designed to make him confess.[8]

Willard Campbell, also detained the next day, confirmed that while being held, he also had not been allowed to call his attorney. He told reporters that FBI agents told him Braxton was being held because someone in his family owed Cash money and the carpenter may have kidnapped the boy for revenge.[9]

In two separate interviews with newspaper reporters, Hoover denied charges that the suspects had been arrested and held against their will, claiming that those questioned were "voluntary witnesses." The fact that no newspaper bothered to question such an implausible assertion confirmed Hoover's status as a "media darling" and the fear some editors felt at crossing the director.[10]

Agents began by questioning Braxton for hours on end. They used all the normal questioning techniques of lawmen in the 1930s: threats of violence; the "good cop, bad cop" routine; and an impassioned plea to bring closure to the heartbroken parents. Sleep deprivation and constant bullying have caused many an innocent suspect to confess, but the carpenter remained firm in his denial that he had anything to do with the Skeegie's abduction.[11]

Braxton became the main suspect for two reasons. First, he seemed to be utterly consumed with the case, even more so than most people in the area. He spent all his waking hours talking about the case or driving to various locations in an attempt to find the boy. G-men suspected Braxton may have been attempting to hide his own involvement by inserting himself into the investigation.[12] His "bad reputation" in the community also worked against him. Agents leaked word to the press that their prime suspect had once been a bootlegger, though there is no record that he had ever been arrested for that or any other major offense. They also repeated the allegations they'd made to Willard Campbell.[13]

One FBI report stated that on the day after the kidnapping, Braxton "picked up [a] cousin of [Skeegie Cash] who was about twelve years old, and drove south about three or four miles to a negro settlement [named Goulds] for no apparent reason and then bought the boy a beer. While down there he contacted a man on the plantation . . . [and] asked the man if he should see the boy down there, would he take him home, and the man said that he probably would." The report said Braxton had displayed an "interest in all that happens [in the case]."[14]

Bureau records listed several other examples of his attempts to insert himself into the investigation. In one instance, two days after Skeegie's abduction, Braxton drove a friend to Henderson's Camp, a small fishing community on the edge of the Everglades. He informed the friend that he knew the whereabouts of a convict's uniform. Leading his friend to a place deep in the woods, there on the ground lay a complete uniform including pants, jumper, and cap. (FBI agents later found the uniform and, after examining it, determined that it was unrelated to the case.) After showing his friend the convict's clothing, the report states that "[Braxton] drove down the road on Allapatta Drive to where a man by the name of Burrichter lives." Braxton told a worker on the farm that if he found the boy he should return him to Bailey Cash and he might receive a reward. Braxton then drove to two deserted shacks in the area and searched them for the boy.[15]

The carpenter had a logical explanation for his seemingly odd behavior—he said he'd simply gone to the quarters in an attempt to get the "negroes" to return Skeegie Cash if they were holding him, or if they knew the boy's whereabouts.

In addition to their relentless grilling of Braxton, agents stayed busy checking other leads. Special agents C. E. Weeks and L. A. Newsom noted in one report that "[o]n the night of the payoff, the homes of certain persons considered to be suspects in this case were observed by various relatives and friends of Mr. [Bailey] Cash in order that the movements of those persons might be determined at the time the pay-off was made."[16]

Asbury Cash spent the night watching the home of a neighbor named A. G. Tripp. The suspect never left his residence, however, and the Feds considered him cleared.[17]

James Herndon, who owned the Last Chance tavern, managed to shake the tail of Wilson Cash, Hal McLaughlin, and D. M. Cooper, and his whereabouts remained unknown throughout the night. For that reason, he remained an off-and-on suspect for a few days.[18]

As soon as Bailey Cash returned home from the second successful payoff attempt, Ellis C. Hollums and Daniel Mahoney gave the go-ahead to their reporters to run with the story. By mid-morning on Tuesday, the presses of both the *Herald* and the *Daily News* were rolling. Shortly after noon, the papers hit the streets, only to be quickly snatched up by curious readers. That same afternoon, the story went national. The Associated Press, United Press International, and many large newspapers sent reporters to Princeton.[19]

Tips soon poured in to the FBI's Washington office, as well as the Miami office. The usual assortment of psychics, informants, and crackpots came out of the woodwork. Running down "hot tips" from Alabama; New York; North Carolina; and Jacksonville, Florida, kept the bureau's local offices busy for several days.[20]

One such tip involved a former resident of West Palm Beach who currently resided in New York City. Immediately after reading the account of Skeegie's abduction, Willie Joe McCants called the New York Field Division of the FBI and gave agents a statement concerning a possible suspect.[21]

McCants, twenty-seven, said that in November 1937 he'd moved up north to join his two brothers and their families. He worked as a gardener while studying the "police course" at Delahanty Institute in Queens, he said. He hoped to become a cop.[22]

Sometime in 1936, McCants recalled that he was hitchhiking from south Florida to Augusta, Georgia. At the Florida Motorlines Bus Terminal in Jacksonville, he said he struck up a conversation with a man who invited him to a party. The man told McCants to call him Buck Newsom, though the informant suspected that was not his real name. He went with the stranger and they met two girls. One of the girls called Newsom "Roy," causing McCants to believe that was his new friend's real name.

After the party, the two drove aimlessly through the streets of Jacksonville in Roy's 1936 Chevrolet coach. During the trip, Roy asked McCants if he wanted to make some money. McCants said he did, at which time Roy explained that he had a plan to kidnap a young boy and ask a ransom of $10,000. If McCants helped, Roy said, they would split the money. Roy showed McCants a .38-caliber blue steel Smith & Wesson revolver that he said he carried everywhere.[23]

Roy stated that his intended victim was named Smith. His father worked as president of either the Chase National or Second National Bank in Jacksonville. According to the plan, Roy and McCants would drive to the boy's residence and kidnap him as he walked to school. Roy had three ransom notes already prepared. At some point, he crossed out $10,000 and replaced it with $30,000.

McCants and Roy spent two nights in a boardinghouse fine-tuning their plan. McCants told investigators that he had become increasingly nervous and wanted no part of the kidnapping but was afraid to leave because of Roy's gun.[24]

On the morning of the second day, Roy dropped McCants off in front of the boy's home. Roy said he would drive around the block several times until the victim came out, at which time McCants should grab the boy and throw him into the back of Roy's car.

As soon as Roy let him out and rounded the corner, McCants sprinted down the street and hitched a ride to a service station. He never reported the incident and caught a ride to Augusta. There he met his brother and eventually relocated to New York City.[25]

Agents from the Jacksonville FBI office spent several days attempting to track down the suspect. Even though G-men knew the suspect's first name; that he was born and raised in Perry, Florida; that he owned or drove a 1936 Chevrolet "coach"; owned a firearm; and had spent time in Jacksonville, they never found him.

This turned out to be just one of hundreds of false leads that kept agents investigating suspects all over the country.[26]

Franklin McCall had known from the beginning that he'd embarked on a risky endeavor, but what amazed him most was how quickly his carefully concocted plan had collapsed. Any chance for secrecy had vanished when Vera Cash rushed to her neighbors in a panicked attempt to locate Skeegie. Then the sudden appearance of hordes of FBI agents had added a dangerous obstacle to his chances of success. Had McCall cut his losses and never again contacted Cash, he might have gotten away with his crime.

But greed got the better of him, and he attempted to salvage the situation with the third ransom note. So far, he'd been able to baffle the fabled G-men, and McCall had no doubt he could continue to keep them in the dark.[27]

Automobiles clogged all the roads in Princeton. Locals had never seen anything like it. FBI agents and Dade County sheriff's deputies swarmed the little town. Citizen volunteers, hoping to be part of the search for Skeegie, streamed in from outlying areas. Newspaper and broadcast journalists huddled in clusters, just waiting to blast each new development onto the airwaves and into print.[28]

By mid-morning, a crowd estimated by reporters to be six hundred men and women huddled together in the area near Bailey Cash's store, each determined to see the drama through to its end.

Most were laborers—men and women who lived on the fringes of society. These "Crackers," as reporters would condescendingly call them, lived day to day by doing the backbreaking work necessary to grow vegetables and fruit, and ship the product to market. Sustained only by a strong religious faith, and a desire to provide their children with a better life, they'd weathered the worst the Depression could throw at them. The despised Crackers had persevered even when the disastrous 1935 hurricane raged its path of destruction through south Florida, killing hundreds and blowing away the livelihoods of thousands.[29]

While some may have been there for the excitement—the kidnapping offered a momentary escape from the daily routine of grueling toil—most of the farmers had stayed as a way of showing support for Bailey Cash. They remembered him as a man who treated them with fairness and dignity, and they felt empathy for the man. Most had asked themselves the question that parents have been pondering since the beginning of time: "Is there anything I would not sacrifice for my son or daughter?"[30]

Northern journalists didn't seem to know quite what to make of the farm-hands. An AP story described them from the reporter's perspective: "Hope apparently had been abandoned that the boy, held for $10,000 ransom, would be returned alive. The temper of the crowd, however, was to start searching regardless of whether the family and authorities were willing. Grizzled, sunburned citrus growers and truck farmers with pistols on their hips and shotguns in their cars voiced grim threats against the men who snatched little 'Skeegie' last Saturday night."[31]

As the day wore on, the crowd grew. The kidnapped boy should have been home hours ago. Some in the crowd would wait no longer. They began driving the back roads in search of Skeegie. If he'd been let off in some remote location, he could be lost and wandering. The thought of a young child floundering about in the swamps of the Everglades prompted many to head in that direction.[32]

Connelley went against Hoover's wishes and concluded that an organized search was the only logical way to make use of the crowds that continued to flood into town.

Preston B. Bird, a county commissioner and former mayor of Homestead, later wrote a report that described the search in detail: "In the beginning this search Wednesday June first the men were gathered in the Chambers' Bus shed at Princeton where they were addressed by Mr. E. J. Connelley, who stressed upon these men the importance of the search and then detailed instruction as to conduct and duty.[33]

"The details [groups] were picked by designated leaders, sixteen men to a crew including the leader.

"A Dade County map was secured and marked 'Original Search Detail Map' and can be so identified.

"Fifty crews were selected and assigned the first day and all crews were supplied with simple food, water and snake-bite anti-venom.

"Beginning with crew one and through crew eight, work was started at Coconut Palm drive west of highway 4A, continuing north to Eureka road and two miles west of highway 4A. Beginning with crew twenty-one through crew thirty they worked from the intersection of Silver Palm drive and South Allapatta road to Coral Reef road on the north two miles east of highway 4A. Then beginning with crew thirty-one through crew fifty they worked from Moody drive south seven miles from Florida City and east of highway 4A. These details are marked in blue pencil on the map.

"On this days search there were approximately sixteen hundred men. A thousand of which were on foot and the remainder being diving units, boat and aeroplane crews."[34]

The first day yielded no substantial leads. But it showed the determination of local citizens to do anything possible to find the missing boy.[35]

As the searchers forged ahead, random calls continued to come in to the FBI and had to be checked out no matter how unlikely they appeared. A woman called G-men stating that she'd had a vision in which she saw Skeegie "rising up from the Everglades" and calling for his "Momma." Agents were sent to interview the woman, and came to the conclusion that she was stark-raving "crazy."[36]

Miami-Dade deputies also investigated a woman named Tessie Gonzalez. According to FBI reports, she was considered "the toughest woman in Dade County." She'd been tried three times for three different murders and had been acquitted each time. She owed a measure of her legal success with the legal system to the fact that she was a stunning beauty, a "black-haired woman of Mexican descent." Around the time of the Cash kidnapping, Tessie had allegedly begun "keeping company" with a known bootlegger.[37]

Lawmen discovered that a woman closely resembling Gonzalez had been spotted near the ransom drop site and quickly brought her in for questioning. But the woman, who had actually been near Princeton, turned out to be the wife of a correctional officer with a legitimate reason for being in the area. Tough Tessi Gonzalez was cleared yet again.[38]

At exactly 9:25 p.m., June 1, 1938, Director Hoover sent a memo to Edward A. Tamm, assistant director of the FBI. Tamm, a native of St. Paul, Minnesota, had graduated from Georgetown University with a degree in jurisprudence. Hoover trusted Tamm to keep his secrets and, except for Clyde Tolson, may have been his only real friend. Tamm's loyalty would be rewarded, in later years, with an appointment to a district federal judgeship.[39]

The memo read:

> I called Mr. Connelley at Miami and advised him that there is a man in Princeton, Florida, who is on probation in New York, who worked for Cash, by the name of Graham. I further stated that I have just received a letter from the Chief Probation Officer in New York City to this effect. I then read Mr. Connelley this letter.
>
> I advised Mr. Connelley that this man should be checked out im-

mediately. He replied that he believes they have something very important there at the present time. He replied that Braxton stands a very good chance of being involved; that yesterday afternoon he picked up a cousin of the [Cash] boy, who is about twelve years old, and drove south about three or four miles, to a negro settlement for no apparent reason, and then brought the boy back. While down there [Braxton] contacted a man on the plantation where he had built some buildings sometime in the past; that he had asked this man if he should see the boy down there, would he take him home and the man had replied he probably would. Mr. Connelley stated that there is a possibility that the boy was taken down in there some where [*sic*] and was left with the idea in mind that he, Braxton, would accidently see the boy there, and he could then say that it looks like the Cash boy and it would appear to be an accidental finding of the boy. Mr. Connelley further stated that he believes they turned the boy loose among some of the negro shacks and that the negroes are afraid to turn him up for fear of being lynched. I stated that this is probably true. Mr. Connelley stated that Braxton was apparently trying to get the fellow working on the farm to get busy and look around for the Cash boy or else have the boy he took down there with him run onto the Cash boy.

Mr. Connelley stated that when the man Braxton had contacted heard of Braxton's arrest he came in and volunteered the information that Braxton had been accompanied by a ten or twelve year old boy. He stated it looks like we have something very definite against this man Braxton.

In addition to this Mr. Connelley advised that they have picked up Willard Campbell, who is a well-known character in those parts, and the subject in several Bureau cases for gun running, etc. Connelley stated that Campbell's brother lives on a corner and within fifty feet of where the payoff was made and that some people say that he left his brother's house about fifteen or twenty minutes after the time of the payoff at four o'clock. He stated that Jimmie Herndon surrendered tonight and that in view of that there is a possibility he is in the clear.

I inquired of Mr. Connelley what he thought of the desirability of my going down there. In reply to my inquiry he stated that my arrival may do a lot of good by putting more pressure on some of the boys down there, although they seem to be going along very well inasmuch as they have about 800 men checking the area today and will have about 1400 out tomorrow morning. I stated that I will try to get a plane out of New York and that in the event I can do this, will make arrangements to go down. I advised Connelley that I will call him back and let him know. Mr. Connelley stated that Heavrin will be on the telephone to receive the call as he was going to question the suspects he has in custody.[40]

On the same night, at 9:52 P.M., Hoover sent a second memo to Tamm. It read: "I called Mr. Vetterli in New York and asked him to get in touch with TWA immediately and get a plane down here to Washington immediately for me. I further stated that I wanted him to try and get Captain Zimmerman, and that when the plane gets to the airport here it should taxie to the EAT hangar which is on the west side of the field. I stated that they should not go in the hangar, but merely over to that end of the field. I stated that if Zimmerman is in charge of the ship he will know where to go. I advised Mr. Vetterli that I want to go to Miami, Florida, and that I do not want any publicity at all. I asked him to call me back and advise me when the plane will be here."[41]

At 10:23 P.M., Hoover wrote: "Mr. Vetterli called and advised that he had secured the plane and it should be there by midnight. He stated further that he was trying to get Captain Zimmerman; that they think he is in the city and are trying to locate him. He stated that the ship is all ready to go and that it is the same kind of ship that I used before. He stated that he would know in a few minutes whether they can get Zimmerman and the exact time the plane will depart. I advised him that I am leaving the office shortly and he should give Mr. Tamm this information when he has secured it. I advised him there will be four passengers out of Washington in the event the airline officials desire to know."[42]

These memos revealed several things about the case. First, after five days, Connelley and Hoover still believed that Braxton had kidnapped the boy and secreted him in the "negro quarters." Although they'd picked up Willard Campbell, the hard-ass, they seemed to have taken him in merely because of his background. Braxton and his family still remained the bureau's prime suspects.[43]

Hoover's theory of the crime presented several problems.

First, since the night of the abduction, dozens of residents and lawmen had checked and rechecked the black section of town, as well as the nearby African American community of Goulds. Braxton's seemingly odd behavior simply mirrored the activities of other white citizens. Living in this era of Jim Crow, few blacks in Florida would have willingly been complicit in the kidnapping of a white child. If approached by a kidnapper, most, like John Emanuel, would have run for the hills—or the Everglades.[44]

Second, why would Braxton have "turned him loose" in the quarters, letting the child wander about until found? If Braxton wanted to collect the ransom, he would have hidden Skeegie in some obscure locale until he'd collected the money.

It was also obvious that Hoover's sense of timing told him to make his move. If Braxton had indeed kidnapped the youth, the director wanted to be squarely in the media spotlight, to take full credit for solving the case.[45]

As midnight approached, J. Edgar Hoover and three agents drove toward Dulles Airport in Washington, DC. It would be an uneventful flight, but the results would have long-lasting effects.[46]

# 6

# "The Greatest Manhunt
# Ever Seen in Florida"

Thursday, June 2, 1938

Newspapers labeled the search for Skeegie Cash as "the greatest manhunt ever seen in Florida." Preston Bird, the county commissioner in charge of the volunteers, wrote: "On this day, Thursday, more than three thousand men were on foot and [adding] the diving detail, the Keys detail, boat and aeroplane details, I would estimate more than five thousand men were searching."[1]

A thudding rain began to fall at mid-morning and continued intermittently for the next three days, making the search a miserable experience.[2]

The posse reflected a fair cross-section of south Florida society. Military veterans made up a large percentage of the searchers; organizations such as Veterans of the Spanish-American War, the American Legion, and Veterans of Foreign Wars were well represented.[3]

Miami city employees and members of the federal Works Progress Administration (WPA) received permission from their supervisors to join in the hunt. Other organizations, as varied as the Isaac Walton League, the Boy Scouts of America, and even the Ku Klux Klan, took part in the hunt for little Skeegie.[4]

The Red Cross established medical facilities and a field kitchen at a nearby abandoned packing shed that also served as search headquarters.[5]

Henry Cypress, spokesman for a group of Seminole Indians who were involved in the search, explained his strategy to a reporter. "We search all sections of Everglades where automobiles go," he said. "Lazy white men not carry boy far from automobile. Him too heavy."[6]

Governor Frederick P. Cone authorized the use of the Florida National

Guard "to guard against the possibility of mob violence." Floridians proudly claimed to have the nation's oldest tradition of a civilian militia, dating back to the original Spanish settlement of St. Augustine. The National Guard had been the primary force that defeated the Native Americans in the last Indian War fought east of the Mississippi River and formed the backbone for the state's Confederate regiments in the Civil War. In modern times they had sometimes served in nonmilitary roles as well. By the third decade of the twentieth century, the Guard had been activated to help evacuate citizens during hurricanes, prevent illegal prize fights, search and rescue missions, and to prevent mob violence.[7]

Men and women with specialized skills also answered the call to hunt for the missing boy. Newspapers reported that "a squadron of bombing planes from the Opa Locka Naval Base, commanded by Lieutenant Commander R. P. McDonald, flew over the town, and observers, [using] powerful fieldglasses, scanned the terrain below." Other privately owned planes, including a crop duster flown by Skeegie's uncle, Ishmael Cash, took to the air in a desperate attempt to spot the youngster.[8]

Local divers and boaters also offered their services. The state fire warden issued a call for volunteer divers to search water-filled limestone quarries. The crews included at least one woman. They searched dozens of pits as well as nearby creeks and rivers. A fleet of seventy-five boats covered 175 miles of Biscayne Bay shoreline and more than 250 miles of Everglades canals.[9]

Bailey Cash's neighbors from the Redlands had a personal stake in locating Skeegie. Not only did they know the Cash family, but also they now knew that they had a monster living in their midst. These hardy farmhands, trappers, and commercial fishermen would still be going when the other volunteers had gone home.[10]

Attorney Fritz Gordon, widely hailed as "one of Miami's best lawyers," worked in the command center with Preston Bird and SAC Connelley. Gordon appears to have been motivated by a sincere desire to help locate little Skeegie, and not simply to use the tragedy in a sleazy attempt at garnering some free publicity.[11]

The evening before, he'd addressed the crowd in a rousing speech. A local writer quoted Gordon in the October 1938 issue of *True Detective* magazine: "Wear heavy boots or shoes and old clothing. The territory which must be searched is probably the roughest and wildest in the whole United States. Much of it is covered with rank palmetto thickets, underbrush and scrub pine. Some of it is rocky and a large portion of it borders on the Everglades, where there are swamps and sinkholes. There is much danger from rattlesnakes. This is no job for weaklings. We will need strong men and this will be no picnic." Each group, he explained, would be assigned a "carefully selected" leader experienced with the terrain.[12]

Gordon then told the men to leave their guns at home. "We are not going to hunt for the kidnappers," he explained. "Uncle Sam will catch them." He might as well have saved his breath. Many of these men usually put on their guns right after they buckled their belts, and few looked to Washington, or even the local sheriff, to take care of their problems. Besides, the attorney had not exaggerated the difficulties involved in the search. The universal sign of distress in the area was three shots, fired in quick succession, and few wanted to waste time searching for a club when confronting a six-foot rattler.[13]

Gordon reminded the men that the abductors might turn the Cash boy loose in the Everglades. If not quickly found, the hostile bogs and marshes would be a death sentence for the five-year-old youth. "He cannot survive many hours," the attorney reminded the searchers, "amid mosquitoes, the tropical sun, snakes, and other dangers to which he would be subjected if he has been turned loose. We must cover the largest amount of territory in the shortest possible time."[14]

Connelley also addressed the group. "We must face the strong possibility this little boy will be found dead," he announced. "If you see signs of freshly disturbed dirt—dig. Take your time and dig deeply. Look into every canal you pass and in every clump of bushes. Don't overlook anything. If [Skeegie is] found alive, take him to the nearest hospital or his home."[15]

Connelley informed the group of protocol in case they discovered Skeegie. "If the boy is dead, under no circumstances touch the body," he said. "Form a cordon around the spot and let no one inside your line. Touch nothing and disturb nothing, until one of you has notified us. At that time an agent will come to the scene and take charge."[16]

With those words, the long lines of men, marching shoulder-to-shoulder, moved to their assigned sections.

Preston Bird, in his role of field general, reported that "one hundred and four crews, composed of from four to one hundred men, were sent out covering areas east and west of highway 4A to Miami, excluding the city limits of Miami."[17]

Various newsmen attempted to describe the search area, but a reader in Seattle or New York City could hardly visualize the terrain being covered. One source stated: "The territory to be searched was sparsely settled. East of the main highway which runs north and south through Princeton, wide winter vegetable fields, weed-grown at this season, cover the flat country to the coast. West of the highway is a district of lime, orange, and grapefruit groves, and west of that lie the Everglades."[18]

While the description was technically accurate, it failed to mention mile upon mile of palmetto scrubs; marshy areas with razor-sharp saw grass that slashed through the toughest denim clothes; alligators gliding unseen through freshwater creeks and canals; and, camouflaged by their colors and sometimes measuring more than six feet long and thick as a weightlifter's upper arm, rattlesnakes laying in ambush for the unwary traveler.[19]

After the kidnapper was caught and convicted, watching the posses slogging through the marshy wilderness J. Edgar Hoover labeled the south Florida terrain "one of the toughest handicaps the Bureau has ever encountered in kidnap investigations."[20]

The Boy Scouts and some of the older Legion veterans served as traffic controllers, an important task with hundreds of buses and automobiles parked haphazardly throughout town. Many local women volunteered to prepare meals for the searchers.[21]

Nine "radio police cars," supplied by Miami-Dade sheriff D. C. Coleman, cruised the roads, picking up information to be relayed back to headquarters.[22]

Throughout the day, a series of incidents occurred that raised the searcher's hopes, only to have them dashed almost immediately.

The first came when a man named Cutler was found dead in his home with a gunshot wound. The searchers initially concluded that he was part of the abduction crew and had taken his own life when he saw the posse closing in on his hideout. However, when lawmen rushed to his cabin, they discovered a suicide note, and the true reason for Cutler's death became apparent. The poor man, suffering terrible pain during the final stages of cancer, found himself unable to stand the agony any longer and ended his own life.[23]

Later, reporters near the packing plant witnessed Wilson Cash and two G-men rush to an automobile and speed south. A woman had found a "croaker sack" (burlap bag) full of decomposing matter. She quickly contacted one of the officers in a radio car, who called headquarters. Upon investigation, agents found that the sack contained only the carcass of a decaying dog.[24]

As the day wore on, rain turned the region into a quagmire. At times, the downpour nearly blinded the searchers. Still they kept on.

Divers at Tavernier, near the Florida Keys, discovered a "blood-smeared fragment of cloth" in a water-filled pit and notified the bureau. Other divers soon arrived and explored the flooded sinkhole and surrounding terrain inch by inch, but found neither Skeegie nor any other evidence. No reason for the presence of the gory rag was ever uncovered. Still the posses pressed forward in their search.[25]

Another "brief flurry of excitement" occurred when one of the search parties brought in two men, handcuffed and under heavy guard. They had been located in a swampy area and, according to a newspaper account, "sullenly refused to answer any questions." Suspecting they might be part of the kidnapping ring, several members of the posse marched the suspects over to the packing shed for interrogation. Sheriff Coleman, however, soon released the "culprits." The two men were well-known moonshiners in south Dade County and had simply been running off a batch of hooch when the posse unexpectedly stumbled upon their hidden lair.[26]

Franklin McCall joined his neighbors in one of the search groups, but he soon proved more of an irritant than a help to his fellow searchers. "I don't think they'll ever catch the kidnappers," he loudly proclaimed to everyone within earshot. "Whoever pulled this job was plenty smart."

McCall's declarations finally became so vociferous that some members of his squad began to suspect that the preacher's son might have had a hand in the abduction.[27]

The day ended without success, and all the posses were called in at nightfall. Fritz Gordon, Sheriff Coleman, and E. J. Connelley explained to the news media that searching in the darkness was too dangerous. Coleman noted the danger of stepping on a rattlesnake as a major reason for stopping, but getting lost, missing an important clue, or suffering broken limbs from falls in the inhospitable territory also argued against a night search. Wet and exhausted, the posse members headed home or found a place on the floor of the packing shed in an attempt to gain a few hours' sleep in their soggy clothes.[28]

The search teams had actually done a remarkable job. More than seventy-five square miles had been covered, and divers had explored every rock pit and quarry in the area.

Lieutenant Commander McDonald informed reporters that naval bombers had covered approximately 750 square miles of territory. Even though the pilots were as tired as the land searchers, they vowed to continue flying the next day.[29]

Calls for additional volunteers filled the airways and newspapers, and more men and boys headed toward Princeton. A reel of film footage shows the street in front of the main section of town clogged with vehicles.

Sam Bennett, district American Legion commander at Fort Pierce, promised an additional thousand legionnaires. As an added incentive, the Palm Beach Town Council voted to pay a $500 reward for information that led to the conviction of the kidnapper. The Dade County commissioners sweetened the pot with an extra $1,000 award, and an unidentified citizen added $500.

Unfortunately for the searchers, during the night, the rain, which had been steady all day, became a torrent.[30]

In Miami, M. F. Braxton had endured a full day of questioning.

John Emanuel, the field worker who'd fled into the Everglades rather than deliver the first ransom note, finally came forward to tell his story. He'd been afraid that police would frame him for the kidnapping, but to his surprise, the G-men believed him. He'd been hiding, he said, first in the Everglades, then with friends.[31]

Agents transported Emanuel to FBI headquarters in Miami. There, according to a report, he was placed "behind a heavy screen listening to the responses of dozens of persons who were being questioned, in an attempt to pick out the voice that he had heard that night." Despite his best efforts, Emanuel would prove unable to identify the voice of the abductor.[32]

G-men arrested Braxton's son-in-law, Brent Rayburn, and his son Pedro, but even the FBI's most experienced interrogators couldn't catch the supposedly disreputable family in a lie or convince them to confess.[33]

Agents needed more space, so the bureau rented a building in Princeton known as the B. L. Mathis Store. Additional G-men quickly moved into the newly leased annex, followed by lab technicians with their forensic equipment.[34]

Throughout Wednesday night and into Thursday morning, Bailey Cash slept little. Even though he'd given up hope of finding his child alive, he paced the floor, always within arms length of the telephone.[35]

Beatrice Cash, Zoe Henderson, and other relatives and friends attempted to console Vera. Her anguish was palpable. She'd lost weight because she

wouldn't eat. Newspapers reported that the bed-ridden mother had been provided sedatives, but still had trouble sleeping. Friends had always considered
Vera to be strong, but now she lay in a fog of despair, a pitiful shell of the
respected, flint-hard businesswoman they knew her to be.[36]

At around nine in the morning, J. Edgar Hoover flew into Miami Munici-
pal Airport with a small entourage that included his right-hand man, Clyde
Tolson. Newspapers reported that no less than fourteen agents stepped off
the plane that morning. Although the director had stated in his memo that
he wanted no publicity, the opposite was true. Somehow the news leaked to
reporters who flocked to the airport to meet the celebrity.

Almost exactly one year earlier, on May 23, 1937, Amelia Earhart had arrived at the small south Florida airport to begin her final flight into history.
The hoopla had been amazing, but reporters who covered that event later
said Hoover's arrival attracted even more reporters.[37]

The media assumed that the famous crime fighter's arrival in Miami meant
a break in the case was imminent. For that reason, reporters focused almost
exclusively on the high-profile visitors, often ignoring local police efforts to
track down the "Madman of Princeton."[38]

The director and his entourage drove directly to the Miami FBI headquarters. Later in the day, he visited Princeton to have photos taken that showed
him in the field. Those snapshots would appear the following day in newspapers across the United States, along with bold predictions that Hoover
would arrest the abductors within a matter of hours.[39]

As step one of the G-men's plan, the bureau flooded the area with lists
of the serial numbers on the bills used to pay the ransom. The itemizations
went to virtually every merchant in South Florida. In addition, newspapers
across the nation, at the FBI's request, also published the currency numbers.[40]

According to FBI files, by June 3, "circularization" had reached 160,000.
Locally, the flyers were passed out to the following types of businesses: automobile dealers, repair shops, garages, and supply houses; filling stations;
bus companies and terminals; railway express offices and terminals; airplane
companies and ticket offices; credit agencies; tourist camps; telegraph companies; doctors; restaurants; dentists; nurses; hospitals; drug stores; grocery
stores; taxicab companies; steamship ticket agencies; and barbers. Civilians
who wanted a copy of the lists merely had to send a postcard to any FBI office requesting one.[41]

Outside of Florida, ransom lists were distributed first to businesses in

New York and Connecticut, then to other northeastern states. Agents never gave a reason for targeting the northeastern states first, rather than those in the Southeast.

The G-men also offered to pay double the face value of each of the first one hundred ransom bills turned into the Feds. (So if a merchant received a fifty-dollar bill, he could receive one hundred dollars by turning it in to the FBI.) The offer stipulated, however, that the person who turned in the bill must be the original recipient of the currency. That way, the G-men could easily identify the person who tendered the note.[42]

A United Press article reported that "shortly after their arrival, radio stations in Miami broadcast at Hoover's request appeals to all persons handling currency to check bills coming into their possession against serial numbers of the ransom currency. With Hoover here, the drive to capture the man or men who kidnaped the Cash boy, collected $10,000 ransom and then failed to return the child, assumed new intensity despite the rain."[43]

The article stated that "printed and mimeographed lists of the serial numbers of the 'hot money' appeared on almost every cash register and on the desk of every bank teller in Florida this morning. It seemed unlikely that any one of the ransom bills could be cashed without quick recognition."[44]

The Feds also examined the Cash home yet again, paying particular attention to the slit screen door. They took photos of the door from every conceivable angle, dusted for prints, and reinterviewed potential witnesses. Although this might have seemed like a waste of valuable time, agents were actually making sure they had covered every base and that nothing had been overlooked.[45]

Other lawmen spread throughout the countryside running down the automobile license numbers of cars spotted by the various watch groups the previous night. Hundreds of drivers were interviewed, but this line of investigation turned up not a single viable lead, as most of the drivers proved to be gawkers, out trying to get a firsthand look at the ransom payoff.[46]

Agent Connelley spent the early part of the day getting the posse into the field. As soon as that was done, he personally directed the search near the Chambers lot.

He and several other agents also had Bailey Cash reenact the ransom drop. This action quickly turned up a couple of pieces of evidence. Roping off the area (in the days before yellow crime scene tape), the Feds discovered a shoe print that "was soon turned into a moulage." (How they found it in the driving rain was not specified in the reports.)[47] Spreading out from the telephone pole where Cash had thrown the shoebox, the lawmen searched Chambers's lot, citrus grove, and a nearby patch of woods. Although the searchers missed the $9,750 dollars in the weeds near the corner of the rock fence, they discovered a second clue in a nearby thicket. An FBI report read: "Pieces of the shoe box in which the ransom money was delivered, found under a rock a few hundred feet away [from the footprint], were carefully wrapped in wax paper and rushed to Headquarters in Miami for minute inspection under microscopes."[48]

The search of the area where the ransom was delivered went on for hours, even after a heavy deluge opened up.

One source indicated that the G-men reinterviewed Franklin McCall during the early morning of June 2. The Feds had only one question. If Preacher Boy had to choose the one local person who most resembled the person he had seen fleeing the W. P. Cash filling station when he found the third ransom note, who would he pick? His answer would have serious repercussions in a very short time.[49]

While the desperate search for Skeegie proceeded apace in south Florida, events occurred in other parts of the nation that were related to the case.

The evening before, a freight agent in Huntington, Long Island, New York, found a leather wallet containing a photograph of Skeegie Cash pinned to a suspicious letter.

The letter read: "Please look for your boy in the Everglades. I broke away from the gang. Man and woman has your boy. Cross railroad track at Princeton to the Everglades. Sixteen miles from boys home." In the wallet was a business card from a Miami restaurant called The Dinner Bell.

Local lawmen turned these items over to the FBI. The G-men dusted the evidence for fingerprints and, finding none, eventually dismissed the spurious clue as a hoax.[50]

In yet another incident, a postmaster in East Islip, New York, turned a letter over to the FBI. Addressed to Mrs. Mary Cash, it had a return address from Miami, Florida. The mailman became suspicious and contacted authorities. The letter turned out to be unrelated to the case.[51]

By now, half the residents of south Florida seemed to be suspects. A man named Williams was, according to Miami police, a "pretty bad actor." While drinking one night in a "whiskey joint," he stated that he was going to get even with Bailey Cash "regardless of what it took to do it." Cash told the

FBI that he'd never even heard of Williams; this lead, like so many others, was dropped.[52]

Even in northern newspapers, the Cash case now eclipsed reporting on the Peter Levine kidnapping and murder. The fact that J. Edgar Hoover had flown south amped up the coverage, and with so few leads coming in from the New York area, even staid newspapers such as the *New York Times* sent reporters down to cover the events.[53]

As the day wound down, there had been no progress in getting Braxton to crack. The affable carpenter continued to answer questions, even when agents got in his face, but would not admit to any wrongdoing.

G-men checked each of Braxton's many alibis and found no discrepancies. In addition, the search had yielded nothing.

Unlike the weather, the case seemed to be going dry.[54]

# 7

# Interrogating the Carpenter

## Friday, June 3, 1938

The hunt for Skeegie resumed the following morning. By now, all hope for finding the boy alive had vanished, and many posse members apparently no longer thought they would even be able to locate the child's corpse. Still exhausted from the previous day spent trudging through miles of swamps, palmetto flats, and piney woods, less than half the original number of searchers returned on the morning of June 3. While planes from the Miami Naval Reserve joined the hunt, the boats along the coast had been sent home.[1]

Having covered the farmlands and scrublands surrounding Princeton the previous day, today's quest extended to more remote areas. One area where volunteers and lawmen concentrated was called Back Bay, two miles south of Princeton. Searchers waded out to the five hundred small, uninhabited islands, said to be a perfect hiding place. One journalist described the area as a labyrinth of "swampy morasses," which, if possible, was an understatement. It had been a hideout for the Seminole Indians during their second conflict (1835–42) with the US government, as well as a haven for bootleggers and rumrunners in more recent times.[2] Other searchers went to the Cape Sable area, the most southwestern section on the Florida peninsula. It seems likely the G-men chose to cover this particular region because Pedro Braxton lived in that locale.[3]

A posse was sent to Buttonwood Key after a navy plane spotted a boat near the tiny island, but it turned out to be only an angler fishing along the shoreline. By mid-afternoon, the FBI called the searchers back to Princeton and told the weary men to go home.[4]

Reporters stressed that the order came directly from the head of the FBI. "This afternoon," a newsman wrote, "J. Edgar Hoover . . . abruptly ordered all searching posses to be called in. The G-man boss telephoned to the field headquarters in Princeton to call off the search at once."[5]

Hoover offered no explanation for his decision. He likely realized that the searchers had no chance of success, and several hundred men, overseen by federal, state, and local lawmen, constituted a waste of his limited manpower resources.

The endless miles of area still to be searched, as well as the driving rain, may also have figured into his decision.[6]

A final consideration seemed to have been the hope that allowing things to calm down might lull the criminals into a false sense of security, and they might start spending the ransom money. Whatever the case, the men likely greeted the order with a sigh of relief. They'd done everything possible to find the missing child and could now go back to their homes, satisfied that they had done their duty for a friend and neighbor.[7]

Even though the search had officially ended, some die-hards refused to quit. Throughout Friday and into Saturday, a remnant continued to doggedly search the area. On his own now, Preston Bird persisted in plotting areas to hunt, concentrating west of the Tamiami Trail. In his report, he made a note that the Seminole tribes had effectively "patrolled the area." Even so, ground crews trudged through the wilderness and airplanes flew over the vast swamps in one last desperate bid to locate clues.

Even though the search wasn't dead, it was on life support. The following day would mark the end of the desperate, unsuccessful hunt for the missing boy.[8]

Meanwhile, various reports from across the eastern United States caused brief flurries of activity, but they all quickly proved to be red herrings. In Fowler, Indiana, a tiny hamlet on the northwestern edge of the state, a short but intensive hunt occurred when a local woman reported seeing a boy who "resembled photographs of the missing Cash child with 'a dark complexioned man who seemed to be a foreigner.'" Indiana National Guard aircraft and G-men joined local volunteers in the quest to locate the boy, but the report turned out to be a case of mistaken identity.[9]

In Oneida, New York, state police sought two women who took a small boy dressed in sleeping clothes to a physician for treatment of a sore throat. Bethesda, Maryland, police devoted most of the day hunting for a car with

Florida plates that allegedly contained two men and a screaming child. And in Lakeland, Florida, almost three hundred miles northwest of Princeton, authorities attempted to find a man and woman spotted driving a beat-up coupe and holding a young child.[10]

At Miami headquarters, G-men continued to grill Braxton, still hoping for a confession. The carpenter's biography seemed to belie his "vicious" nature, as journalists described it. He originally hailed from middle Georgia, but had lived in the Florida Redlands for about twenty-five years. Most recently he worked as a carpenter for the International Fruit Company, of Peters, Florida, during 1937 and the early months of 1938. On February 23, Braxton had stepped on a nail, and that accident had briefly disabled him. He returned to work on April 24, at which time he'd taken a job with August Brothers, a packing company owned by two men of German extraction.[11]

The FBI's first priority involved establishing a timeline for Braxton's activities during the period immediately preceding the kidnapping. The carpenter had numerous friends and acquaintances and, as it turned out, there was barely a moment in the past week that he hadn't been accompanied by some member of the community.[12]

On Saturday night, May 28, Braxton left his home at around seven thirty and went to Bailey Cash's general store, where he and his friends were in the habit of meeting to discuss the day's activities. He spent the evening with Mr. Walker, a Princeton farmer; Bob Barlow, who worked at a local packing plant and lived nearby with his sister and brother-in-law; Franklin McCall; and a Mr. Waters, who worked for the WPA. Braxton related that the nightly get-together had been a common occurrence. When interviewed, Braxton's friends confirmed his alibi.[13]

When the meeting broke up, Braxton drove Jim Mizell, an employee of Bailey's filling station, to his (Mizell's) residence, which stood next door to the carpenter's house. Braxton estimated he got home around ten, at which time he went inside and began to read the newspaper.[14]

About 10:15 Mrs. Mizell rushed over and announced that Skeegie Cash was missing. Frampy, as his friends called him, and his wife, Flo, joined Jim Mizell's wife and hurried to the Cash home, where a crowd had begun to gather. Braxton recalled that the Cash child (whom the carpenter called "Skeets" rather than Skeegie) often played with the Garrett child, and he hurried over to the Garrett house to make certain that Skeets had not wandered over to his playmate's home during the night.[15]

This was the first of many attempts to help find the boy that would eventually lead to Braxton becoming the G-men's main suspect.

Returning to the Cash service station, he volunteered to help Bailey in any way possible. As the crowd began walking toward the "quarters" in their first search of the black section of town, Bailey asked Braxton if he was carrying his pistol. The carpenter assured the desperate father that he was indeed toting a gun. Braxton assumed, but didn't know for sure, that Cash was also armed.[16]

Later, when the increasingly distraught father drove over to check out John Emanuel's cabin, Braxton accompanied Cash, a Mr. Smith, and Bob Barlow in the search of "the negro shack." In fact, more than twenty-five people drove or were passengers in automobiles that used their car lights to help Bailey find the note. Between 1:30 and 2:00 A.M., Braxton finally returned home and went to bed.[17]

Except for fifteen minutes, when he was alone with his wife, the carpenter had an airtight alibi. He couldn't have left the notes.

As their interrogation dragged on, the G-men realized they couldn't pin the actual kidnapping on Braxton, so they revised their theory. In this new version, the carpenter became the mastermind of the crime, while one or more members of his family pulled off the actual abduction.[18]

On the following day, May 29, Braxton spent the entire day and evening in the crowds that gathered around Cash's filling station. Literally dozens of witnesses could attest to his whereabouts throughout the entire day and night. Sometime after nine that night, Braxton went home and remained with his wife the rest of the evening. They retired sometime before midnight.[19]

On May 30, Braxton and his friend Bill Bethea drove to the home of Mr. Loren Roberts, two miles south of Homestead. The carpenter had heard that Roberts planned to build a boat, so Braxton offered his services to construct the vessel. He and Bethea remained with Roberts for a couple of hours before returning to Princeton.[20]

Braxton hung around the Cash store for the rest of the afternoon. Knowing that his friend Bailey was raising money for the ransom, he took the opportunity to pay part of the credit account he owed. (Cash and his wife had gone into virtual seclusion, but his clerk, a Mr. Singer, kept the store open.) Braxton paid seven dollars of his seventeen-dollar tab, plus five dollars on his gas bill. The carpenter left word with Singer to tell Mr. Cash "he would be willing to do anything to help recover Skeets at any time."[21]

An FBI document reported that "on Monday afternoon [Braxton] was down around the filling station again, and there was a considerable number of people there."

During the evening, Braxton apparently talked with Charlie Chambers, who convinced the G-men's chief suspect that "it was best for everybody to get away [from the Cash store] . . . in order that the boy could be brought back." As a result, the carpenter went home and went to bed.[22]

Unable to sleep, Braxton got up and went outside in his underwear. He sat on the front porch, enjoying the night breeze, but he worried about the boy.

According to the bureau's report, "he saw a car slow down about one and one half blocks south of his house headed east. This car then turned on the road leading to the highway. Because the Cash child had not been returned, Braxton said he thought possibly this car contained the Cash child. He dressed and went to the service station where he saw Albert Watson, a local farmworker and acquaintance, who told him the car he'd seen belonged to George Cooper of Princeton. Braxton told Watson, 'There is too big a crowd here,' and went home alone. He retired for the evening around 2 A.M. and stayed in bed until after daylight."[23]

The G-men apparently hoped to prove that Braxton had used the time he spent on the porch to slip off and meet his accomplices in the kidnapping, but their test balloon crashed and burned almost immediately. It turned out Braxton had been spotted by "several cars [that] passed, including the 1933 or 1934 Ford sedan which belongs to the boy who delivers the *Herald* newspaper." (That boy, Walter Fisher, would soon become the next victim of the FBI witch hunt.)[24]

The next day began like the previous three with Braxton joining the mob that milled around the Cash Service Station. While there, the carpenter heard a great deal of speculation about the case. Many wondered aloud who could have committed such a horrible crime. While everyone seemed to agree that the kidnapper was a local citizen, no one wanted to point a finger at a neighbor or friend.[25]

By now, law enforcement, which rarely came into the area, was a massive presence. Even though they attempted to conceal their identities, federal agents could always be spotted by the fact that they were strangers wearing suits and ties. In addition to the G-men, Sheriff Coleman's deputies descended onto the village en masse.[26]

After noon on the third day, Braxton suggested to a friend, V. D. Smith, that they drive out toward the Everglades to look for Skeets. Smith initially agreed to accompany the carpenter, but found that he couldn't get off from his job.

Despite this setback, Braxton determined that he would head toward Goulds to check out a group of "nigger shacks" he had recently built while working for August Brothers. Like J. Edgar Hoover and many of his agents, Braxton had become obsessed with the idea that the kidnappers had let "Skeets" loose among the African American community near Princeton, and that the blacks were too frightened to turn the boy over to the lawmen.[27]

As Braxton drove southeast, he spotted Walter McVickers, nicknamed "Junior." Twelve-year-old McVickers was the son of Vera Cash's sister. Braxton pulled up beside the youth and announced: "I'm riding out here looking for Skeets; the kidnappers may have dropped him off around here." The boy asked to ride with Braxton and they proceeded to the homes Braxton had built.[28]

Finding the shacks deserted, Braxton and McVickers carefully checked each of the buildings. After a few minutes, the carpenter concluded that Skeegie was not there, and they drove out Pine Island Drive and went to Webb's Camp, also called Henderson Camp. While there, Braxton showed McVickers the old convict suit he'd found.[29]

An FBI report of the Braxton interrogation stated that the carpenter "saw some fellow working there whom he knew from having seen him before at this place and he asked him where Webb was; that he intended to tell them if the boy was found they should bring him in; that he believed the negroes had become frightened and might hesitate to bring the boy in if he were left there."[30]

Thinking they had caught the carpenter in a lie, investigators asked why Braxton had omitted mention of his discussion with a man named Hansen. Braxton admitted that he might have spoken to Hansen, who was a native of Germany and foreman of the August Brothers operation near Princeton, but suggested it was just an unimportant few moments in the afternoon excursion. "He advises that Hansen asked him what was happening in the kidnapping and he advised him that he had heard nothing definite," but "he told him Cash would be glad if he [Hansen] brought the boy in."

Braxton admitted he had bought the boy a beer, but supplying a twelve-year-old a brew seems to have raised no eyebrows, even among the Feds.[31]

After this bizarre excursion, Braxton dropped McVickers at home and returned to his normal routine—lounging around his house and milling about at Cash's Service Station.[32]

During this lengthy interrogation, John Emanuel sat behind a wire divider where he could listen to the voice of Braxton. Although not specifically mentioned in the files, it seems certain that Emanuel did not recognize the suspect's voice.[33]

The G-men spent hundreds of hours beating the bushes in an attempt to disprove Braxton's alibi. They interviewed dozens of residents but couldn't shake the carpenter's story.[34]

Florence "Flo" Mabel Sowell Braxton (Frampy's wife) and Mary Ellen Braxton Rayburn initially cooperated with the Feds, even allowing the agents to search their houses. Mrs. Braxton, in particular, seemed astounded that her husband could be a suspect. She repeatedly told the G-men that they were close friends with the Cash family. (The knowledge that close friends were suffering may go a long way to explain Braxton's near obsession with trying to help locate Skeegie.)[35]

As the relentless interrogation of Frampy continued, agents repeatedly questioned Mrs. Braxton and Mrs. Rayburn about their husbands' alibis. Both confirmed these accounts.[36]

Florence Braxton had had a rough life. Born in 1890 in Screven County, Georgia, she'd lost a baby shortly after her marriage to Braxton, which may have led to the couple's decision to relocate to Florida. She appears in news photos as a thin, wrinkled, dour-looking woman. Any attractiveness she may have possessed had been worn away by the ravages of the Depression, childbirth, and a husband who often came home without a paycheck. Her life had not been easy, but she had a fierce loyalty to her family and friends, as well as a sure knowledge of her husband's innocence.[37]

Mary Ellen Rayburn, in her early twenties, beamed with the vibrancy of youthful beauty. She and her husband, Billy Ray, had one child. Flo Braxton seemed to think they wasted their money on extravagant pleasures. For example, she informed the lawmen that one night during the previous week, even though she thought they shouldn't spend money on such frivolities, they had all gone to Miami to view *The Guns of the Pecos*, a Western shoot-'em-up. Mary Ellen described the movie in general terms, admitting that she had not really enjoyed the talkie but stayed because her husband liked that kind of show.

Another night, Billy Ray and his wife went to a seafood restaurant. They appeared to be a young couple, very much in love, and not always frugal with their money.[38]

G-men checked, then double-checked the Braxton and Rayburn stories. Their alibis could not be shaken. Still the bureau kept the men confined and continued to grill them, trying to find some discrepancy, no matter how minute, that would allow them to charge one or both men with kidnapping.[39]

In an effort to break their stories, the FBI used a newfangled "forensic" tool, a "lie detector," on Braxton, Rayburn, and Willard Campbell. This was indeed a long shot.

The first modern lie detector had been created in 1885 by Cesare Lombroso, an Italian. American William Marston had used a polygraph of his own design to interrogate German POWs during World War I, but Marston's device used only blood pressure to check the person's veracity. Marston, who claimed to be the "Father of the Lie Detector," continued to improve and publicize his contraption. Dr. John Larson, of the University of California, created a device that, like the modern polygraph, measured both blood pressure and galvanic skin responses. His and Marston's lie detectors found only limited acceptance among law enforcement agencies and had been labeled "pseudo-science" by almost all courts and state legislatures. (Courts and lawmen recognized early on that sociopaths, habitual liars, and those who choose to believe a lie can, and do, beat the machine.) As a result, the machine could not have been used in most courts of law.[40]

However, the contraption gradually gained acceptance as a "psychological tool" among American police agencies. Lawmen used the device as a way to coerce confessions from those who "failed" the test. The FBI subjected Braxton to the test several times in an effort to coerce him into admitting his guilt.[41]

After her husband had been detained in the Miami FBI office for three days, and having been turned away when she attempted to see him, Flo Braxton made a fateful decision.

On the afternoon of June 3, she and Mrs. Rayburn appeared at the doorway of the FBI Miami office and demanded the release of their husbands.

The two women may have seemed like country bumpkins to the G-men, but they were smart enough to make sure several reporters were present when they issued their ultimatum. Mrs. Braxton loudly proclaimed that the two wives would take "legal action" against J. Edgar Hoover and the Federal Bureau of Investigation unless the G-men released their spouses.[42]

This was the last thing J. Edgar Hoover wanted. If it ever got back to his detractors in Congress that he had arrested two innocent men, held them for days on end, and tried to force them into confessing, the director's days at the FBI would have been in jeopardy.[43]

The women were sent away, but two hours later Marshall Frampton Braxton and his son-in-law walked out of the offices of the FBI. Journalists photographed the joyous family reunion, and Braxton even invited the newsmen into his house. There he and his family posed for pictures around the kitchen table.[44]

Willard Campbell had been released before Braxton. Unlike the carpenter, he had an extensive criminal background. Only thirty-seven, his long rap sheet showed convictions for conspiracy to smuggle aliens into the country, violation of probation, bootlegging, and gunrunning ("conspiracy to export arms"). He'd served two years in the federal penitentiary in Atlanta after a conviction for smuggling.[45]

Campbell had also been arrested for writing worthless checks, and he'd served thirty days in the local jail for "tapping wires." In addition to these charges, he'd been investigated for the murder of another bootlegger, but he was never charged.

Campbell currently owned a popular dance hall and barbecue restaurant in Miami. The Hi Lo Inn, located on the corner of 62nd Street and 27th Avenue, did a brisk business, particularly on weekends. The place served southern-style food while an orchestra provided music for dancing. (Rumor also had it that illegal gambling activities took place in the restaurant's back rooms.)[46]

On June 3, two Miami sheriff's deputies walked into the restaurant and handcuffed Campbell. Spiriting him to the FBI high-rise, agents immediately accused him of kidnapping Skeegie. Campbell had been through the game before and his reaction was more of amusement than fear. Like Braxton, he knew he was innocent and could prove it. He'd been either at his restaurant or his home next door the entire weekend.[47]

As Campbell related the names of people who had seen him, agents spread out over south Florida to interview them. The following employees vouched for his whereabouts on Saturday night: three curb girls named Dot, Peggy, and Catherine; Pop Eason, the night watchman; and Michael McLaughlin. In addition, Campbell recalled a "gambler" named Woody Woods, and a woman named "Mrs. Jenkins," who spent several hours in the restaurant.[48]

Shorty Davis and his orchestra played from 9:00 P.M. to 3:30 A.M., and the entire ensemble could place Campbell there. In addition, more than two hundred paying customers ate, danced, and drank at the Hi Lo Inn that night.

In fact, the only time Campbell left for the whole weekend was Monday afternoon when he drove to the Economy Cash Shop to buy cigarettes and supplies for the restaurant. On the way home he stopped at Charlie Sirkins's Used Auto Parts store to purchase two tires. He made a couple of additional stops, then returned home.[49]

As person after person vouched for the restaurateur, it became obvious even to the FBI that Willard Campbell didn't have the time to drive to Princeton and kidnap the boy, then place three notes in different locales and transport Skeegie to a safe hiding place.

After only a few hours of interrogation, agents asked Campbell to take a polygraph test. Like Braxton, he agreed. Although the G-men never made public the results, agents quickly released Campbell.[50]

Because of his reputation, however, local residents viewed the former bootlegger with suspicion. His name continued to pop up as a possible suspect throughout the investigation.

No report mentioned J. Edgar Hoover's reaction to this setback, but the director must have been livid. He had gambled his reputation and the prestige of his agency on solving the Cash kidnapping, but they still had no good suspects. The maddening thing was that the abductor lurked somewhere in those crowds that walked the streets of Princeton, yet he might as well have been a million miles away.[51]

As night began to fall across the swamplands of Dade County, G-men began casting about for another suspect.

# 8

# The Paperboy

## Saturday, June 4, 1938

Saturday dawned on a community shaken to the core. Exactly one week earlier, in the no-stoplight town of Princeton, Florida, an innocent child had been snatched from his home. It was the type of crime small-town residents naively believed only happened in big cities.

In rural southern Florida, people tended to live harsh but simple lives, and not many stuck their noses in their neighbors' business. Under normal circumstances, that was the best way to keep the peace. Few things, however, remained completely hidden, and now that residents knew a monster walked among them, they opened up to investigators. These country folk revealed buried secrets and dragged skeletons from long-closed closets in an attempt to ferret out the identity of the kidnapper. In some cases, this offered them a chance to get back at old enemies.[1]

Even though he'd been officially cleared, Willard Campbell's name kept coming up in the investigation. On the previous evening, William Johnson of West Haven, Connecticut, had called the local office of the US Secret Service and told agents that he had information about the Cash kidnapping in Florida. Johnson said he thought a local man named Willard Campbell might have taken the boy.[2]

The caller informed Secret Service agents that in 1921 he'd been a bootlegger in south Florida and that Campbell was his supplier. He described Campbell as a "daredevil, very tricky, [and] capable of committing almost any crime; that in addition to being a bootlegger, he has smuggled aliens into the United States."[3]

Johnson said that on one occasion he and Campbell drove to a house Campbell's father owned. The building had been unoccupied at the time, and Campbell told Johnson that he stored illegal liquor there. The house had a secret trapdoor in the ceiling and other hidden entrances and concealed compartments.

Johnson informed the agent that Campbell may have snatched the Cash boy and hidden him in one of those secret rooms.

Unfortunately, it had been more than fifteen years since the caller had been in Florida, and he was unable to pinpoint the exact location of the house.[4]

The FBI recorded this information but spent little time pursuing the lead.

Having struck out with Campbell and Braxton, the G-men now turned their attention to the most unlikely suspect of all—an eighteen-year-old churchgoing paperboy named Walter Augustus Fisher.[5]

This unlucky teenager became a suspect for one reason: he drove a car that looked exactly like one that had allegedly been spotted near Asbury Cash's house early on Monday morning, about the time Bailey Cash paid the ransom.[6]

Beatrice Cash told G-men that she'd seen a car circling her home sometime between three and four that morning. Several streets connected with each other to form a circle around her residence, she said, and the car kept driving around and around on those roads. She described the vehicle as an older model Ford with a fog light attached to the front bumper. The first time it passed her house, she recalled, the auto had on its front lights, rear lights, and fog light. Later, after the sixth time it drove by, all the lights were off except for the fog light and the taillights. Beatrice claimed that she later saw the Ford parked near a grove opposite her house.[7]

The story seemed odd, but the G-men took it seriously.

According to the FBI files, "[Walter Fisher] was taken into custody and was questioned at the temporary headquarters at Princeton, Florida, regarding his activities on the night of the payoff."

When interrogated, Fisher, naive to the ways of hardened investigators, proudly proclaimed that he'd been "making his way" since he was twelve years old. By that, he meant he'd been working and making money to help support his family.[8]

He stated that he lived with his father, Franklin, a carpenter, his mother, Ethel, and a brother and sister. He had a route delivering the *Miami Herald* newspaper. Fisher informed agents that he'd worked for the *Herald* for three years and had never missed a day. He also worked odd jobs, depending on the season. He'd finished the eleventh grade but had decided not to complete his schooling this year and hadn't reenrolled.[9]

Fisher regularly attended the Methodist Church, he said, and had a twenty-year-old girlfriend named Cleo Clubb.

The FBI asked for permission to search his car, and Fisher consented. A report states that the paperboy's car was "a 1932 Ford V-8, four-door sedan, green in color; that this car has three tail lights in the rear, one on each bumper and one to the left of the spare tire; that it has a V-shaped bumper guard with a fog light on the front." Fisher stated that he'd bought it for $225 and still owed $90 on it.[10]

On the night of the payoff, the teenager said that he and his family had attended a party at the home of Ole Peterson, near Princeton. Members of the local congregation had thrown the affair to honor the local Methodist preacher, who had been assigned as pastor to another church. Fisher said he drove his Ford into town, picked up his girlfriend, and went to the get-together. There he met his family, including his twenty-year-old sister, Mary.[11]

The teenager told the agents that he left the party at about 11:45 P.M. and drove Cleo home, after "taking a short ride." He then drove to the Sinclair Service Station in Princeton and hung out with four friends until 2:00 A.M. He had to deliver his newspapers at four so he went home.

(It seems that the fact that all his customers received their papers should have eliminated him as a suspect since Bailey Cash dropped off the ransom shortly after four.[12])

When he got home from the party, he told investigators, his father informed him that Mary hadn't returned. Franklin Fisher asked his son to go find her and bring her home. Walter left the house and drove back into town. When he couldn't locate Mary at the typical teenage hangouts, he began stopping at the homes of friends who might know his sister's whereabouts. Still unable find her, he drove home again, thinking she might have arrived while he was gone.[13]

She hadn't, and by now Franklin Fisher had progressed from being merely concerned to highly upset. Even though the clock read 3:00 A.M., Fisher's dad insisted that he go back into town and try again to find Mary.

During his second trip toward Princeton, something happened that shook Walter Fisher to the core.

The teenager had learned about the kidnapping of Skeegie Cash on Sunday morning. He'd driven into Princeton to get gas, where the station attendant told him about the abduction. At first, he didn't believe the boy had been snatched, he said.[14]

After several people confirmed the kidnapping, Walter, like Frampy Braxton and others, became obsessed with the case. It was all people talked about, he told the agents. He listened to the speculation, even going so far as to drive by Bailey Cash's home. He said that before he delivered the *Herald* to his customers, he read every article about the case.[15]

From local gossip, young Fisher knew that Bailey Cash planned to attempt a second payoff before dawn on Monday morning. As the teenager drove toward town to look for his sister, he kept his eyes open for the kidnapper's car.

From his home, Fisher could get to Princeton by two routes. One route went directly by Asbury Cash's home, but he said he rarely took that road. However, on the second trip into Princeton that night, he took the highway that led him by Asbury's residence. He informed agents that when he drove by the house, at about three o'clock, he saw a car parked at the edge of a grove about three hundred yards from the residence. Fisher said he thought the automobile was a Plymouth or Chevrolet sedan and that it had only one taillight on the left side.[16]

At any other time, he would have barely noticed the car. But on this night, his imagination ran wild. The teenage boy decided that the parked car might belong to the kidnapper. He stated that he became frightened and turned his car around to head back home. As Walter passed Asbury's home again, he said he saw another car pass him. He informed the agents that he believed it was Bailey Cash's Plymouth. He knew the car because his father had done several carpentry jobs for Cash.[17]

Walter said that as the vehicle passed, he thought Skeegie's father was on his way to drop off the ransom money to the car sitting near the grove. He assumed that Cash would retrieve the boy after the payoff.

The paperboy arrived home thoroughly shaken. He told the story to his father, but Franklin Fisher could have cared less. Mary still hadn't returned home, and by now Franklin had worked himself into a rage. He ordered his son to get back in the car and go find his sister. Fortunately, his father soon realized how frightened the teenager was and decided to accompany him.[18]

On the way back into Princeton, Fisher took the route that did not go by Asbury Cash's house. Once in town, Franklin Fisher spoke with several people, including Hal McLaughlin, Harry Wright, and Wilson Cash. None had seen Mary.

Agents fanned out across town to check out the teenager's story. They soon learned that almost everything he said could be verified.[19]

Still not knowing what to make of Beatrice Cash's story, investigators re-interviewed her. She insisted that the car did indeed circle her home on six different occasions. Later, she said it had been parked beside another car near the area where Walter had seen what he called "the kidnapper's car." The Feds discovered, however, that Beatrice's story contained a major flaw. Agents checked and couldn't see the car Walter said he saw from the spot where Beatrice claimed to be standing.[20]

The G-men also questioned Bailey Cash again. He denied being in the area during his drive on Monday morning.

Agents decided to ratchet up the pressure on young Fisher. They transferred him from the Princeton warehouse to FBI headquarters in Miami. They also brought in the top guns to interrogate him: Earl J. Connelley and J. Edgar Hoover.[21]

By now, Hoover was seething. He'd come to this one-horse town to make a statement to his detractors, and now his best leads had dried up. To avoid incurring the director's wrath, agents stayed in the field as long as possible. When unsuspecting Walter Fisher walked into the office, there was no preliminary discussion: the G-men immediately accused the paperboy of being the kidnapper.[22]

While the flabbergasted teenager sat in stunned silence, Connelley laid out the case against him.

Walter once again told his story to the skeptical agents, trying to explain what he'd done Monday night.

The interview now became farcical.[23]

Connelley informed the teen that agents had found "hundreds of rubber bands" scattered throughout his car. They had taken samples of the rubber bands to Beatrice Cash who identified them as being similar to the one found on her doorknob. (She had thrown away the original rubber band.)

Walter explained that he used them to wrap his newspapers. According to the files, the boy said "that when delivering his papers he has a habit of rolling the papers and using rubber bands to hold them in place, which is his reason for having the rubber bands strewn all over the car."[24]

Next, Connelley presented a handwritten note to Walter. It had been found in his home, the agent in charge said, and the writing looked similar to the ransom note. Scrawled on a page from an ordinary writing tablet, the "note" consisted of a series of numbers showing how much American money it would take to exchange for English farthings.

Connelley and Hoover seemed hopeful that this might be the clue needed to solve the case. If the kidnappers were thinking of changing the ransom money into foreign currency, this is how they might have figured out the exchange rates.

But Walter had a logical explanation. His father, he said, had been born and raised in the Bahamas, and occasionally enjoyed showing his children the difference between the value of American and English currency.[25]

What looked like sinister plot to the G-men turned out to be just an unusual pastime.

They next questioned Walter about a flashlight found in his car. When turned on, the light shone dim and needed new batteries. It seemed to be similar to the one Bailey Cash said he'd seen at the drop-off. Again, Fisher claimed he used it when delivering papers.[26]

Finally, the agents advised the teenager that they had uncovered a bottle of ephedrine sulfate pills in his room. Connelley and Hoover insinuated that Walter was a drug addict who had devised the kidnapping scheme to obtain money for drugs. Fisher responded that he had asthma and had used the drug for two years to relieve his breathing problems. He informed the interviewers that he obtained the drug from Burns Pharmacy in Homestead, and that Robert Brown, the pharmacist, could vouch for him.

The agents interviewed Brown, who told them that "Fisher was a regular customer of his drug store. He stated that he knew Fisher suffered from asthma and that he generally purchased one of two different remedies in order to relieve his condition. One remedy is Dr. R. Schiffman's Asthmador. This is put up in a three-ounce tin and is used by inhaling the fumes created by burning this powder. . . . Brown also informed that Fisher purchased, from time to time, capsules containing 3/8 gr. Ephedrine Sulfate."[27]

In just a few hours, Hoover had seen another promising lead crumble into dust. Walter obviously had nothing to do with the kidnapping. In fact, he seemed to be a clean-living, hard-working teenager with a bright future ahead of him.[28]

So the G-men reversed course. They asked the teenager to name people he thought might be the kidnappers.

Walter had obviously thought about this and listed the names of several individuals. Willard Campbell, naturally, topped the list. Fisher stated that Campbell possessed a generally bad reputation, and everyone knew he operated a "juke joint" in Miami. The law-abiding folks in town, Fisher said, felt confident that Campbell had his fingers in the crime, one way or another.[29]

A second group of "undesirables" Fisher named included Hal McLaughlin, Franklin McCall, Clarence Mullins, Harry Wright, George Singer, Kenneth Bryant, Bob Barlow, and Harry "Red" Graham. Fisher claimed these men had a reputation for playing poker and gambling in an old boxcar near the packinghouses. His father had warned him to steer clear of them.

During his interview, Walter dropped a few more tidbits of information.[30] He stated that most people felt the kidnappers had thought the federal government wouldn't be interested in investigating the abduction of a little "cracker" boy in a small Florida town.

Fisher then described the following episode as something the FBI should check out: "He . . . cited an incident of a negro by the name of Gerald, who works for Cash, who about two weeks before Christmas last year was working at the Farmers Service Station operated by Cash in Miami, and he, Fisher, was running the cement mixer; that the child, "Skeets," got close to the mixer and this negro did not make any effort to get him out of the way and made some remark to the effect that the child was hard to get along with."[31]

Fisher related that a member of his search party had told him that the pinewoods north of Silver Palm contained a number of moonshine stills. The teenager thought that area might be a good place to look for the boy.[32]

Walter's father, mother, and sister were all interviewed and confirmed his accounts. Other witnesses mentioned in his narrative also verified his story.

Late that afternoon, the frustrated agents released the paperboy. Even the hardened interrogators had been impressed with him. He may, in fact, have caused some to recall a more innocent time in their own lives.

Agents never determined whose car Fisher had seen on the night Cash paid the ransom. They also never identified the owner of the vehicle Beatrice Cash saw. G-men spent hundreds of hours checking out this incident. They finally concluded that "gawkers" had driven the cars seen by Beatrice and the newsboy. It's likely that Beatrice saw Walter's car pass by, turn around, and head back in the other direction. Agents thought this may have inflamed her own imagination and caused her to exaggerate the number of times she saw the car.[33]

Mary Fisher finally arrived home at around four o'clock that morning. She told her father she'd spent the time with a girlfriend. The FBI files say nothing about his reaction.[34]

Later in the afternoon, the Miami field office received a teletype from the FBI office in Los Angeles. An anonymous letter had come in postmarked El Centro, California. The writer claimed he "was in Princeton, Florida last winter; that he was a poker player and acquainted with J. B. Cash, that he overheard Hal Pahlmer [later identified as Hal Parham] of Florida City, Florida and the Bagget Brothers of Princeton remark that the Cash boy was pay dirt and that they were waiting for the right time to cash in." The letter writer also stated that one of Cash's employees comes "from the north [and] may have an underworld contact."[35]

Agents rushed to interview Bailey Cash.

Skeegie's father stated that he was indeed acquainted with Herman and Fred Bagget. The brothers hailed from Georgia, Cash said, and were opposites of each other. Fred Bagget, the younger of the two, worked in South Carolina for part of the year, then returned to Princeton during the vegetable season. He usually rented a room from Cash, who described him as a decent man who never drank or gambled.[36]

Herman, on the other hand, "drinks considerably and gambles," but had never been in trouble with the law. He was sometimes called "Google-eye" because he had "pop eyes." Herman left Princeton around March or April and as far as Cash knew was currently residing in Dania, Florida.[37]

G-men launched an investigation into this lead but it turned out that the two brothers had been nowhere near Princeton when the kidnapping occurred.

Cash told agents that he also knew Hal Parham and considered him to be "a sensible man when sober, but that he became crazy when drunk." In 1936, while Parham was renting a room from Cash, he received a large sum of money from a "bonus." Parham decided to use the money to set up a "chicken business," Cash said. He rented a place in Florida City and bought lumber from Cash to build chicken coops. Parham built the structure but then spent most of his money drinking and couldn't afford to buy the chickens.[38]

About a year later, Parham drove up to Cash's store, walked inside, and without saying a word, grabbed Cash's shirt and ripped it. Cash said that he "remonstrated [Parham] for doing this, whereupon Parham had gotten back into the car and driven off."[39]

Cash said he didn't hold that against him, and they still greeted each other when they met. Cash said he hadn't seen Parham since September or October of 1937 and assumed he had moved away.[40]

Agents asked Cash if he knew anyone who resided in El Centro, California, the origin of the anonymous letter. It took a while, but Skeegie's father finally came up with a name.

He said he'd known a man named Windy Davis who had once lived in Princeton but later moved out west. Windy got his nickname, Cash said, because he "is an inveterate liar and bragger." Cash stated that "he would attach no significance and little credence to any statements made by Davis, inasmuch as from his experience, he knew that Davis was given to loud brags."[41]

G-men questioned Cash about whether he had ever gambled with any of these men. He denied it, although he "tacitly admitted" that he played cards occasionally.

Bailey Cash, always sensible, then made a statement that was recorded in the files: "Mr. Cash stated that he had reached the conclusion that the subjects of instant case were persons who were well-known in the community, so well-known that their presence would not attract any undue suspicion, and for this reason, stated that had either of the Bagget brothers or Parham, or in fact, any [who hung around with them been] present during the time of instant kidnapping, that their presence would have attracted some attention."[42]

As another day faded away, the vaunted G-men had once again been stymied. Walter Fisher had turned out to be just an average teenage boy, maybe a little more responsible than most, and certainly not a prime suspect for a child abduction. Most of the leads coming in by mail, telephone, and teletype seemed to be from crackpots or persons who wished to be involved in the case in some way.[43]

At seven at night, in Charlotte, North Carolina, commentator William Winter took to the air as he usually did on WBT radio. One of the oldest and most popular radio stations in the south, it had broadcast its first program in 1920. By 1938 the station combined a menu of local and national news, as well as "hillbilly" music shows. Music historians have concluded that WBT's Carolina Hayride provided the inspiration for Nashville's world-famous Grand Ole Opry.[44]

That night, Winter had a special guest. Edward Schneidt, special agent in charge of the Carolinas office of the FBI, was scheduled to speak about the Skeegie Cash kidnapping. As always, when an FBI agent appeared on any radio show, writers approved by J. Edgar Hoover scripted the entire broadcast. Hoover himself purportedly reviewed every script, and the director would not allow agents to deviate from the document in the slightest detail.[45]

Schneidt's main purpose in appearing on the show was to advise the audience that they could receive the list of serial numbers of the ransom bills. Citizens could call their local FBI office or send a postcard requesting the list.

The WBT radio signal went out to most of the East Coast and all over the South, making it a prime propaganda machine for the FBI. Schneidt mentioned that several kidnapping cases had been solved when citizens noticed ransom serial numbers on currency and alerted police. For example, the Lindbergh case, as well as the kidnapping and murder of businessman Charles Ross by Henry Seadlund, had been cracked as a result of help from sharp-eyed citizens.[46]

Just one year before, in 1937, Seadlund had kidnapped the Chicago businessman at gunpoint and, with his partner, collected a $50,000 ransom. Once he had the money in his hands, however, Seadlund shot and killed both Ross and his own partner.[47]

Seadlund then began spending money all over the country. He finally landed in Los Angeles where ransom bills began showing up regularly. Clerks at the Santa Anita Race Track discovered several of the "hot" bills. The FBI staked out the track and arrested Seadlund when he came to bet on the horses.[48]

The killer paid the ultimate price for his crime in 1938, not long after Franklin McCall received his death sentence.[49]

William Winter stuck by the script. Schneidt refused to comment on the Cash case, but as always, gratefully acknowledged Hoover's "personal leadership."

Over the years, G-men continued to use radio broadcasts for propaganda.[50]

Franklin McCall continued to blend into Princeton society. Danger now lurked around every corner, and he knew he had to be careful. His wife hadn't yet returned from Jacksonville, so he continued hanging out with his old cronies.[51]

Normally confident, even brash, McCall's sudden realization that the ransom money couldn't be spent for many years had shaken his self-assurance.

By now, he and Claudine should be in some big city living the good life. Instead, he was still stuck in this backwater town with the same dismal financial prospects he'd had when he committed the crime.[52]

Even though he knew he couldn't spend the money, no one suspected him of being the kidnapper. The local cops were dumb, and the G-men even dumber, he thought.

He couldn't believe Braxton had talked his way out of custody. McCall had hoped the cops would pin the kidnapping on him, but Braxton seemed to have come out of it a hero. Everybody around town wanted to talk to the carpenter and find out what happened during the three days he spent in FBI custody. The son of a bitch continued to bask in the glow of his newfound fame, being interviewed by local as well as national newspapers.[53]

Preacher Boy knew Willard Campbell had also been released. McCall had only met Campbell once and was afraid of him, though he'd never admit it to himself. The man's eyes were like steel, devoid of human sympathy. He's the one they should have charged, McCall thought.[54]

McCall figured he could be questioned again, but thought he was slick enough to outsmart the Feds. He'd made sure to have alibis for most of Saturday night and early Monday morning. He'd mingled with townspeople before and after the kidnapping and the payoff. Lots of folks could vouch for his whereabouts.

After thinking about it, he began to feel pretty good about his prospects. No eyewitnesses could place him at the scene of the abduction. And even though he'd thrown away most of the ransom money, he'd kept back several hundred dollars in the oil drum at McLaughlin's service station. When things cooled down, he might drive to Jacksonville and get rid of the cash. He'd give it some thought, maybe read a couple of stories in his crime magazines about how the underworld launders money. After the FBI left Princeton, he might even go back to Chambers's fence and retrieve the rest of the cash.[55]

For the first time in days, the skies over Princeton had cleared. McCall looked out into the darkness and saw the stars twinkling high in the sky. One week into the case, the world continued to turn just like it always had. No one suspected him. No one would.

Franklin McCall went home, dropped onto the bed, and sank into a heavy, dreamless sleep.[56]

1. Photograph of Skeegie Cash taken just weeks before his abduction and murder. (FBI)

2. Home of James Bailey Cash, his wife, Vera, and son, Skeegie. (Critical Past LLC)

3. Home of African American laborer John Emanuel, where the second ransom note was found. (Critical Past LLC)

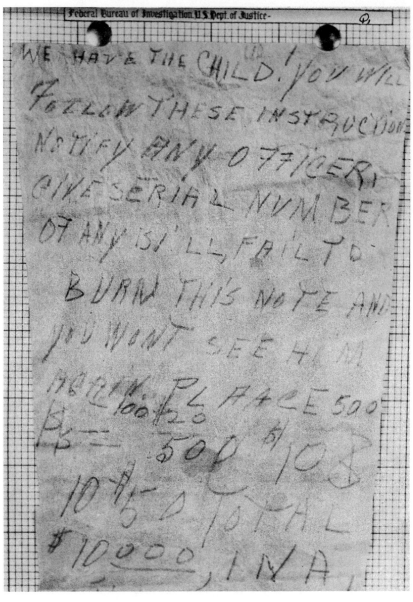

4. Page of the ransom note confiscated at the home of John Emanuel. (FBI)

5. Grief-stricken parents Vera Cash and James Bailey Cash attend the funeral of their murdered son. (Miami-Dade Office of Records Management/Archives Unit)

6. J. Edgar Hoover, pictured in his office in 1940, had an ulterior motive for becoming personally involved in the Skeegie Cash kidnapping. (Library of Congress)

7. Franklin Pierce McCall is led to court to stand trial for the kidnapping of Skeegie Cash. (Miami-Dade Office of Records Management/Archives Unit)

8. Miami-Dade sheriff D. C. Coleman fingered the kidnapper, but Hoover and the FBI took credit for solving the case. (State Archives of Florida, *Florida Memory*, http://floridamemory.com /items/show/23171.)

9. Counsel for Franklin Pierce McCall. Attorney C. A. Avriett (right) worked valiantly with Paul Brinson (left) to spare the life of McCall on appeal. (State Archives of Florida, *Florida Memory*, http://floridamemory.com/items/show/155842)

10. "Old Sparky," Florida's electric chair. Photo is dated 1939, the year McCall was executed. (State Archives of Florida, *Florida Memory*, http://floridamemory.com/items/show/137112)

# INFORMATION
# WANTED

## CONCERNING
## PETER DAVID LEVINE

Peter David Levine was last seen at 3:30 P.M., February 24, 1938, in the vicinity of North Avenue and Hamilton Avenue, New Rochelle, N. Y. The pictures reproduced on this circular are good likenesses of him.

Photograph taken December 1937

Photograph taken (Date Unknown)

**PETER DAVID LEVINE** is described as follows:

| | |
|---|---|
| Age: | 12 years (born 2/2/26) |
| Height: | 4' 8" |
| Weight: | 80 pounds |
| Build: | Average |
| Eyes: | Blue-green; deep set |
| Hair: | Dark brown; straight |
| Face: | Round |
| Complexion: | Fair. |
| Teeth: | Brace on upper teeth. |
| Nose: | Normal |
| Mouth: | Small |
| Ears: | Small and flat to head. |
| Head: | Large |
| Hands: | Large |
| Feet: | Slight bow legs. Flat feet |
| Birthplace: | New Rochelle, N. Y. |
| Education: | Student, 7th grade, Albert Leonard Junior High School, New Rochelle, N. Y. |

Photograph taken December 1936

When Peter Levine disappeared, he was wearing: Tan oxfords, size 4½; high stockings; brown corduroy knickerbockers; shirt, possibly blue, with tie; blue sweater patched at elbow; red melton cloth wind breaker, with hood, with zipper front, with picture of Indian head and letters "C.W." high on left chest; brown leather belt.

If you are in possession of any information concerning the whereabouts of Peter David Levine or the persons responsible for his disappearance, it is requested that you communicate by telephone or telegraph collect with the undersigned, or with the Special Agent in Charge of any Field Division of the Federal Bureau of Investigation, the addresses and telephone numbers of which are set forth on the back of this notice.

JOHN EDGAR HOOVER, DIRECTOR,
FEDERAL BUREAU OF INVESTIGATION.

11. New Yorker Peter Levine's unsolved kidnapping and murder occurred the same month as Skeegie's abduction, and the cases ran parallel in the media. (FBI)

# 9

# Sheriff of Dade County

## Sunday, June 5, 1938

D. C. Coleman, forty-six, had been the sheriff of Dade County for five years, replacing colorful veteran sheriff Dan Hardie in 1933.[1] Hardie came to Miami in the 1890s, in an era when outlaws brazenly roamed the city. Opium dens and bawdy houses were commonplace, and local lawmen often turned a blind eye to these illegal activities. In "Wild West" style, Hardie often took the law into his own hands, busting up illicit operations. He served as sheriff from 1908 to 1916.[2]

Hardie had only a third-grade education, but during the boom days in the 1920s he became a millionaire. Like many wealthy Americans, the stock market crash of 1929 wiped out his fortune, leaving the former lawman virtually penniless.[3]

In 1932, Hardie ran for sheriff again, and won, after Dade County's previous top lawman had been removed for corruption. Modern historian Blaise Picchi reported: "No one could accuse Hardie of dishonesty, but he was hotheaded and melodramatic and . . . 'stepped on too many toes.'"[4]

When Governor David Sholtz ordered his removal, Hardie was still basking in the glory of the arrest and conviction of anarchist Giuseppe Zangara for murdering Chicago mayor Anton Cermak. The diminutive Italian anarchist had attempted to assassinate president-elect Franklin D. Roosevelt in Miami, but missed, and instead shot Cermak.[5]

Despite the positive publicity he received from this case, the sheriff's "take no prisoners" style and innate honesty made him a plethora of important enemies. He irritated some by "arresting prostitutes and their clients, many of whom were respectable citizens, closing betting parlors and in general, some said, making the city look bad and hurting tourism." He detested the media, particularly the *Miami Herald* and its then-editor, Frank Shutts. Once, when Hardie threw the switch to execute a convicted murderer, a *Herald* reporter asked if the sheriff had any regrets for doing his duty. The sheriff quipped that his only regret was that Frank Shutts "had not been sitting in the condemned man's lap."[6]

It was not surprising, then, that the area's major newspaper would lead the charge to unseat the elderly lawman.

Hardie's true "sin," however, seems to have been his determination to enforce Florida law as written and not pander to special-interest groups and the politically powerful. Eight months after the conviction of would-be assassin Zangara, Sholtz removed Hardie for "misfeasance and nonfeasance because of 'lack of sound judgement and mental stability.'" The governor allowed stories to circulate in the press that Hardie groped and fondled women who came to the sheriff's office to file complaints.[7]

Such rumors amounted to a political kiss of death in the Deep South (still an apt description of Florida in the 1930s). Hardie labeled the charges as lies and distortions, but his enemies in the press, as well as state leaders, made sure that his rebuttals sounded like the ranting of a lunatic. According to Picchi, the *real* reason he received the axe was that Hardie hated the gamblers and showed them "the way out of town at the end of a .38. . . . Hardie was eventually exonerated, but by then his political career was over."[8]

Governor Sholtz quickly appointed D. C. Coleman, the Dade County chief deputy sheriff, to finish Hardie's term of office. Coleman hailed originally from Dodge County, Georgia, and had moved to the Miami area when he was twenty-five years old. Unlike many Florida lawmen of the time, he was well educated, having attended Atlanta Medical College and Emory University before moving to south Florida.[9]

Florida's chief executive publicly ordered the new sheriff to "clean out every racketeer and gangster in your county forthwith." This rhetoric was aimed at appeasing his Bible Belt constituents in north Florida and the Panhandle regions, but Sholtz, in reality, believed that establishing Miami as a mecca for gambling would improve the state's economy. (Like many politicians, before and since, Sholtz apparently thought the state could run mobster-free casinos.)[10]

The initial crisis of Coleman's first term came not from criminals but from "an act of God." In September 1935, a hurricane roared through the Florida Keys, killing hundreds of workers (primarily World War I veterans) who were constructing the Key West to Miami highway. Coleman and his officers directed rescue operations in the lower Keys, but the body count soon rose to more than 350 men. With decomposing corpses littering the area, state health officials quickly declared them a health hazard and recommended the bodies be cremated to prevent the spread of disease. President Roosevelt asked state and local officials not to burn the bodies, but Coleman ignored FDR's call, believing that further delay would put the citizens of south Florida at risk.[11]

Deputies, health officials, and volunteers gathered the remains into huge piles. After appropriate prayers by Protestant ministers, Catholic priests, and Jewish rabbis, lawmen put the sad remains to the torch. Defying the president of the United States seemed not to have caused Coleman to lose any sleep.[12]

Unlike J. Edgar Hoover, Sheriff Coleman always took pains to give credit to local officials and lawmen for any success he enjoyed. With this tact and political savvy, he easily won his first election for a full term as sheriff.[13]

Mob-related killings in Dade County made headlines across the country, but Coleman's star continued to rise as he brought criminal suspects to justice and shut down known gambling establishments and houses of prostitution.

The sheriff took heat, however, from the liberal media for instituting his "hobo train" scheme. Every year, during the winter season, thousands of vagrants made their way to Miami to escape the cold weather in the north. Petty crime skyrocketed during their stay in the area, and providing food and shelter for the idlers drained the public treasury. Coleman sought to solve both problems by rounding up the hobos and putting them on trains headed north. When his operation became public knowledge, it brought screams of outrage from newspapers and some politicians, but local residents generally backed these extreme measures.[14]

Sheriff Coleman also disliked putting prisoners to death. While he wasn't completely opposed to the death penalty, he hated the state law that required him to pull the switch. All in all, Coleman did a good job, making the hard decisions, even if those actions made him some very powerful enemies.[15]

Coleman was also known for his kindness to inmates. During the Christmas holidays, he sometimes took presents and food to destitute families of prisoners.[16]

While newspapers concentrated on the FBI's investigation into Skeegie's abduction, Sheriff Coleman and twenty deputies had been beating the bushes, looking for that one big break in the case. They retraced the route Bailey Cash had earlier traversed, interviewing literally hundreds of area residents. Coleman knew his county and its people (black and white) intimately, and he put pressure on informants to reveal the whereabouts of the kidnapped youth. Despite their best efforts, local lawmen had come up as empty as the G-men.[17]

Sheriff Coleman's first contact with Franklin McCall came on the morning after the preacher's son "found" the third note. The FBI requested the Dade County lawman to bring McCall to headquarters to be interviewed about what had occurred at the W. P. Cash store. McCall not only convinced the agents of his innocence, but also had thrown them a red herring by inferring that he'd seen his friend Frampy Braxton running behind the filling station. Preacher Boy was, as he had said all along, a pretty smart fellow.[18]

Sheriff Coleman located McCall sitting on the front porch of his residence. (In the days before air conditioning became commonplace, a rocking chair or swing on the porch provided one of the few places to find some relief from the steamy south Florida heat.)

Coleman casually took a seat on the top step, making small talk while he took his measure of the man. Hoover's agents considered Preacher Boy to be merely a friendly witness, but Coleman quickly came to a different conclusion. The sheriff later said he got goose bumps while listening to the slick-talking, arrogant McCall.[19]

The sheriff waited for a time before casually mentioning the case. Once Skeegie's name came up, McCall enthusiastically recounted his part in finding the third ransom note. Coleman quickly determined that McCall enjoyed being the center of attention and seemed delighted to be considered an integral part of the kidnapping investigation.[20]

McCall gave a straightforward account of his actions on the night the payoff had been scheduled. He'd told the story so often that he'd virtually memorized his version of events.[21]

He spoke of borrowing his father-in-law's truck in order to get three gallons of gas. He and his friend Harry Wright had driven to Hal McLaughlin's Sinclair station and stopped in front of the pumps. It was at that point, he said, that he saw a dark figure running away. The form ducked behind the station and disappeared.[22]

Sheriff Coleman asked McCall if he'd told FBI agents that he thought the shadowy figure running away was Braxton.

McCall looked sheepish, and nodded. "But I wouldn't want to get anyone in trouble," he said. "It was dark and I couldn't see very well."[23]

The sheriff asked McCall to ride in the front seat with him as they drove toward Miami. When Coleman asked McCall about his whereabouts on the night of the payoff, the preacher's son stated that he'd just been hanging around Princeton. He had plenty of witnesses to confirm the first part of his alibi. He'd been just one of at least five hundred others waiting for Skeegie's father to return from the first, unsuccessful, attempt to deliver the ransom money.[24]

After that, McCall said he went to his father-in-law's house to return the truck and discuss the day's events with Mr. Hilliard. Then he retired for the night. He said he was sure that he went to bed at exactly 3:30 A.M.[25]

Along the way, Coleman stopped at a café and bought lunch for McCall. With Claudine away, it may have been the first decent meal he'd eaten in a week. McCall enthusiastically thanked Coleman while wolfing down his food.[26]

The sheriff may not have liked McCall, but at this time there is no indication that he suspected the truck driver of kidnapping Skeegie. It would take Coleman another day and a half to realize that he had been riding, talking, and dining with a fiend.

After their meal, Coleman dropped McCall off at FBI headquarters. G-men questioned him for three hours before releasing him. Since other witnesses and suspects had been interrogated for hours on end, and sometimes even for days, this indicates that agents had bought the truck driver's story.[27]

In his career as a south Florida cop, Coleman had dealt with wife beaters, moonshiners, human traffickers, gunrunners, and rumrunners. He'd also battled gangsters, cold-blooded killers, and had even investigated the attempted assassination of a US president-elect.[28]

Newspaper accounts reported that "the Cash family first became suspicious of McCall, and alerted Sheriff Coleman of their suspicions." While that may have been the case, Bailey and Vera would almost certainly have discussed their suspicions with the agents living in their home. Nowhere in the FBI files is there even a hint at such a conversation.[29]

Exactly when he first began to suspect McCall is a matter of conjecture. The FBI files provide no help here since they completely wrote Sheriff Coleman out of the case. (In the more than 4,200 pages of documents detailing the investigation, Coleman is barely mentioned.)[30]

Two clues led Sheriff Coleman to zero in on McCall. First, the sharp-eyed lawman noticed that virtually every major event in the case had occurred within a four-block area of "downtown" Princeton. He and his deputies had traversed the area many times, and the compact area of the crime suggested that the culprit had limited mobility. Coleman then made the logical deduction that the kidnapper lived within that very restricted geographic locale.[31]

McCall fit the suspect profile, because he had no automobile. Coleman knew that the preacher's son had borrowed his father-in-law's truck on the night of the ransom payoff, but several sharp-eyed "spies" confirmed that Hilliard's pickup had been sitting in the driveway by 3:00 A.M. So, if McCall were indeed guilty of the crime, he would have been on foot when Bailey Cash delivered the ransom. That fit the geographic contour.[32]

The second strike against McCall involved the finding of the third ransom note. How, Coleman wondered, did the kidnapper know the service station would be reopened for a few minutes at around midnight when it had already closed for the day? By setting the new drop-off time for 4:00 A.M. that same night, the kidnapper must have known the station would open before then. Or maybe the culprit himself decided to make sure the manager opened the store.[33]

Finally, the sheriff noticed that the butcher's paper the message had been written on was badly crumpled. Preacher Boy had repeatedly stated that Harry Wright had difficulty opening the door of the filling station because the note had been jammed into the tight space between the floor and the door. The lawman wondered how a wrinkled wad of paper could have been wedged into that tight gap?[34]

Coleman decided that this incongruity deserved further investigation. What if McCall had brought a prewritten note, the sheriff wondered, and dropped it on the floor once he and Wright entered the building? If that were the case, then the preacher's son either kidnapped Skeegie Cash or knew who did.[35]

As a result, on the morning of June 6, Coleman again picked up McCall and took him to FBI headquarters in Miami.[36]

A pool of almost fifty newsmen, bored and discouraged, milled around in the lobby of the Biscayne Building. What had started as an exciting investigation, with a fair-haired boy kidnapped, grieving parents, a huge manhunt, the nation's "top lawman," and the possibility of blood and murder, had devolved into a waiting game. Perhaps because there was nothing else to do, one photographer snapped a picture of Sheriff Coleman escorting Franklin McCall into FBI headquarters. While it didn't run in any of the following day's newspapers, that snapshot would enjoy wide circulation in the days to come.[37]

Coleman took his charge up to the thirteenth floor of the "skyscraper" and explained his suspicions to the agent in charge (likely Earl J. Connelly). With McCall safely in federal hands, the Dade County sheriff headed outside, certain that he had identified at least one of the kidnappers.[38]

Two days later, the press asked Coleman about the federal contribution in the case. The sheriff issued a gracious statement, noting that "the federal men have been of invaluable help to the local authorities throughout, and I'm deeply appreciative of the fine work they have done." Director Hoover responded in kind. "Sheriff Coleman has given the most magnificent cooperation we have received anywhere in the United States."[39]

This period of good feeling did not last long, at least on the part of the director.

After McCall confessed, the FBI took full and complete credit for identifying the suspect. Hoover's "pet" newspapermen systematically excluded any mention of Sheriff Coleman while building the legend of J. Edgar Hoover.[40]

Sheriff Coleman seems to have brushed off the slight, as if he expected it. His goal had been to catch the kidnapper, and he had succeeded.

Local newspapers, however, and many south Florida citizens recognized Coleman's immense contributions toward bringing the culprit to justice.[41] Within a week, he would receive numerous letters from the public as well as civic organizations disputing the FBI's version of events leading to McCall's arrest. Groups as diverse as the Knights of the Ku Klux Klan (headquartered in Jacksonville) and the League of Southern Women against Lynching wrote congratulatory letters rebuking Hoover for claiming that the G-men had solved the case, and congratulating Dade County's "high sheriff."[42]

While many American citizens never doubted Hoover's lies about how his agency had single-handedly cracked the Cash kidnapping, a substantial minority (particularly Floridians who had followed the case closely) knew the truth and unsuccessfully attempted to set the record straight.[43]

# Politics and Peccadillos

## Monday, June 6, 1938

Franklin Delano Roosevelt won the presidency in a landslide victory in 1932, sweeping into office in 1933. A progressive, he quickly began implementing programs designed to stem the Depression. For several years, until America's entrance into World War II, the economic situation maintained a steady, though not spectacular, improvement. By 1938 the Great Depression still persisted in many areas of the country, including Princeton, Florida, where most people eked by on the bare essentials.[1]

Married to his fifth cousin, the former Anna Eleanor Roosevelt, FDR hid several illicit sexual affairs that would have jettisoned his political career had the public known.[2]

In 1918, Eleanor discovered letters proving that her husband had been unfaithful. FDR's mother, however, demanded that she keep her son's long-term affair with Lucy Mercer secret. Although Eleanor was heartbroken, she agreed to a marriage of convenience for the sake of her husband's political career.[3]

Even though this affair nearly ruined Roosevelt's marriage, he continued to correspond with Mercer for years. Sometime in the late 1930s, while he was president, FDR and his former lover resumed their sexual dalliance. The Secret Service even had a code name for Mercer—"Mrs. Johnson." Mercer, now Mrs. Winthrop Rutherfurd, sat with FDR when he died in 1945 in Warm Springs, Georgia.[4]

It appears that Roosevelt may also have had an intense twenty-year affair with his private secretary, Marguerite "Missy" LeHand. In fact, he left half his estate to her when he died.[5]

J. Edgar Hoover made it a point to ferret out those secrets and others from the wall of silence erected to protect the president. To the director, this information meant job security. It may have been because of Hoover's knowledge of FDR's sexual affairs, or simply because the president supported a strong national police force, but the FBI invariably received special treatment from President Roosevelt. (In fact, FDR showed no compunction in using the director's spy network for his own political agenda. In one instance, he enlisted Hoover to gather illegal information on Louisiana governor Huey Long, whom Roosevelt viewed as a potential threat to his presidency. Even ordinary citizens, who posed no particular political threat to FDR, were not immune to presidential snooping.)[6]

In addition to the president's peccadillos, Hoover's spies quickly discovered that the First Lady also had a few secrets of her own. More radical in her political beliefs than even her husband, the bureau's dossier on Eleanor was one of the thickest in its archives. And this didn't include items that may have been in Hoover's personal files. (The director's loyal personal secretary destroyed those documents on the day he died.)[7]

Eleanor's close friendship with known communists certainly got Hoover's attention, but her alleged lesbian affairs may have been more damning had the public known. Many historians believe that the First Lady had a long-term sexual relationship with reporter Lorena Hickok. Correspondence found after Eleanor's death revealed intimate longings for her friend. "I want to put my arms around you & kiss you at the corner of your mouth," she wrote. In another letter, Eleanor said, "I can't kiss you, so I kiss your picture good night and good morning."[8]

The director would have been privy to these and other such indiscretions. (One biographer claims that Hoover owned nude photographs of a younger Eleanor that he allegedly obtained from actor W. C. Fields.)[9]

In fact, just the knowledge that Hoover had proof of certain secrets that could have ruined his political career certainly made FDR more likely to grant favors to Hoover.

In the first week of June 1938, as the Senate continued to debate the deficiency appropriations bill, FDR requested that Congress provide funds to the FBI specifically for the Skeegie Cash case. The Associated Press reported that "President Roosevelt has asked congress to appropriate $50,000 for the search for the kidnappers of James Bailey Cash, Jr. The five-year-old Cash boy was abducted from his Princeton, Fla. home [on] May 28. His father paid $10,000 ransom, but the child was never returned." The chief executive vigorously lobbied to have this appropriation inserted into the pending deficiency bill.[10]

FDR also requested a total of $308,000 for the FBI, nearly half of that to be set aside as an emergency fund for "whenever unexpected crime waves" occur. An AP story reported that "the FBI was caught short-handed recently when a large number of its agents were on furlough because funds for their expenses were lacking. . . . [Pro-Hoover] legislators said this seriously handicapped the agency when the Peter Levine and Jimmy Cash kidnappings increased its work. One Democratic politician claimed that the Budget Bureau was "starving" the FBI.[11]

Many journalists agreed. An *Omaha World Herald* columnist wrote: "To hamstring the FBI with inadequate support would be the worst sort of economy. It would be a mere pittance of thousands in an era of billion-dollar outlays. Crime never sleeps and there is no prospect that the arch-criminals would take a furlough just because G-men are doing so."

On the publicity front, Hoover, an inveterate reader of newspapers, must have been pleased with the way things were stacking up.[12]

Several months before, in an address to the Association of Life Insurance Presidents, the director attempted to convince the American public of his agency's importance. An AP story reported that Hoover announced "dividends to taxpayers of $7 for every dollar spent on the bureau. He said that during the last four years the cost of operating the FBI amounted to a little more than $18,000,000, while it was able to return in savings, in fines, and in recoveries of stolen goods a total of more than $135,000,000, or more than $116,000,000 above what it cost to operate the bureau."[13]

Those head-spinning numbers proved only a preface to what soon became a full-fledged diatribe by the diminutive director. He attacked shyster attorneys, the parole system, "venal" politicians, soft treatment of criminals, the court system, police agencies that refused to provide statistical data to the bureau, and other alleged weaknesses of the criminal justice system.[14]

Hoover informed his listeners that in the last four years, "of every 100 persons charged by the G-men and tried, 94 were convicted." Finally winding down, he claimed that there was a "criminal army" in America, consisting of

300,000 lawbreakers. Two hundred thousand murderers roamed America, he said. "American crime begins in the American home," Hoover concluded. "The only way it can be cured is by a re-establishment of respect for law by the heads of our homes."[15]

The statistics and opinions of Hoover had been published without question by nearly every major newspaper in America. Now, six months later, his hard work seemed to be paying off.[16]

In a unanimous vote, the committee approved FDR's request for $308,000 in the deficiency appropriations bill. The full Senate would vote on the FBI bailout later in the week.[17]

Even with the outpouring of public and political support for the FBI, events in south Florida left Hoover frustrated. The Cash case began to resemble a pit of quicksand, and the harder the agents floundered, the more they sank. Worse yet, the suspect pool was drying up.[18]

More than a hundred agents toiled on the ground, and another half-dozen lab technicians scoured every piece of evidence brought to them. Hoover, like most local residents, knew the kidnapper walked among them, but he couldn't seem to find the clue he needed to solve the puzzle.[19]

The abduction had virtually destroyed the Cash family and their close friends. Vera, who would later say that she "died" along with her son, lay in her bedroom in a near catatonic stupor. Bailey had given in to a spirit of bitterness and rage. Rumors even ran rampant through the Cash clan that a member of the family might have masterminded the crime.[20] But Hoover, with cold-blooded detachment, viewed the case as simply business, and as a way to impose his will upon those who opposed him. *If* he could solve it.

Hoover had not yet been informed, but Miami-Dade sheriff D. C. Coleman had once again brought Franklin Pierce McCall to headquarters. When Coleman explained to SAC Connelley his reasons for suspecting that the preacher's son might be involved in Skeegie's abduction, the agent agreed to subject McCall to another round of questioning.[21]

In the last week, G-men had interviewed hundreds of local residents. These included possible suspects and individuals affiliated with them in some way. Other interviews originated from tips, such as individuals who may have seen a strange car at the time Skeegie was abducted or the ransom picked up. Letters from psychics and assorted crackpots continued to arrive unabated.[22]

FBI agents in other parts of the country also got in on the act. On June

6, the Washington field office received a call from the Virginia State Police reporting that E. G. Wilson, representative of the Shell Oil Company in Roanoke, had been traveling on Route 58 near Hillsville, Virginia, when he came across a car containing several "suspicious" characters.

The automobile was a black 1935 Plymouth sedan, with District of Columbia license tags. Wilson wrote down the number and gave it to investigators. Inside the car, one man drove while two others held a child in the back seat. What made Wilson suspicious was the fact that the child had a bandana on his head and face and the men were "heavily suntanned," as if they'd been to Florida. When the men spotted Wilson showing an interest in them, he said, they turned off the main road onto a street "not connected with any main highway." This spurious tip wound up on the desk of an agent in the Richmond field office.[23]

Police in Grafton, West Virginia, also contacted the Washington field office concerning an informant who had hitched a ride with three men driving a blue and black Buick bearing Florida tags. The car allegedly contained pistols and a machine gun.

The understated FBI report noted that "the information does not seem particularly useful," but they referred it to an agent at the Huntington field office.[24]

J. C. O'Connor reported a lead to the Chicago field office. He claimed that he was driving back to Chicago from Athens, Georgia, when he stopped at the Blue Ribbon Café north of Nashville, Tennessee. There he met two men, one of whom asked him the distance from Cleveland to Detroit. The stranger stated that he planned to drive to Grand Rapids, Michigan, to see his brother who had been injured in a car accident. The man told O'Connor that he'd lived in Miami, Florida, for the last two years.

The affable diner drove a "1930 or 1931 Model A, four cylinder, Ford roadster, black in color with large 'air wheels' which O'Connor characterized as super-balloon tires."

O'Connor left the Blue Ribbon Café a few minutes before the talkative stranger and "expected for these two men to pass him on the road since he was driving only thirty-five to forty miles an hour, and when they failed to pass he became suspicious of their activities and thought possibly they might have some connection" to the Cash kidnapping.

The Grand Rapids field office handled this rather odd tip.[25]

On it went. No less than five patrons reported a "suspicious-looking" man and boy eating in an Elyria, Ohio, restaurant. A nurse having lunch at the Smorgasbord Restaurant in Washington, DC, described a man and boy who entered and asked directions to the National Zoological Park. She thought the boy looked like Skeegie Cash, so she called the Washington field office.[26]

Dozens of such reports were received each day and had to be checked out. The G-men dutifully investigated each tip, but none had any connection with the kidnapping of little Skeegie.

# "A Roll of Money as Big as My Head"

## Tuesday, June 7, 1938

FBI files on the Cash case contain dozens of newspaper clippings. Not only did the New York, Washington, and Los Angeles dailies come under the scrutiny of J. Edgar Hoover, but so did the weekly journals of rural county seats in the southern and midwestern hinterlands. Each day the director would examine these newspapers, and a single negative comment about him or his agency might bring an angry note to some unsuspecting editor. A pattern of criticism would incur the undying wrath of the vindictive lawman.[1]

The reports he read on Tuesday morning must have infuriated him. Many of the newspapers pulled no punches. An article in the *Charleston Daily Gazette* in West Virginia was typical. It noted that "for the first time since they began their investigation of the kidnapping [of Skeegie Cash] nine days ago . . . G-men had no known suspects in custody tonight. The two men longest held by the federal agents, M. F. Braxton, 55-year old Princeton carpenter, and his son Pedro, were released without comment late today after Braxton's wife threatened to take legal action against the FBI unless they were freed.[2]

"Because of the absence of any announcement from FBI headquarters in Miami, some observers were of the opinion the investigation . . . was back where it started a week ago and that all authorities were without any clues.

"The G-men neither confirmed nor denied the report, turning away all inquiries with the usual 'no comment.'"[3]

The press corps, as well as the citizens of Princeton, had thought Hoover's arrival signaled an imminent break. His picture graced nearly every newspaper in the nation, and a spirit of optimism radiated from south Florida.

Instead, the case had gradually sucked the director and his bureau into what must have seemed like a bottomless mire. Throughout it all, agents worked tirelessly.[4] The *Miami Herald* reported that a five-dollar bill from the ransom payoff had been recovered at a Dade County filling station, but that report quickly proved erroneous. Some harried gas station attendant had transposed the numbers and called the G-men. Reports of ransom bills surfaced in all areas of the country and kept agents busy tracking down false leads.[5]

Perhaps the most futile attempt to breathe new life into the floundering investigation involved another full-scale search of the Cape Sable region. Describing this new effort, the *Daily Gazette* reported: "Carrying food and other provisions sufficient to last them a week, four men left here today to undertake a thorough search of the desolate Cape Sable region south of here for a clue in the kidnapping nine days ago of James Bailey Cash, Jr."[6] No agency had sanctioned or authorized this expedition. It appears to have been a private mission undertaken by four individuals who had decided that little Skeegie might be buried in that marshy, inhospitable region of southwestern Florida. The bureau's initial interest in the area had come from the presence of Frampy Braxton's son at the Cape, but by now, the carpenter's family had been cleared. Still, readers in Pocatello and Poughkeepsie would assume it was a bureau operation, which made Hoover's men look desperate.[7]

Then, out of the blue, after having chased phantoms for a week, a lead came in that sounded promising. Rumor had it that the year before, a local teenager had attempted to extort $3,000 from a Homestead banker. Agents thought it likely that the youth may have reverted to his old ways and snatched Skeegie.[8]

Special agents N. D. Willis and M. E. Gurnea investigated.

Their report reads: "On either January 17 or January 18, 1937, on a Monday night, Mr. A. A. Paine, President of the First National Bank at Homestead, Florida, received an extortion note tied to a rock about 7:00 P.M. . . . This extortion note had been thrown into the house of Mr. Paine, and Mrs. Paine, and her daughter, name unrecalled, located this note and called the same to Paine's attention, who at that hour of the evening was in the First National Bank at Homestead.

"The note demanded that Paine get $3,000 and place same at 7:30 P.M. the same date, on the steps of the City Swimming Pool, Homestead, or his whole family would be destroyed."[9]

Paine's daughter saw a red car, possibly a Buick, racing away. It had yellow license plates, she said, unlike Florida's white plates.[10]

Willis and Gurnea spoke with Jack Hennessey of the Miami-Dade Sheriff's

Department. The veteran cop had investigated the case a year before and told agents that he and Paine felt it was a childish prank.[11] Hennessey said he had met with officials at the Redlands School. There the superintendent gathered specimens of handwriting from each student. As the samples were being collected, one girl, Irma Griffin, became nervous and asked to be excused. As soon as she left the room, she placed a call to James Gibbs, a student at Homestead High School.[12]

Griffin's handwriting appeared to match that on the extortion message. Further investigation revealed that she had a friend who owned a red Buick with yellow New York license plates, and witnesses reported Griffin, Gibbs, and two high school friends had been joyriding the night the rock was thrown.

Gibbs was taken to the sheriff's office and questioned, but denied everything.[13]

The next morning, Irma Griffin returned to school where she got a phone call from James Gibbs. He told her deputies had questioned him the previous night. According to the superintendent, Griffin dropped the phone, became hysterical, and left the school in an extremely agitated state.[14]

Hennessey arrested Gibbs, but under questioning he continued to deny that anyone in the car had thrown the note. With no confession and minimal evidence, he was again released.

Two days later, a repentant Gibbs walked into Paine's office and tearfully confessed. He said that Irma Griffin wrote the note and he'd thrown it at the front window of the house. Gibbs stated that it was "done as a joke because Mr. Paine had a daughter who was a teacher at the Redlands School."[15]

Paine accepted Gibbs's apology and refused to press charges. He told Hennessey he had been relieved of anxiety by the confession and he was certain it was just a childish stunt.

Gibbs later moved to Georgia, married, then returned to Homestead. Six months after the incident, Paine died of a heart attack.[16]

It was the type of event that occurred often in small towns. Paine knew that a conviction for a serious offense could jeopardize the futures of two young people, so he chose to show charity and mercy in dealing with the juveniles.

After hearing the tale, Willis and Gurnea realized they had once again struck out.[17]

Franklin Pierce McCall showed no particular emotion when Sheriff Coleman picked him up on the afternoon of June 5 and delivered him to FBI headquarters in downtown Miami. The truck driver likely felt confident as they drove north from Princeton. He'd hoodwinked the G-men three times. The vaunted G-men had gunned down John Dillinger and Pretty Boy Floyd, but they'd never matched wits with master criminal Franklin Pierce McCall.[18]

While D. C. Coleman spoke with Agent Connelley regarding his suspicions, McCall relaxed in a nearby room used for conducting interviews. Coleman shared his observation that McCall seemed to always be around when a clue popped up.[19] Low-ranking agents began the questioning. The G-men scribbled copious notes and periodically turned them over to the lead investigators. They made it a point not to confront the suspect on inconsistencies—that would come later.

For the first twenty-four hours, guards allowed McCall to eat, exercise, and even sleep. The questioning continued in a cordial, relaxed atmosphere.[20]

Finally, on the evening of June 7, SAC Connelley entered the room, joined by special agent H. B. Dill and director J. Edgar Hoover. Their stern faces may have rattled McCall. He certainly recognized that Hoover's presence would ratchet up the questioning.[21]

Suddenly, the interrogation became tense, the questions hard-edged.

McCall continued to deny any guilt in the abduction of Skeegie Cash. This time, however, the Feds were relentless, showing their suspect no mercy. There is no indication that the agents resorted to physical violence—they simply questioned each inconsistency and generalization, poking and prying until McCall could not keep his lies and distortions straight. Soon he found himself admitting things he never thought he would ever say aloud.[22]

According to FBI documents, the initial interview lasted from 7:30 p.m. until 9:00 p.m. After a fifteen-minute break they resumed the interrogation.[23] At 10:40, McCall finally cracked.

But even as he gave the first of three confessions, his primary objective was self-preservation. So McCall used the age-old strategy lawbreakers have employed since the beginning of time—he laid the blame for his crime on an innocent party.[24] The real culprit, he claimed, happened to be Asbury Cash.

The first confession read in part: "I, Franklin Pierce McCall, make the following statement . . . in order that the truth may be known as to what happened." According to the document, it was given "voluntarily, of my own free will, and without promise of any kind having been made to me."[25]

The suspect wrote: "About one week before James Bailey Cash, Jr. was kidnapped from his home . . . Asbury Cash, approached me as to whether or not I wanted to make a roll of money as big as my head. He told me we could make this money by kidnapping J. B. Cash, Jr., and holding him for $10,000.00. Thereafter, on either Tuesday, 8 or 9 a.m. and Friday, which would be May 24 and 27, 1938, Asbury Cash, when he left his house between 12:00 and 1:00 a.m., came over to my house on Tallahassee Road where I was staying alone, my wife being in Jacksonville. At this time we discussed fully the proposition of kidnapping J. B. Cash, Jr. He came to my house . . . [and] discussed fully the plan we would use in kidnapping the boy."[26]

In order to minimize his guilt, McCall attempted to portray himself as the unwitting dupe of a monster. He had fooled the G-men before and felt certain he could do it again.

He continued: "The arrangement was for me to write the notes and take the payoff and Asbury would kidnap the boy and take care of him during the time he was to be here. On Friday morning, May 27, 1938, at about 12 and 1 a.m., we prepared the ransom note in full on brown paper. I printed this note first on some scratch paper which I had in the house which was similar to the paper I used in writing my wife in Jacksonville. I thereafter copied the ransom note upon a piece of brown paper taken from a paper bag such as you get in a grocery." He then described the contents of the first ransom note page by page, as well as the second note he had to write when John Emanuel refused to deliver the first.[27]

The story he quickly concocted to enmesh Asbury Cash showed some imagination. "In accordance with our plan," he wrote, "at about 9:30 p.m., on Saturday night May 28, 1938 I walked into the grocery of J. B. Cash . . . Vera Cash . . . and a Mr. Singer. I asked them what time it was and I believe Vera said it was 9:30 and that it was time I was in bed. In accordance with the arrangement I had with [Asbury] Cash I then went outside at a point along the highway between the grocery and the house of Cash and pushed my hat on my head and lighted a cigarette. This was the signal we had arranged to make [Asbury] Cash, who was supposed to be somewhere in the rear of the Cash home, that Mr. and Mrs. Cash were in the grocery store and it was time he should go and get the child and take it away." McCall added, almost as an afterthought: "The money was to be divided half and half between us."[28]

In agonizingly precise details, McCall described his activities since the abduction of Skeegie. Asbury Cash had taken the child, and he [McCall] had gone to deliver the ransom demands. John Emanuel's refusal to deliver the note had thrown him into a panic, but he quickly recovered and wrote the second message, which he placed on Beatrice Cash's door handle. When they had to amend their plans, due to the presence of spies and the volunteer "posses," he'd written the third note and made sure it got into Bailey Cash's hands.[29] On the night of the payoff, he had signaled Bailey with the flashlight, collected the ransom money, and then hidden it along the fence in John Chambers's orange grove. Finally, he'd destroyed the shoebox and various notes before going home to get a little sleep. In all of that time, McCall said, he assumed that Asbury had Skeegie and was keeping him safe in some unspecified cabin.[30]

One inconsistency in this story glared out at the questioners. Why did McCall hide all the money except for $250 along the rock fence? If Asbury Cash was entitled to half the payoff, why did McCall not set aside $5,000 to pay to his cohort in crime?

For the time being, Connelley and Hoover ignored these discrepancies. Now that they knew who had snatched the Cash boy, they could go slow and make sure the confession covered all the bases. The G-men would continue their interrogation throughout the night and the following day.[31]

If Hoover ever questioned his G-men about their inability to peg the slick-talking truck driver as the kidnapper in the early stages of the investigation, he never mentioned it. Instead, he joined in the interrogation with a vigor rarely seen, except when criticizing his political opponents.[32]

# 12

# Found

## Wednesday, June 8, 1938

At midnight, in an upstairs room at FBI headquarters, Franklin Pierce McCall sat fidgeting like a rat in a cage. As SAC Connelley interrogated him, the noose slowly tightened around the suspect's neck. Special agent H. B. Dill assisted in the questioning.[1]

Director Hoover stood in the back of the room. The top G-man almost never participated in questioning suspects, and his presence indicated the importance of the case to the future of the bureau. McCall's demeanor differed greatly from former suspects Frampy Braxton, Willard Campbell, and Walter Fisher. Each had unshakable alibis and repeated the same story over and over. On the other hand, McCall's recollections of his whereabouts on the night of the abduction and the night the ransom was paid changed with each telling.[2]

The inconsistencies raised red flags to the experienced agents, who continued to press McCall until he broke.

If McCall thought that placing the blame for the kidnapping on Asbury Cash would alleviate his guilt, it showed his lack of legal knowledge. Like most southern states, Florida legislators had long ago enacted the felony murder rule. This law explicitly stated that if a death occurred during the commission of a felony, both offending parties were equally guilty, even though one had not actually "pulled the trigger."[3]

Either McCall didn't know the law, or he simply hoped that shifting the responsibility for Skeegie's abduction would make him appear less like a monster to the G-men.[4]

Richard Asbury Cash seems to have been a strange choice for the truck driver's imaginary partner in crime. Cash and his wife Beatrice had four boys, Ishmael, Ormond, Lloyd, and Oliver, and one daughter, Josephine. Asbury, as his friends and family called him, had a close relationship with his older brother, Bailey, and by all accounts, doted on his nephew Skeegie.[5]

The FBI had already interviewed Asbury. He informed the G-men that "he has always been of the opinion that Franklin Pierce McCall is a worthless young man, too shiftless to work steadily." Asbury stated that the previous month, the preacher's son had obtained twenty-seven crates of tomatoes from him on credit, then refused to pay for the produce. Asbury had threatened to have McCall arrested if he did not settle his debt.[6]

According to FBI files, the bitterness went deeper than a few crates of tomatoes. "Mr. Cash . . . state[d] that he [Asbury] is on unfriendly terms with the Hilliard family due to the fact that he, Cash, has been associated with various growers in the community in selling their produce; that the business nets him from three to four thousand dollars a year; that Joseph Hilliard, father in law of McCall, has attempted to take this business away from him several times, unsuccessfully; that Hilliard had indicated to him that if he could get half the business from Cash he could employ his son in law."[7]

But perhaps the most important reason McCall attempted to blame Asbury was that Preacher Boy had somehow learned a secret that Cash's brother had attempted to keep hidden. For several months, Asbury had been having an affair with an attorney's wife.[8]

FBI reports described Thelma Hill as "a very attractive woman." Her husband, C. Malcolm Hill, had practiced law in Tarpon Springs, Florida, until about two years before the kidnapping of Skeegie. Seven years earlier, he'd married "a very pretty brunette girl [Thelma] who came from the Keystone section of Hillsborough County, Florida, and that from that union there was one boy, who was described as being five or six years old."[9]

On hearing about Asbury's alleged infidelity, G-men quickly opened up an investigation, surmising that Hill might have snatched little Skeegie in retaliation for Asbury's affair with his wife. A witness suggested that Mrs. Hill liked to "party" and could be responsible for the abduction. On a fishing trip to Anclote, the witness claimed to have heard Thelma complaining about her own child who was crying. "If we get rid of this damn kid," she allegedly said, "we might be able to catch some damn fish."[10]

It turned out that the couple had recently moved to New Port Richey where Hill planned to open a law office. According to an informant, the local police chief was spending a lot of time at the lawyer's house when Hill was away.

It's interesting to note that many of the informants the G-men used in this investigation were "contract mail carriers."[11]

Looking for any sign that Skeegie might be hidden there, agents staked out the Hill home. Neighbors said they'd seen no one other than the couple and their son.

After several days of furtive snooping, G-men dropped their investigation into the Hill family.[12]

Agents called Asbury Cash back to FBI headquarters and interrogated him as a possible coconspirator. He admitted to a "brief" affair with Thelma Hill, but claimed he no longer had any contact with her.[13]

Like so many of the suspects, Asbury quickly eliminated himself from suspicion because numerous witnesses could account for nearly every minute of his life at the time of the kidnapping and the delivery of the ransom money.[14]

Journalists covering the case knew the FBI had a suspect, but up until now Hoover's men had refused to announce any details. The embarrassment the bureau had suffered in their public arrest, and equally public release, of the Braxton clan and Willard Campbell made them cautious.[15]

Hoover knew that reporters needed to fill a certain number of inches of copy each day. They would write about something, and another day of rehashing the G-men's ineffectiveness did Hoover's reputation no good. So at this time, the bureau issued a written statement naming their suspect.[16]

They released the following information around noon on June 8: "Franklin Pierce McCall was born in Jasper, Fla., on March 31, 1917. His parents were the late Franklin Pierce McCall and Lillie Taylor McCall. The latter [is] now residing at Jasper. McCall graduated from high school at Jasper in June, 1934 and came to Princeton, Fla. to live with his parents, where his brother is pastor of the Nazarene Church.

"Since that time he was employed by various farmers in driving trucks, grading, packing, and selling tomatoes.

"He married Claudine Evelyn Hilliard at Fort Lauderdale, Fla. on January 9, 1936. McCall was employed by the state highway [department] at Dania, Florida as a rodman.

"During the past two tomato seasons in the vicinity of Princeton, Fla. McCall and his wife have occupied an apartment in the house of James B.

Cash, the father of the victim. On or about 1938, McCall and his wife moved to the home of Red Lambert, located at the intersection of Tallahassee road and Sunset avenue, where the ransom payoff was effected."[17]

Finally, after several days of little news, newsmen had a bone to sink their teeth into. They quickly began digging into the suspect's background.[18]

McCall had confessed, albeit only to being a "minor" part of the abduction scheme. He dictated a statement laying the lion's share of guilt on Asbury Cash. Despite Preacher Boy's protestations of innocence, G-men ignored his self-serving drivel. They knew, with a certainty based on experience, that they had their man. Despite McCall's yarns to the contrary, Skeegie Cash would never come home alive. Their suspect, they knew, had murdered the innocent child.[19]

At about two thirty in the morning, on a blustery night, a team of G-men rolled into Princeton to search for the ransom money.

The search party contained a distinguished cast of lawmen: FBI director J. Edgar Hoover; assistant director (and Hoover's special friend) Clyde A. Tolson; inspector E. J. Connelley; Mr. Frank Baughman; and the hired gun from Texas, special agent S. K. McKee.[20]

They gathered at the Chambers estate.

McCall had informed the Feds that the payoff money could be located at "the west corner of the rock fence along Sunset Boulevard" at the Chambers lot. Despite these fairly specific directions, darkness confused and disoriented the veteran officers. After an hour and a half of scrambling around the yard with flashlights and lanterns, the searchers admitted defeat. They called headquarters in Miami and ordered that McCall be brought to the scene.[21]

While they waited, the lawmen went to Joseph Hilliard's home. From there, they proceeded "into the palmetto and pine growth directly north, across the road from the . . . Hilliard home." Their landmark was a "rock which . . . McCall [had] indicated the pieces of the shoebox in which the ransom money had been delivered" could be located. G-men had better luck here. McKee, and reportedly Hoover, found the cardboard debris with little difficulty. McKee bagged the material and marked it for later identification and use at the McCall trial.[22]

About an hour later, five agents arrived with the preacher's son. Accompanying McCall was R. G. Danner, J. A. Robey, E. McNamara, W. T. Morton, and agent in charge M. E. Gurnea. Hoover, Gurnea, and McKee led the handcuffed suspect "inside the stone wall on the Chambers' property, at

which time he [McCall] walked practically immediately to the spot where . . .
Gurnea picked up a package containing $2250.00 of the ransom money. At
a spot about four feet to the south of this point . . . the second package was
picked up by Inspector Connelley and contained $7500.00 of the ransom
money. Both of these packages were taken by Inspector E. J. Connelley and
sealed in an envelope." Connelley turned the package over to Robey, who returned to headquarters and placed the evidence in the safe.

After retrieving the money and shoebox remnants, McCall and the lawmen returned to Miami.[23]

Apparently, the suspect was given a break from his interrogation.

After this brief respite, the grilling of McCall resumed. The suspect still
insisted that Asbury Cash had masterminded the abduction.[24]

Interrogators hammered away at McCall throughout the morning. G-men
brought the preacher's son a transcript of an interview they'd had with him
earlier, on the night of June 7. The suspect went over the document carefully,
made several corrections, and signed each page.[25]

The bureau's report stated that "it is significant to note that at the time
this statement was presented to him for correction and signing, he was reclining on the bed in a rather nonchalant, careless and resting manner, and
did not seem particularly concerned as to the gravity of the situation confronting him. He went about signing and correction of this statement in a
careful manner. He read same thoroughly and made numerous corrections."[26]
Throughout the interrogation, McCall never expressed any remorse for his
part in the kidnapping and murder of the boy.

The big prize for the bureau would be locating Skeegie's remains. McCall,
understandably, seemed reluctant to give up this information. He continued
to lay the blame for Skeegie's abduction on Asbury Cash, pretending that
he'd only gotten hints from his coconspirator regarding the youth's resting
place. According to the official reports, Director Hoover took the lead in
grilling McCall about where the boy's body had been hidden.[27]

McCall finally admitted that he "thought" Skeegie was dead, and that
Asbury had killed him.

In this confession, McCall stated: "I did not believe [Asbury] would kill
the child. He was going to blindfold the child as soon as he got him out of
the house. I discussed this on Friday morning, but he did not say how he
was going to blindfold him. He could have put his hands over his eyes until
he got him outside. He said he was going to hide him. He said we will keep

him two or three days and turn him loose. He has as much or more sense than I have. My job was to write the notes and collect the money. He said he would take care of the part as to the keeping of the child."[28]

The FBI official report gives an excellent account of the afternoon and evening's maneuvering. "On the afternoon of June 8, 1938, Mr. J. Edgar Hoover had a lengthy talk with the subject, Franklin McCall, in an endeavor to have him point out to us the location where he believed the body of the boy might be at this time. Subsequently, on the afternoon of June 8, 1938, further conversation was had with McCall by Inspector E. J. Connelley and the Director, Mr. J. Edgar Hoover, and he [McCall] offered several suggestions to us as to where we should search for the body, and in this connection indicated that he believed along certain points which he indicated on the map we should have about twenty-five Agents move forward abreast of each other, covering the area on both sides of the road."[29]

The G-men knew that McCall was playing games with them but allowed him to continue in hopes that he might slip up or have a change of heart. An agent wrote "that his [McCall's] first contention as to this was that these would be places he would think that the body might be concealed, rather than stating they were places where the body was actually located. He first suggested that we make such a search, proceeding to the north from a house located back off the road in the northeast corner of Silver Palm Drive and Newton Road. He suggested that we cover that area on both sides of the road; that there was a house located here, back off the highway, partially concealed by Australian Pines. The next search he suggested he designated the starting point as the northeast corner of the McVickers property, which is located to the east and north of the intersection of Sunset Drive and Bay View Road. He suggested we proceed to the northeast from this point to the Glades; that thereafter we should search from that point on both sides of the Glades to the north and northwest until we reached a point about two squares south of Coconut Palm Road along the Glades just to the southeast of Princeton."[30]

The idea of having twenty-five Feds stumbling around in the Everglades at night likely appealed to McCall's perverse sense of humor. Connelley and his team may have looked down on the Crackers, "Negroes," and other denizens of that godforsaken area, but they had developed a healthy respect for the swamplands that formed the western boundary of the Redlands. As a result, Hoover hammered away at McCall to provide a more specific locale for finding Skeegie's remains. Finally, the suspect admitted that Asbury had told him the approximate location of the body.[31]

The bureau report continued: "McCall . . . agreed to take us to the points designated in order to point out the place he believed the body would be found, and thereafter at about 10:30 P.M. we proceeded from Miami with the prisoner . . . in an automobile, [with] Mr. J. Edgar Hoover, Inspector Connelley, SAC Gurnea, and Special Agent McKee being in the automobile with the prisoner. We were followed in a second car by Frank Baugham, of the Bureau; Assistant Director Mr. C. A. Tolson; Dr. Thomas O. Otto, of Miami, and Special Agents Dill and Jahn. In the third car were Special Agents Danner, Robey, Blackburn, and Special Agent in Charge Rutzen." The document conspicuously left out Sheriff Coleman, who also accompanied the search party.[32]

The report continued: "We proceeded from Miami on Highway 4-A to Allapattah Road [sic], then we proceeded to Coconut Palm Drive, then west on the latter road a short distance to the east of the Nazarene Church on Coconut Palm Drive, and then proceeded to the south along the Glades to the second rock road [a country road paved with a mixture of granite pebbles and tar] which comes into this place."[33]

"Franklin Pierce McCall stopped us at the first rock road and looked around to determine whether there were negro shacks at this point. He stated definitively, after a very brief observation that this was not the place; that it was the next road below. We then all proceeded to the next road below, which is identified as the Rock Road, leading to the east from Bay View Road along the Nelson Pear Grove. A short distance on the south of this road from the Glades were a number of negro cabins all built together. At the southwest corner of this road where it reaches the Glade[s] is a hammock of thick pine and palmetto, in the center of which is a prominent crooked pine tree with little in the way of green growth on same. This particular spot is more or less known as a landmark in designating the place in question."[34]

"When we arrived at this place McCall led us to these negro shacks and then, with us, very eagerly searched these various shacks, presumably for the location of the body." (It is interesting to conjecture whether McCall's choice of a hiding place constituted an attempt to throw suspicion on the area's African American community.)[35]

An FBI report stated that "we then started a search of the road to the north and south of this rock road, McCall proceeding to the north side of the road and indicating Agents should cover the south side of the road for a distance of possibly twenty-five yards. . . . [I]t is significant to note that if we had proceeded definitely along this route on the south it would have taken us to the place where this road joins the Glade where the body was located. We proceeded to the Glade at this time and did not find the body immediately."[36]

A dark wind rustled the palm fronds, causing even the lawmen to shiver. They knew the boy was close by—a faint smell of death somewhere in the distance drifted on the night breeze.

The report then gave Hoover credit for coercing McCall to reveal the location of the child's body. "Mr. J. Edgar Hoover then took Franklin Pierce McCall off to the side alone for a private conversation and asked him to definitely tell us where the body was in order that we could get same and get out of the area before we attracted attention of the public and particularly newspaper men. At this time Franklin Pierce McCall stated to Mr. J. Edgar Hoover, and it was overheard by Inspector E. J. Connelley, 'The body is in the center of that thicket at the corner there,' designating the place previously above described; in the center of which is the lone crooked pine tree."[37]

Again, FBI reports leave out what Hoover actually said. He emphatically informed McCall that daylight was approaching and journalists and citizens would soon follow the FBI trail into the Everglades. If local citizens learned that the boy's body had been found, Hoover informed McCall, the G-men would be powerless to stop them from lynching him.[38]

This certainly sent a chill up McCall's spine. He'd heard the talk around town. Bailey Cash's friends and neighbors wanted a quick and final justice, without shyster lawyers, appeals, and "bleeding hearts" in the press trying to create sympathy for the killer. Self-interest finally motivated McCall to give up the location of Skeegie's remains.[39]

The FBI report continued: "About the time he had made this statement Special Agent in Charge M. E. Gurnea, who had proceeded through the center of this thicket or hammock, called out that he had found the body. He was immediately joined at this spot where the body was located, [by Dr. Thomas O. Otto]. . . . The body was lying at the base of this one lone pine tree with the head facing approximately north and the feet to the south along the west side of this pine tree. The body was apparently fully clothed in the pajamas the child wore on the night he was kidnapped. The body was badly decomposed."[40]

Dr. Otto moved up to join Agent Gurnea and begin his preliminary examination. A graduate of the prestigious University of Virginia Medical School, Otto had the reputation of having seen more dead bodies than anyone in south Florida. He was a competent, highly experienced forensics expert and surgeon.[41]

Dr. Otto recorded his first impression of viewing the sad remains: "The body when first viewed . . . in a dense palmetto pine thicket approximately three-quarters of a mile south and east of Princeton revealed the following findings: The body appeared to be that of a child five to six years of age lying in a supine position with the lower extremities flexed at the groin and knees, the lower legs resting on a vine entanglement approximately six to eight inches above the ground level."[42]

This explains why the searchers, within a mile of their starting point, failed to find Skeegie's body. He'd been placed in a natural cavity created by a mass of vines and foliage growing above the ground. A member of the posse might have actually walked directly over the child without ever realizing what was beneath his feet.[43]

"The middle portion of the torso," Otto wrote, "rested close to a large pine tree, and the long bones of the upper extremities lying at the sides of the body with the right forearm crossing the lower half of the torso. The body was in an advanced state of decomposition, disintegration and the exposed skeletal portion completely disarticulation. The torso and upper portion of the lower extremities were enveloped in a single garment of a child's pajamas which were found to be completely buttoned along the front and across the back; however, ingestion of remaining integumental structures remaining chiefly on the left thigh and lower legs by myriads of maggots was in progress."[44]

In his trial testimony, the surgeon marveled at the number of larva at the disposal site. The "body," he testified, "[was in] an advanced, very advanced state of disintegration. It had been destroyed by maggots. They were there by the millions."[45]

"Under the completely denuded skull," he continued, "was found a large mass of matted short-lengthed distinctly blond hair with no remaining evidence of scalp. Upon coroner's release the above described body structure was carefully removed to a sheet and taken to the Turner Funeral Home at Homestead for further and more careful examination."[46] Twelve days earlier, Skeegie had been spirited away from his home and dumped beneath a lone, gnarled pine tree.

As Skeegie's remains were being removed, Connelley observed McCall. "At this time," the G-man wrote, "Franklin Pierce McCall observed the body intently for several minutes. He apparently showed no deep emotion, but did state: 'Why, that dirty son-of-a-bitch,' referring to Asbury Cash. [Otherwise] McCall showed no nervous emotional reaction."[47]

Carefully, almost tenderly, the G-men and Dr. Otto placed the pitiful corpse of James Bailey Cash Jr. into the trunk of one their automobiles.[48]

"Florida's Lindbergh case," with all the twists and turns of a dime novel, and the tragedy of a Shakespearean play, had finally been solved.

# 13

# Skeegie's Funeral

## Thursday, June 9, 1938

Dr. Otto accompanied the sad corpse of James Bailey Cash Jr. to Turner Funeral Home in Homestead. There he performed a meticulous autopsy on the remains.[1]

While the resulting postmortem analysis revealed little information about the cause of Skeegie's death, it added a great deal of horrifying detail. Dr. Otto later testified: "I first saw the body after entering this pine thicket where it had been designated, lying at a stump or the base of a large pine tree in a dense thicket of palmettoes, vines, [and] undergrowth."[2]

"The body when first seen was lying in a supine position, flat on its back, head turned to the left, arms at the side, fore arms lying across the body and the legs bent at the groin and the knees. It was in an advanced, very advanced state of disintegration. It had been destroyed by maggots. They were there by the million[s]. It had almost been completely eaten away by maggot action.

"The position of the body with the arms lying to the side and the hands across the body, lying on the back, would indicate that the body had been placed there after death. There was no evidence of locomotion or turning over."[3]

In other words, Skeegie never moved after being tossed into the palmetto thicket.[4]

Otto continued his testimony: "The head and neck of the body were virtually a skeleton. The torso was encased in a suit of pajamas, child's pajamas, and that was very nearly walking around with maggots. The legs were not completely destroyed. In fact, they were in a remarkably good state of preservation, but they were probably six or eight inches off the ground, hanging in vines."[5]

Otto described the condition of the bones, concluding that Skeegie's remains had been there for at least a week. Finally, he addressed the cause of death. "I then carefully examined the bones of the skull and face," he said, "with particular reference to the jaws and bones of the nose, the facial bones, for evidence of any blow or injury to the skull or to the face, [for] violence. I found none. I then carefully identified all the long bones, the arms, legs and all of the ribs, collar bones, all the bones of the skeleton, and found no evidence of any violent injury."

He concluded that "this body did not contain sufficient organs, viscera, and somatic structure to determine an exact cause of death."[6]

At around one thirty in the morning, two agents arrived at the door of the Cash residence. Entering, they informed Bailey and Vera that Skeegie's body had been located.[7]

An hour later, about forty members of the Cash family arrived at the funeral home in Homestead. Newspapers reported that Vera Cash, supported by a nurse, sobbed, while Bailey Cash appeared "dry-eyed but grief-stricken."[8]

Otto and funeral home proprietor George Turner refused to show Skeegie's skeletal remains to the grieving family. Instead, Turner and his staff carefully washed the white-and-rose-colored pajamas and presented them to Bailey Cash. For the first time, the distraught father broke down. The facade of emotional control he'd maintained for the past two weeks dissolved in a flood of tears as he lovingly clutched his son's death shroud.[9]

Wilson Cash made the arrangements for little Skeegie's burial. He announced to the press that the funeral would take place later that morning and that it would be private. Only members of the family and a few close, trusted friends would attend. He asked journalists to respect their wishes so that the family could mourn privately.[10]

By mid-morning the family gathered in front of the funeral home. A newspaper announced that "four white-clad cousins of the dead boy carried the tiny casket to the waiting hearse for the thirty-one mile trip to Graceland Memorial Park in Miami."[11]

Citizens of Princeton, who had stood firmly behind their friend throughout the ordeal, paid one last tribute to the boy and his family. As the funeral processional passed through the town, the citizens—black and white, male and female, and young or old—again showed their respect. "The entire populace," a source related, "stood with bared heads beside the road." Motorists along the route stopped until the motorcade had passed.[12]

The funeral proceeded north along Highway 1-A to the cemetery. As they walked to the grave, Vera, still accompanied by a nurse, leaned on Bailey's shoulder.[13]

A tent provided some protection from the sun. Reverend Dr. Everett S. Smith, of the First Christian Church of Miami, tried hard to console the heartbroken clan. After quoting from scripture, Smith said, "A full life depends not on the number of years we live, but on how they are lived."[14]

Enterprising reporters somehow infiltrated the gathering. An AP article described the scene: "A kind relative plucked a spray of pink and yellow rosebuds from the blanket of flowers on the coffin and pressed it into the mother's hand—a last lingering token to help her remember laughter that would be heard no more; to comfort her in the darkness of the room where there would no longer be a light burning as a beacon for a blond-headed boy."[15]

The *Brainerd Daily Dispatch* published a photograph of the Cash home on the front page. "Over this house today hung a pall of sorrow," the caption read. "It is the combination service station and home from which Jimmie (Skeegie) Cash was kidnaped. But today the boy's body was found. And no more will his boyish laughter, his scampering feet, resound within its walls."[16]

Bailey and Vera returned to a home filled with food provided by neighbors and friends. But a void existed in the rooms of the house, an empty hole that would never be filled. (They would never have another child, and would dedicate the rest of their lives to accumulating wealth. In the end, Bailey and Vera Cash would become more prosperous than they could ever have imagined.)[17]

In the next days, though, as they learned more about the cruel murder of their child, pain and sorrow would transform to a rage that never went away.

Asbury had not attended the funeral. In a final twist of the knife by Franklin Pierce McCall, the FBI was questioning him. The preacher's son had taken away his chance to grieve with his brother and sister-in-law.[18]

At least a few newspapers carried interviews with the lawman who fingered McCall. Local journalists, in particular, acknowledged Sheriff Coleman's part in solving the case.[19]

One editorial compared him to Sherlock Holmes.[20]

Thereafter, the sheriff became a forgotten man. Those in his department and many residents of Dade County knew the truth. However, J. Edgar Hoover's campaign to grab the glory for solving the Cash kidnapping proved an overwhelming success. Most Americans believed that brilliant detective work by the vaunted G-men had once again apprehended a brutal kidnapper and killer.[21]

Throughout the morning of June 9, Connelley, Hoover, and Agent Dill continued hammering away at their suspect. As night turned into morning, McCall's lingering resolve finally crumbled. He admitted that he'd known all along where Skeegie's body had been hidden, but said he had taken the lawmen to various other places in the vicinity so it would look as though the evidence did not point directly at him.[22]

With that hurdle crossed, agents bluffed McCall to finally obtain an admission that he'd acted alone. Connelley informed the suspect that the bureau owned a machine that could definitively tell if he was lying. From his reading, McCall knew about the polygraph. In stories published by pulp magazines of the time, the magical machine seemed to allow lawmen to read a suspect's mind.[23]

McCall, exhausted and beaten down, turned to Hoover and said: "Well, I guess you want to get a stenographer up here."[24]

The final confession of Franklin Pierce McCall revealed a self-absorbed, psychopathic personality. As such, he lacked any feelings of regret for taking a child's life; destroying the lives of Bailey, Vera, and the Cash family; and disgracing Claudine and his own family. His only remorse was that he'd been caught, and that he couldn't spend the ransom money.

An edited version of the confession read:

I, Franklin Pierce McCall of Princeton, Florida, make the following statement in the presence of Mr. J. Edgar Hoover, Director, Federal Bureau of Investigation; [and] E. J. Connelley, Inspector; of my own free will without promise or threat of any kind. I wish to make the statement because I wish to tell the truth of things which have occurred in the recent past.

For the past—well, ever since we were married—we've done without things and my wife did without things which she should have had. I thought of practically everything to get money. I guess I was desperate. I don't know. I tried to get a job until about two weeks before the kidnapping took place. The idea popped into my mind to kidnap somebody, and then I did not know who. I did not have a car. I knew it would have to be some one [*sic*] in Princeton, but I did not know who had the most money. I did know Bailey Cash, Charles Chambers, and Charles F. Eichenberger were, what I thought, in the position to arrange that much money, but Eichenberger's boy [Charles Jr.] was away at school so that was out. Charles Chambers' boy [Charles Jr.] is always with his mother, so all that was left was Bailey Cash's son.

About a week after I made up my mind, I wrote the first ransom note in my house. I told no one of my plan. I wrote the first note on a scratch pad and later copied it on a piece of paper that I cut from a brown paper bag. I left the note in the pocket of a gray coat hanging in my home. On the night of May 28th, I went to James Bailey Cash's store and asked what time it was. Mrs. Cash said it was 9:30. I turned and walked behind the store and up to the rear door [of the Cash home]. The screen of this door was locked and I cut it with my knife.

I had two large handkerchiefs in my left hand. I picked up Skeegie with my right arm and placed the handkerchiefs over his mouth, eyes, and nose. I didn't know I had his nose covered. I went out the back door and through the underbrush to my home. I thought he was asleep. He never made any movement at all. Going through the woods it took me fifteen to twenty minutes to get home. I went in the back door. The house was dark and I knew Skeegie could not recognize me in the dark and I tried to wake him up. I shook him and called his name but he didn't answer. I knew then that he was unconscious and I heard that people who had been strangled could be restored by artificial respiration. I tried this. I tried a damp cloth, but I knew he was dead because I couldn't wake him up. . . . I didn't know what to do. I picked him up and went out the back door running some and walking fast when I couldn't run, back toward the thick clump of bushes where he was later found. I forced my way through the bushes to the old crooked pine and placed him there, then ran back home, which was about a half a mile.

I got the note [I'd written] and went to John Emanuel's house. I talked in a low voice and told him I had placed a note on his front steps, for him to deliver it and get five dollars, then went home. I knew Emanuel did not have any way to ride and I waited to hear him walking toward Princeton. He would have to walk past my house to get there. When he did not go by, I tore a strip of paper from some meat in the ice box and wrote the second note, which I left at the home of Asbury Cash (only a few hundred feet from McCall's home).[25]

McCall had displayed more than a little animal cunning in his activities after the kidnapping, blending in among his neighbors and joining the searchers on their trip to John Emanuel's residence. Even when he had to modify his plan and deliver a third note, he had been skillful enough to fool the FBI.[26]

His account of the ransom money drop continued in the same unemotional, matter-of-fact tone. He stated:

> In a few minutes a car came south on the Tallahassee Road and almost passed the spot where I was in the grove which was about three or four trees north and three or four trees west of the grove. The car almost passed before I recognized the fact that it was Bailey Cash's car. I flashed the flashlight twice and he stopped the car as quickly, I believe, as he could, and got out. I think he left the motor running, I know he left the lights on, walked around the front of the car and tossed the money that was in a shoebox somewhere across to the telephone pole that is in the corner of John Campbell's property. I waited until he got back in his car and proceeded south on the Tallahassee road. I then walked directly to where the shoe box was. [I] picked it up, went back into the grove and took almost the same route I took coming into the grove. I opened the box while in the grove and took $250.00 from the stack of money, and in doing this the band around this $250.00 was broken and I placed the bills loosely in my pocket. I kept the shoe box and newspaper around it and came back in to Sunset Drive almost directly in front of Mr. John Campbell's house. At the corner of the rock fence I threw the money over the fence and I thought up into the corner. I carried the shoe box and the newspapers around in back down to Mr. Hilliard's. I tore the box in several pieces. I don't remember how many, and placed the pieces under a rock in the Palmetto Grove about thirty yards in front of Mr. Hilliard's home on the north side of Sunset Drive. I took the newspaper the money had been wrapped in and placed it in the toilet in Mr. Hilliard's and placed some other papers down on top of it.[27]

The only person McCall showed any concern for was his wife, Claudine. The preacher's son steadfastly denied her involvement in, or knowledge of, the crime. "I told no one of my plans," he stated emphatically. At another time he admitted: "I did not plan on having my wife go to Jacksonville while I did this, but after she was gone I decided this would be a good opportunity to do the kidnapping."[28]

After daylight on June 9, the G-men brought Claudine and her mother to headquarters. (They had hurriedly returned to Princeton after hearing that McCall was being questioned.) The FBI questioned them for six hours before releasing the unfortunate women. Newshounds took several photos of the two as they left, surrounded by stone-faced G-men.[29]

No record has been found regarding what the women said or did at the FBI headquarters. However, on June 20, after McCall's conviction and death sentence, Hoover's shill Walter Winchell wrote an article describing several aspects of the case.[30]

For some reason, Hoover had developed an irrational hatred of Claudine McCall, as the Winchell article demonstrates. She had nothing to do with the crime, but the journalist went out of his way to besmirch her reputation. Winchell wrote: "It isn't true, as reported, that McCall's bride refused to see him, or that she is 'thru with him.' . . . When McCall asked if he could see her G-men agreed. . . . They embraced long and affectionately. . . . McCall told G-men: 'My wife is hungry, ain't slept or eaten for two days.' . . . So Hoover brought in enough food and soft drinks to fill six people. . . . To everyone's amazement the McCalls devoured it all, indifferent to onlookers and the crime he committed."[31] The reason for Hoover's incomprehensible contempt for Claudine McCall remains a matter of conjecture. Perhaps she had the temerity to question his tactics or express her doubts as to the guilt of her husband. Or maybe the answer lay deeper, in some unexplained flaw in Hoover's own troubled psyche.

On the other hand, Hoover sympathized with Bailey's brother, Asbury. Winchell wrote: "G-men say that pitiful was Asbury Cash, a kin of the child, put on the spot by McCall. . . . McCall accused Asbury of plotting the snatch. . . . McCall could look Hoover straight in the eye and say: 'So help me God, Mr. Hoover, I'm innocent.' . . . But, ironically, the innocent Asbury Cash couldn't look anyone in the eye when he denied any part of it. . . . 'It was awful,' said a G-man, 'We had to put a guilty man in the [electric] chair and at the same time save an innocent man from being put in it. McCall is the lowest, rottenest, meanest person we ever encountered. Not only did he kill a child, but he did all he could to involve innocent people in the crime."[32]

McCall's decision to name Asbury Cash as a coconspirator had nothing to do with business rivalries or an attempt to heap more tragedy on the beleaguered Cash family. The reason for McCall's choice was simplicity itself, and threefold. First, McCall knew that Asbury had gone home and likely retired to bed while his wife and daughter went to the movies in Homestead. As a result, he thought Bailey Cash's brother would have no alibi. The second reason involved the grudge he held against Asbury. And finally, he may have assumed that telling the G-men about Asbury's affair would lead to an intense investigation by the Feds, and might even break up the younger Cash brother's marriage.[33]

After McCall's final confession, Hoover called reporters into the FBI offices for a press conference. In his usual authoritarian manner, the director informed the group that no one would be allowed to leave the room until he had completed his statement. Then, while reporters scribbled on their notepads, Hoover read an abbreviated version of the confession.[34]

The game had played out exactly as he wished. The director knew he would become a national hero and that his name would soon be praised throughout the land. Now Senator McKellar and his cohorts would be forced to give him the funding he needed to expand his empire. And that thought likely brought him more pure joy than having solved the murder of an innocent child.[35]

J. Edgar Hoover's picture did indeed grace the front pages of nearly every newspaper in America. The successful conclusion of the case brought about the publicity goldmine the bureau so desperately needed. It also brought desperately needed funding when Congress passed FDR's appropriations bill and handed the director a check for $308,000. Hoover immediately reopened his shuttered offices.[36]

While all Americans seemed happy the kidnapper had been caught, a few questioned the appropriateness of federal involvement in kidnapping cases. On June 9, the *Charlotte News* published an editorial titled "Laws and Parents."[37]

It read:

The G-men seemed to have cracked the Cash kidnapping case wide open in record time. But the little boy, Skeegie, is dead. Perhaps he would have been dead, in any case, whatever. No one can say with any certainty. But the suspicion still will persist in many minds that he might have been saved had it not been for the Lindbergh law and similar laws passed by the states—laws imposing the death penalty for kidnapping—and the relentless determination of the G-men to enter the case regardless of the wishes of the parents. Certainly, when one remembers the Mattson case and the Levine case, it begins to look as though murder has got to be the usual accompaniment of kidnapping, and it used not to be so.

The question here is not one easy to decide. So far as the law goes, the G-men have been perhaps bound to enter these cases regardless of what the parents wanted, to attempt to close on the criminal even though it might mean death for the child. And certainly, a kidnapper would seem to deserve the death penalty if anybody ever did. More than that, it is possible to argue that the practice must somehow be broken up, and that in the long run ruthless methods are best—that for one life sacrificed many others will be saved. But it is a hard doctrine, truly, if you imagine the child as your own, and one which must afford small comfort to the Mattsons, the Levines, and the Cashes.[38]

After his final confession, agents took McCall upstairs to the thirteenth floor—the cellblock—and allowed him to bathe and shave. (Walter Winchell also claimed they had to "de-louse" him.) They distributed photos of the confessed kidnapper dressed in a gray suit, open-necked white shirt, and reclining on his cot reading the Bible. His belt and shoestrings had been removed, as a matter of course, to prevent any attempt at suicide.[39]

In Princeton, coroner S. L. Kendrick impaneled an inquest jury of six men to determine the cause of Skeegie Cash's death. The jurors had rushed to Turner Funeral Home before the family arrived in order to examine the bones and clothing recovered at the disposal site. Circuit judge Arthur Gomez would soon call a special grand jury to consider the case. Despite FBI involvement, no federal laws had been broken, and the state of Florida would try the preacher's son. Since both charges of kidnapping for ransom and first-degree murder carried the death penalty in the Sunshine State, it hardly mattered which choice state's attorney George A. Worley made.[40]

On the day McCall confessed, reporters located his mother, Lillie, at the home of her daughter in St. Augustine. "I never dreamed of such a thing,"

Mrs. McCall said. "The boy has been in no trouble before in his life. His Daddy was a preacher and as good a man as ever lived on this earth."[41]

Reporters said she appeared dazed. She informed journalists that she learned of the arrest while listening to a news broadcast on the radio.[42]

Lillie McCall would stand by her son to the bitter end, hiring the best attorney possible, visiting him in prison, and attempting to save his soul by suggesting he study the Bible. In one of the most poignant acts of the whole case, McCall's mother would even attempt to sway the heart of Vera Cash, begging the heartbroken mother to intercede for her son.[43]

## 14

# "The Most Cold-Blooded Thing
# I Ever Heard Of"

### Five Days Later—June 14, 1938

The wheels of the Dade County justice system began turning almost as soon as J. Edgar Hoover announced the FBI had secured a confession. S. L. Kendrick, serving as both coroner and Homestead's justice of the peace, impaneled a six-man jury for the coroner's inquest. They assembled in a room of the Turner Funeral Home, right down the hall from where Bailey and Vera Cash had earlier grieved for their lost child. State's attorney George A. Worley demanded swift justice, and he resolved to bring Franklin McCall to trial as quickly as possible.[1]

The coroner's inquest is a relic from antiquity that wormed its way into American jurisprudence via the English common law. Many modern legal scholars believe this judicial tradition is unnecessary, but the Homestead coroner cared little for ancient history or the opinions of law professors. Justice Kendrick charged his jury with hearing testimony regarding the Cash abduction and murder to decide if the facts warranted taking the case to trial.[2]

Several newspapers claimed that the six men would have difficulty returning a formal verdict since the exact cause of death was inconclusive. In fact, finding out how Skeegie Cash expired was not really necessary. No federal law had been broken, so the state would try the suspect. As noted, Florida law allowed the death penalty for both murder and kidnapping for ransom (the so-called Florida Lindbergh law), and George Worley intended to see the preacher's son die in "Old Sparky," come what may. After a quick consultation with Dr. Otto, the prosecuting attorney decided to sidestep the homicide indictment and charge McCall with kidnapping for ransom.[3]

The inquest required that jurors observe certain formalities. Kendrick took the panel to visit the location where McCall had dumped the body. As the breeze fitfully swished among the trees and palmetto fronds, members of the jury caught a lingering odor of decomposed flesh.[4]

Worley then drove the group to the Cash home where the crime occurred. Journalists at the scene reported that "fifty spectators and six jurors heard unemotional, monosyllabic testimony from Cash senior that his only child, [aged] 5, was dead and [heard] the G-Men's account of McCall's kidnapping confession."[5]

As if Bailey Cash had not been through enough, he was forced to publicly recount how he had come home to find his son gone, how he'd received three ransom notes, and how he'd delivered the $10,000 to the kidnapper. SAC Connelley followed, describing how Franklin Pierce McCall had led them to the dumpsite and confessed to taking the child.[6]

The panel then retired to an undisclosed location, and in less than fifteen minutes returned with the verdict: "We, the jury find that James Bailey Cash Jr. came to death at the hands of Franklin Pierce McCall." Kendrick notified the prosecutor, and Worley set plans in motion for a quick trial.[7]

The press had a hard time reading the mood of the small crowd still milling around downtown Princeton. Many seemed as drained of emotion as the Cash family. Some reporters described the mob as "more sorrowful than vengeant [vengeful]." Others noted that whispered hints of a "possible lynch party" still circulated through the crowd. The FBI took no chances with McCall. They sequestered him in a "sunless" room on the thirtieth floor of the Dade County Jail.[8]

Determined to leave no stone unturned and no victim of the tragedy to their private grief, newshounds cornered McCall's father-in-law. Joseph Hilliard expressed his desire to see justice done. In addition, he commented that Claudine "never expects to see him [McCall] again and she wishes nothing more to do with him." (Hilliard's daughter, however, loved the scoundrel, and would later do everything in her power to keep him from receiving the death penalty.)[9]

For a legal proceeding, the case was progressing at white-hot speed.

State's attorney Worley received the grand jury indictment, dated June 14, 1938, and set the initial phase of the trial for the following day. Circuit court judge H. F. Atkinson would preside over the case. Atkinson had moved to Miami from Titusville, Florida, in 1896. He quickly established a reputation as one of the finest legal minds in the area, though due to his extreme sensitivity to harsh sunlight, many residents of south Florida considered the judge something of an eccentric. None doubted his integrity.[10]

Worley hit his first snag when he attempted to locate a defense attorney who would agree to represent the accused kidnapper. Several refused to accept the case, citing "extreme prejudice against the defendant." Their decision was almost certainly based more on economics than personal aversion to McCall. Dade County residents, almost to a man, considered the defendant a monster, and anyone representing him might lose present or potential clients. With that in mind, they refused to take the case. Jack Kehoe, a veteran Dade County attorney, finally agreed to defend the former truck driver.[11]

Kehoe faced a number of seemingly insurmountable problems. It would be almost impossible to question McCall's guilt since he'd admitted the crime and led lawmen to both the body and the ransom money. The biggest obstacle Kehoe faced, however, involved the accused killer's insistence on instructing the experienced attorney on how he wanted his case tried.[12]

McCall apparently never quite grasped the idea that the state didn't need to prove he intentionally killed his victim to send him to the electric chair. (An admission of kidnapping for ransom would also put him on death row.) Instead, he demanded that Kehoe mold his defense solely to show that the child's death had been an accident.[13]

On the afternoon of June 14, Franklin McCall, Jack Kehoe, and G. A. Worley stood before Judge Atkinson. McCall surprised many reporters by entering a plea of guilty on the charge of kidnapping for ransom. The judge set the evidentiary hearing to begin on the following day.[14]

The presentation of proof began the next morning at exactly 9:30 A.M., exactly nineteen days after the crime occurred. State's attorney Worley called the long-suffering father as his first witness. Grimly, Cash yet again recounted the events surrounding the abduction of his child and his role in paying the ransom. Near the end of Bailey's testimony, George Worley handed him the pink-and white-striped pajamas, and asked if they were the nightclothes Skeegie had been wearing the evening of the kidnapping. "Yes, sir," he muttered, then turned away.[15]

The next witness brought a note of comic relief, though unintended. Worley called Mrs. Cash to the stand, expecting to examine Vera. The woman who took the stand, however, was Beatrice Cash. After a bumbling attempt to question her about the kidnapping, Worley realized his mistake. With tongue in cheek, Judge Atkinson pointed out the obvious—the witness was not Vera Cash. "I know she is not," a flustered district attorney replied, "It was just a mistake made somewhere. I don't know where. The [list of witnesses] shows that a subpoena had been issued for Mrs. J. B. Cash at Princeton, and somehow or another, somewhere, the praecipe [order to appear] was written for Mrs. W. P. [Cash]."[16]

John Emanuel took the stand next and recounted the events of the night when McCall demanded that he deliver the ransom note to Bailey Cash. Kehoe finally roused himself, asking two questions of cross-examination. Neither seemed particularly important, but at least the defense attorney seemed to be trying to defend his client's interests.[17]

FBI SAC Earl J. Connelley followed Emanuel. His direct testimony lasted longer than any other witness. Carefully avoiding any mention of Sheriff D. C. Coleman's contribution to the capture of the preacher's son, the G-man delineated the pertinent details involving the interrogation of Franklin McCall. Worley led Connelley through the three days of interrogation, through McCall's various stories, and finally to the discovery of the ransom money. For the final nail in McCall's coffin, the FBI man related in detail the midnight excursion to the edge of the Everglades and the discovery of Skeegie's body.[18]

The prosecutor asked Connelley whether physical brutality or psychological intimidation had been used in obtaining the confession. Connelley vehemently denied the allegation. Since convicted criminals often claimed on appeal that their confession had been obtained through coercion, having a witness deny this charge in open court often saved convictions on appeal.[19]

One after another, Hoover's agents followed: Samuel McKee, with his Texas twang; Walter G. Blackburn; Harold P. Turner; Norman D. Wills; and Richard G. Danner all corroborated Connelley's testimony. Kehoe, hamstrung by the facts of the case and by his client's wishes, had no cross-examination for any of the Feds.[20]

Dr. Thomas Otto followed the agents to the stand. Using the clinical language of physicians, he described the condition of Skeegie's body after it had lain in the Florida rain and heat for ten days. Worley established that Otto had been on site when McCall led agents to the child's body, that the physician had given the remains a cursory examination in the dark palmetto patch, and that he had performed a complete autopsy at Turner's Funeral Home. The physician mentioned that he and Mr. Turner had removed the pink-and-white pajamas from the corpse. The district attorney then recalled two G-men to establish chain of custody for the garment.[21]

Finally, Vera Cash, pale and tearful, testified that her child had worn the pink-and-white garment on the night of the abduction. Mercifully, the prosecutor kept the examination short. Defense attorney Kehoe, as usual, had no questions, and Judge Atkinson dismissed the court for a lunch break.[22]

When the trial reconvened, Kehoe began his direct examination of Franklin Pierce McCall. After establishing the defendant's identity, his attorney asked: "The indictment that was read to you in this court yesterday, charging you with the offense of kidnapping—to that indictment you entered your plea of guilty; is that correct?"[23]

"Yes, sir," McCall answered.

Kehoe then walked the preacher's son through the crime from beginning to end. McCall still claimed that little Skeegie's death had resulted from accidental suffocation. "As I got out the back door," he told the court, "I carried him [James Bailey Cash Jr.] in both arms and held the handkerchiefs over his mouth—I guess over his nose. Then I didn't know it. I walked across Coconut Palm Drive and in through the woods to my house. It was dark there and I came in through the back door into the bedroom, and placed Skeegie on the bed and shook him to wake him up; called his name and he didn't answer. I tried—then I knew something was the matter with him. I knew he was unconscious. I tried artificial respiration. I had heard of people that was unconscious could be brought back to consciousness that way. I tried this, and I run to the Frigidaire [refrigerator], and got some cold water that was there, with a towel, and bathed his face and hands with cold water, and he still didn't wake up, and I knew he was dead."[24]

After McCall testified about writing the ransom note and retrieving the money, Kehoe inquired: "During the time that you were in the Federal Bureau of Investigation's headquarters how were you treated by the agents there?"[25]

"They treated me very nice," McCall answered. "Only on two occasions were there any hints at all of any violence mentioned. At other times they were very, very nice."

"Did the two hints of violence you refer to, did they influence you or anywhere bear upon you making this statement?"

"None whatever," McCall said.[26]

George Worley took his turn, pressing McCall regarding the kidnapped child's cause of death. The defendant steadfastly maintained that he had not tried to end Skeegie's life, but that the child had suffocated by accident. The district attorney knew that the defendant had already condemned himself by his own testimony, so he didn't press the issue. His cross-examination lasted less than twenty minutes.[27]

Defense attorney Kehoe delivered a brief summary of his reasons for taking the case and emphasized that he "followed his [McCall's] wishes in presenting every fact he has for the Court's consideration." (This certainly explains the strange tactics the defense employed, which seemed designed to convict the kidnapper rather than lessen his criminal culpability.) One of McCall's uncles, Rev. A. C. McCall, a minister from Manatee County, sat at the defense table throughout the trial. The defendant's uncle made a brief, but impassioned plea, for mercy.[28]

Kehoe also introduced C. A. Avriett [called "Avery" in the court documents], a Jasper, Florida, attorney hired by McCall's wife and mother. Avriett requested that Judge Atkinson put off sentencing until the next day, and the Dade County jurist agreed. With that completed, the court was dismissed.[29]

The trial resumed the following day at 10:00 A.M. According to news accounts "two hundred or more persons, half of them women, thronged the corridors outside the courtroom, which holds only 150. Officials herded them into line for admittance singly. Inside, two policemen searched each man and two matrons 'frisked' the women, even removing their hats and peering into their handbags." Two armed, uniformed police officers sat on either side of Judge Atkinson, with "a commanding view of the whole room." As if that weren't enough of a circus atmosphere, journalists wrote that "State Attorney Geo. A. Worley, suffering from boils, was accompanied by a nurse."[30]

Reverend McCall, one of the defendant's brothers, and Jack Kehoe sat at the defense table with Franklin. In the long-standing tradition of American criminal trials, as the circuit court judge began reading the sentence, Franklin Pierce McCall and Jack Kehoe stood.[31]

Declaring the crime "the most cold-blooded thing I ever heard of," Judge H. F. Atkinson found McCall guilty of kidnapping for ransom and sentenced him to death. The jurist directed Sheriff Coleman to transport the preacher's son to the state prison at Raiford. Governor Fred P. Cone would set the date for the execution.[32]

"May God have mercy on your soul," Atkinson concluded. As newsmen noted: "The 21-year old prisoner stood erect with clenched fists resting on the desk and heard his fate without a word or change of expression."[33]

Reporters discovered that on the previous evening Harry Wright, his friend from Princeton, had come to visit his poker-playing buddy. On interviewing Wright, he stated that McCall seemed to be at peace with the situation. The preacher's son told Wright that he preferred death to life in prison. When asked if he thought he had been fairly treated by the lawmen and judiciary, McCall said: "I guess I got what was coming to me."[34]

McCall's attitude, however, would soon change.

The following day Sheriff Coleman drove McCall to the state prison at Raiford. The trip from Miami would require a minimum of six hours by automobile. After their arrival, prison superintendent Leonard P. Chapman reported that "[McCall] appeared stunned. I think he hardly realized what had happened to him, and that his act had brought him here so quickly. He made no requests and he did what we asked automatically." He was housed on death row, where fourteen other condemned men awaited their date with "Old Sparky." (In the 1930s, the electric chair actually had several nicknames, including "Old Smoky," "Old Sparky," and "Flat Top.")[35]

Meanwhile, McCall's mother, Lillie, and wife, Claudine, shifted into high gear in their efforts to save him. Using their meager funds, they'd hired Avriett, who would make up for Kehoe's lackluster defense by fighting to the bitter end to save the convicted kidnapper.[36]

The next hurdle for prosecutors to cross was the state pardon board, which could recommend clemency. Worley knew the committee didn't need to find extenuating circumstances and often operated on whim and their own beliefs and opinions.

The pardon board had been established by the 1885 state constitution, after the former Confederates had "redeemed" the state from carpetbagger rule. The legislature, realizing that law could be as inflexible as iron, attempted to create an agency that allowed Florida officials to act with equity and justice. Their noble dream failed in its practical application. The governor and his cabinet composed the clemency committee, and often they presided over more than a hundred pardon applications in one day. "This," according to journalists, "resulted in hurried or capricious release procedures by overburdened officials."[37]

On the day the board was to hear McCall's plea for clemency, the condemned man's mother met Vera Cash in Governor Cone's Tallahassee office, with newsmen futilely straining to hear what they said.[38]

The two brokenhearted women sobbed and whispered. After the meeting, Lillie McCall told reporters: "[I asked Vera Cash to] please ask the pardon board to grant Franklin commutation of his death sentence."[39]

Skeegie's mother, however, could not bring herself to forgive the monster that had taken her only child. "Your son not only killed my son," she said, "but he has figuratively killed my husband and myself. No penalty imposed on him can expiate the crime, or relieve us of our misery and grief." Bailey Cash concurred. He informed the governor and cabinet that "anything less than the maximum penalty will be unsatisfactory for me and my family."[40]

C. A. Avriett eloquently presented the plea for McCall's family. But with the grieving mother and father's words still ringing in their ears, the pardon board confirmed the sentence of death.

On July 8, 1938, Governor Fred P. Cone signed the death warrant for the preacher's son.[41]

The decision found almost universal approval. An editorial in the *Zanesville Times Recorder* provides a typical example. "It is gratifying to note that the Florida state pardon board has refused clemency to Franklin Pierce McCall, kidnap-slayer of little Jimmie Cash. . . . In Florida kidnapping is punishable by death even if the victim is not slain. McCall's life is doubly forfeited. Like all murderers he holds life cheaply until his own life is at stake, then life to him becomes something to be cherished. . . . To grant clemency to this kidnap-slayer would be to make a mockery of justice and to invite other criminals to perpetuate like crimes."[42]

On July 11, McCall's attorney filed a writ of error with the Dade County Circuit Court. This automatically halted the execution of Franklin McCall until all avenues of appeal had been exhausted.[43]

C. A. Avriett, the Jasper attorney, proved an inspired choice to lead the campaign to save Franklin McCall. He had earlier defended a client considered more heinous than McCall. George Courson, the acting captain of the Sunshine Work Camp (near Jacksonville), somewhat resembled the northern journalist's caricature of the typical southern lawman—big-bellied, swaggering, hard drinking, and violent.[44]

The state tried and convicted Courson of torturing a prisoner to death in a sweatbox. The case became a cause célèbre in the North. Hollywood made a movie depicting the heroic prisoner abused by sadistic guards, and news journals rushed exposés of the Florida prison system into print. As a result, the state undertook a complete overhaul of work camp operations. Despite the revulsion the incident created, Avriett managed to get Courson, who could have received a death sentence, off with a virtual slap on the wrist. In fact, the convicted prison captain served no actual jail time.[45]

In McCall's case, the Jasper attorney launched a two-pronged legal attack. State law provided that a person convicted of kidnapping for ransom "shall be punished by death, unless a majority of the jury shall recommend the defendant to the mercy of the court." As a result, McCall's attorney contended, the defendant's rights had been violated when a nonjury tribunal in Dade County sentenced him to death. In other words, Avriett maintained, the death penalty could only be imposed in a trial by a jury of his peers.[46]

Avriett also asserted that McCall's trial attorney had been incompetent. This is often the final refuge for a desperate lawyer but perhaps represented McCall's best opportunity for a mistrial. Kehoe, an able, veteran advocate, had advised his client against trying to prove that the death of Skeegie Cash had been an accident. McCall persisted, however, and Kehoe had reluctantly followed his client's wishes.[47]

While the legal appeals progressed slowly, a defrocked minister entered the fray on behalf of McCall. Elder E. H. Crowson had been the prime mover in establishing the Apostolic Methodist Church (Holiness) in 1932. The mother church, the Methodist Episcopal Church, South, had excommunicated the maverick minister and his son, F. L. Crowson, for teaching premillennialism (that there would be a literal thousand-year reign of Christ on earth). Elder Crowson preached at a church in Kissimmee, Florida.[48]

Aided by Avriett, no doubt, Crowson presented a petition to the court that contended that the former truck driver had revoked his previous confession of guilt. Driven by a desire to keep the case alive, journalists reported that "the petition was sent by E. H. Crowson . . . who said he had received McCall's repudiation of the kidnapping and his statement of innocence 'in that sacred confidence which is often imparted to a minister.'" (This would be just the first shot McCall would fire in his attempt to avoid dying for his crime.)[49]

The petition asserted that McCall told the minister that his plea of guilty had been obtained by "torture, duress, and fraudulent misrepresentation of the facts involved."

The petition further insisted that McCall's trial had been in violation of his constitutional rights. The Florida Supreme Court was asked to grant a jury trial to the condemned man. This would include "freedom to subpoena witnesses in his favor; a change of venue through 'an atmosphere removed from mob-violence, fear, or other cause of misapprehension'; and the freedom from self-incrimination." Crowson's specious document carried no legal weight but represented an attempt to change the public's perception of Franklin McCall.[50]

Dade County Circuit Court judge H. F. Atkinson, predictably, rejected Avriett's argument, and the matter proceeded to the state supreme court. On January 4, 1939, Florida's highest court also rejected the Jasper attorney's twin arguments and denied a rehearing of the case.[51]

Regarding ineffectual counsel, the court stated: "A defendant convicted of kidnapping could not complain that he had been denied assistance of counsel, where an able, active, and conscientious lawyer of many years of experience was appointed for defendant and defendant reasserted on examination that he pleaded guilty and clearly told in detail every step of the kidnapping."[52]

Avriett based his argument that a trial by jury was required to confer a death sentence upon a defendant upon a similar ruling by a New Jersey state court.

The Florida Supreme Court, after summarizing the Garden State's decision and the US Constitution's guarantee to right to trial by his or her peers, wrote: "Upon the right of one charged with crime to waive a trial by jury, and elect to be tried by the court, when there is positive legislative enactment, giving the right so to do, and conferring power on the court to try the accused in such a case, there are numerous decisions by state courts upholding the validity of such proceedings."[53]

Finally, as dicta, Justice C. J. Terrell took judicial notice of Elder Crowson's campaign. The justices decreed: "The convicted petitioner for the first time in the record denies his guilt of the offense charged. The record of his own testimony and of corroborating physical circumstances show beyond any question of reasonable doubt that he did commit the crime of which he stands convicted and that his present belated denial of guilt is false and untrue."[54]

Unlike baseball, three strikes did not necessarily mean Mr. Avriett had struck out. Appeals to the federal courts remained.

On February 3, 1939, senior judge Rufus E. Foster of the Fifth United States Circuit Court of Appeals, located in New Orleans, refused to issue a certificate of probable cause to save Franklin McCall from the electric chair. Avriett's cocounsel, C. E. Rutledge, presented his plea to the court of appeals while the Jasper attorney made the rounds in Washington, DC.[55]

Twenty days later, Washington attorney Paul Brinson and Avriett proceeded with their last-gasp effort to save Franklin McCall from the electric chair. The two men made an application for a stay, pending an appeal to the US Supreme Court. Justice Felix Frankfurter heard the plea first and quickly rejected the application. He issued the denial "without prejudice," and the two lawyers quickly made their plea to Justice Hugo Black. Although they spent three hours pleading for the stay, in the end they left disappointed.[56]

With the two darlings of the nation's political liberals refusing to halt the execution, Avriett knew he had no options left. He'd done everything in his power, but all doors were closed. Franklin Pierce McCall would die—and soon. Governor Cone had already signed, on February 9, a new death warrant.[57]

The new date of execution was set for February 20.

# 15

# Time Runs Out

## 8 Months Later

On the morning of February 20, 1939, prison officials had scheduled three executions at Raiford. The condemned men, Clyde Hysler, Paul Fried Bunge, and Franklin Pierce McCall, waited in their cells for Superintendent Chapman to appear and lead them one by one into the death chamber.[1]

When he did arrive, the superintendent announced that Governor Cone had suspended Hysler's date with the chair in order to assure that all his legal appeals had been exhausted. A career criminal, Hysler and two cohorts had gunned down a Jacksonville businessman and his wife while robbing them. (His appeals would drag on until 1942 before he finally met his doom.)[2]

Ninety minutes before McCall's execution, Chapman met with the condemned man and informed him that his death sentence had been postponed until Friday, the twenty-fourth. The superintendent then explained to reporters that he'd spoken "long-distance with the governor who agreed with the decision." McCall's family had requested the delay, Chapman announced, saying they planned one final appeal to the United States Supreme Court.[3]

The postponement caught even McCall's lawyer by surprise. C. A. Avriett had been at the prison waiting to meet with his client before the death walk. Now, with a gleam of hope glistening through the darkness, he rushed past reporters and shouted that he was headed to Washington, DC, to meet with court officials.[4]

Guards informed journalists that McCall broke down and wept after hearing the news. Disappointed reporters, who had gathered to cover a triple execution, wrote that the reprieved prisoner seemed to be ecstatic.[5]

While McCall rejoiced at the temporary reprieve, Paul Fried Bunge cele-
brated the fact that his sentence would finally be enforced. Some witnesses
claimed that he literally skipped from his cell to the death chamber. Newspapers across the country proclaimed that no one in recent memory had welcomed death more readily than the guilt-ridden triple murderer.[6]

Approximately ten months earlier, on May 2, 1938, Hillsborough County
sheriff J. R. "Jerry" McLeod received a strange telegram informing him that
he would find three bodies at a certain apartment in Palma Ceia, near Tampa.
Ingebord Bunge, living in Pennsylvania, told the sheriff that her father, Paul
Fried Bunge, had called her claiming to have murdered her mother and two
younger sisters.[7]

Deputies rushed to the dilapidated home. There they discovered Marie
Larsen Bunge lying dead in the bathtub. An autopsy later revealed that she'd
been smothered with chloroformed rags and her throat cut. She'd also been
held down in the bloody half-filled tub. An autopsy revealed that Marie had
actually died of drowning.[8] When lawmen made their way into the bedroom, they discovered two more bodies. Bunge's children, Edith Ann, nine,
and Nina, six, had been posed on their beds, each holding a doll. Cotton had
been stuffed up their noses, and both had died of chloroform poisoning.[9]

Sheriff McLeod organized a massive manhunt. Neighbors told investigators that Bunge, a native of Germany, had moved to Florida six weeks
earlier, coming from Pittsburgh. A self-described "poet and piece of drift-
wood," Bunge rarely sold any of his writings and stayed perpetually destitute.

Arrested by police, the unemployed writer readily confessed to the murders, claiming that he and his wife had made a pact to kill his family and
then himself. But he said that after slaying his wife and children, he lost his
nerve and fled.[10]

Tried only for the murder of Marie, Bunge was convicted and sentenced
to die in the electric chair. The killer informed the court that he welcomed
death. In later media interviews, he reiterated a desire to end his suffering. The
guilt was eating him alive, he said, especially his own cowardice, which had
prevented him from ending his miserable existence. He also railed against a
capitalistic society that placed little value on poetry.[11]

At 10:10 A.M., on February 20, Bunge, wearing a handkerchief woven to
resemble a homemade yarmulke, entered the death chamber.

A fly buzzed around his face as prison guards strapped him into the chair.
Sheriff McLeod, nonchalantly smoking a cigar, pulled the lever before the

staff was ready—a guard scrambled away from the chair and screamed: "Not so fast, Sheriff!"[12]

An eyewitness described the scene: "Some of the spectators, finding their view obstructed, climbed on a window sill and viewed the grim spectacle. Several of those in the room turned deathly pale. The sheriff started to turn a wheel on the wall behind the chair. Somebody shouted '25', then '30', then '35', and finally '40' as the amperage rose. 'Turn it the other way, Sheriff,' said prison superintendent L. F. Chapman. McLeod obeyed."

The chaotic scene might have been comical had the occasion not been so serious.[13]

At 10:19, the prison doctor pronounced Bunge dead.

Guards reported that as Bunge walked from his cell to the death chamber, Franklin Pierce McCall turned his head away.[14]

To any neutral observer, little doubt existed as to McCall's guilt. However, as Judgment Day approached, the convicted kidnapper and killer of little Skeegie Cash began to proclaim his innocence. He rarely offered details, but claimed someone else had committed the crime. The truck driver now hinted that a vast conspiracy of law enforcement officials and politicians had framed him.[15]

That statement conflicted with an undated letter he wrote to his mother:

> Darling Mother, I haven't written because I did not know what to write. But I know that I must write you now to give you the words that you want most to hear. Uncle A. C. was here just now. We had prayer and I do believe that if I do have to die, I will go to be with Dad. Try not to take it so hard Mother. I have confessed my sins and believe I have been forgiven. They are very kind to me here, for I know that they know, that I did not mean for it to be as it was. If I have to go, the separation won't be so very long, so think of meeting me there. I'm so sorry dear Mother, for causing you the pain I have. If there was only some way to take it back. You know I would. I don't know anything else to write except to tell you that I'll meet you some day. Your Baby Boy, Franklin[16]

This cryptic confession seemed to be yet another attempt to manipulate those closest to him. In the letter, McCall showed no remorse for the suffering he'd caused Skeegie, or the lingering misery of the victim's family and his own family. His religious references contrasted with every action he'd taken in the last ten months.[17]

In addition to conning his mother, McCall had also laid a masterful guilt trip on his wife. Claudine now told anyone who would listen that her husband had kidnapped little Skeegie so he could afford to buy her some of the finer things in life. (After his execution, she even appeared on a national radio show extolling her husband's virtues and advising other wives to inform their husbands that material things were inconsequential.)[18]

McCall didn't stop with hoodwinking his family. He worked tirelessly to convince the media that poverty had provoked him into kidnapping Skeegie, and that the killing of the child had just been a tragic accident.[19]

One reporter, Harold S. Cohn, editor of the *Jacksonville Journal*, fell for it hook, line, and sinker. The journalist finagled a five-hour interview with the condemned man, then announced that he had the answer to why McCall committed the atrocious crime.[20]

"In attempting to analyze the social aspects of his kidnaping of five-year-old Skeegie Cash," Cohn wrote, "one must not lose the mental picture of McCall in Princeton—Princeton with 50 or 60 inhabitants, destitute of many things considered essential by modern civilization—Princeton nestling in the shadow of Miami, a glamorous city of glittering tinsel, beautiful women, races, night clubs, magnificent residences, and gaudy display[s] of wealth."[21]

McCall saw this dazzling city firsthand every day as he delivered tomatoes to Miami, Cohn wrote. His longing for the finer things finally overwhelmed him, causing his descent into madness.

"My father was a Methodist preacher," McCall informed the journalist, "whose major prayer was that someday the conference would give him a church. . . . He never got a church, and just as I am condemned, so was he to the life of an itinerant evangelist. The most money he made was $150 a month and he gave most of that away."[22]

McCall stated that his father shared his wages with others because of a great love for humankind. On the other hand, the condemned man told Cohn: "My sharing has been of the Huey Long kind of sharing. I never had much to share except poverty." So destitution and hardship, the journalist concluded, had precipitated the kidnapping.[23]

Cohn's article was published in many newspapers, and reaction was swift. In most cases, the condemned man's whining fell on deaf ears. Outraged letters to the newspapers that carried the piece flooded editorial rooms. One wag summed up the controversy for the vast majority of readers when he wrote that if poverty caused kidnappings and murders, there wouldn't be anyone left because 98 percent of the people in America were impoverished.[24]

By the time June 21 rolled around, McCall had changed his tune. He was innocent, he told anyone who would listen. He'd been coerced by law enforcement into taking the rap for an unnamed perpetrator.[25]

Superintendent Chapman had developed a reputation for treating all death row inmates with dignity and respect. McCall was no exception. The warden allowed the condemned man to speak with anyone he wished, to have writing pads and pencils, and to receive and send mail. On June 20, Chapman himself, with the approval of the governor, had made the decision to give McCall's lawyers a few more days to file their appeal.[26]

One spurious claim surfaced in local newspapers during the days leading up to McCall's execution. On June 21, an Associated Press story claimed that Bailey and Vera Cash, along with Wilson Cash, visited McCall in his cell. "They remained with the confessed kidnaper for nearly half an hour," the reporter wrote, "and later declined to discuss their call." No other wire service picked up on what would have been stunning news.[27]

It was well known that both Bailey and Vera wanted McCall to die for what he'd done to their son. Not long after McCall had been identified as Skeegie's killer, Bailey had asked Sheriff Coleman if the state would allow him to pull the switch. The lawman informed the grieving father that only the local sheriff could legally execute a condemned man.[28]

As the day of McCall's scheduled execution approached, Bailey and Vera Cash remained in Princeton. Asked if they planned to travel to Raiford for the execution, Bailey glared at the reporter and said, "No."[29]

On the morning of February 24, Franklin Pierce McCall ate a breakfast of bacon, eggs, toast, and coffee. He and Claudine spoke for about an hour, then she left the prison sobbing.

His brother, Byrd McCall, and his uncle, Reverend A. C. McCall, also visited with him.[30]

An Independent News Service article stated that "in the past 21 hours, McCall's lawyers were exhausting every effort to block the execution. At New Orleans, Judge Rufus E. Foster, of the U.S. Circuit court of appeals, denied an application for a writ of probable cause. At Washington, two Supreme Court justices rejected appeals by Attorney C. A. Avriett for a stay of execution so that the case could be appealed."

At about ten o'clock, C. A. Avriett sent a telegram to Superintendent

Chapman asking him to inform McCall that there would be no additional stays. All appeals had been turned down and no other judicial avenues remained open for his attorneys. The execution would proceed.[31]

McCall dressed for his last hours of life in a dark gray suit, white shirt, and blue tie. He wore a hat and slippers. Prison guards informed reporters that he was ashamed of his shaved head, and he kept the hat on until guards ordered him to remove it.[32]

Sheriff Coleman and Superintendent Chapman met McCall in his cell. All three stood as Coleman read the death warrant. It took five minutes. McCall shifted from foot to foot, looking at the floor.[33]

Once they completed this formality, McCall said, "Well, Mr. Coleman, I want you to know that I understand your position and you just take it easy."[34]

They walked into the death chamber as a chaplain shuffled behind the condemned man reciting the Lord's Prayer.[35]

As Chapman and several guards stood nearby, McCall seated himself and read a statement. "This case has aroused intense public interest," he read, "consequently the public is very much interested in learning my final statement concerning it.

"Last Saturday, Feb. 18 1939, by placing my signature on a petition for a writ of habeas corpus and on a petition for a writ of coram novis, the final statement was made.

"Perhaps the newspapers who have so consistently presented only one side of the case will accommodate the above mentioned interested public by presenting those writs in their entirety. They may be obtained from anyone at several courts. Records are available to anyone wishing to see them."[36]

McCall then stated that many were benefiting financially from his execution.[37]

Pausing, he continued: "According to the decisions rendered relative to this case, one may now be electrocuted within the bounds of the world's greatest democracy without trial by jury, which is directly contradictory to the constitution of the these United States of America.

"I maintain that the public is the law and vice versa. Therefore, a recurrence of this tragedy can be prevented.

"I would be despicably unappreciative if I failed, at this time, to give eloquent praise to Supt L. F. Chapman for the most humane act in Florida's criminal history—the temporary postponement of my execution.[38]

"Col. Chapman has been severely criticized for this act. But mark my word—the word of a man who will be dead in a few short minutes—a day is coming when he will be praised for it.

"Although the following remarks are perhaps irrelevant, I would like to say my beliefs concerning capital punishment coincide with those expressed by Warden Lawes of Sing Sing Prison, and they are: 'Did you ever see a rich man go the whole route through to the Death House? I don't know of any.'"[39]

McCall continued his self-serving diatribe for several more minutes. Finally, he concluded: "I have repeatedly asked to be taken into any court before any judge and jury and be injected with truth serum and to be given lie detector tests, have my fingerprints compared with any found at the scene of the crime, and my handwriting compared with that of the alleged ransom notes. To be put through any known examination to determine guilt or innocence. All this has been denied.

"Yesterday morning I was given alienist examination and was adjudged quite sane. I am glad of this. Perhaps that fact will lend credit to some of the above allegations.

"From hearing some of these remarks, it might be supposed that I am very bitter toward my persecutors and my executor. Such is not the case. I have found that for one to be forgiven he must first forgive.

"I did both when I wholeheartedly accepted the teachings of Jesus Christ and claimed the countless promises made in the Holy Bible as my own."[40]

When he completed his statement, McCall handed the sheath of papers to Chaplain Leslie Shepherd and requested that it be given to Bill Matthews of the *Miami Daily News*. Then McCall noticed the reporter in the visitor's gallery and said: "You can have it word for word. This is because of your fair treatment of me."[41]

After the execution, attendants from the prison hospital removed McCall's body and placed it in an ambulance. A few minutes later, the ambulance driver pulled out of the prison yard and headed toward Jasper, where McCall's long-suffering mother gave her son a proper Christian burial.[42]

The execution of Franklin Pierce McCall made headlines in newspapers all across the country. McCall was the first person sentenced under Florida's so-called Lindbergh Law, which made kidnapping for ransom a capital offense. For many, it was a final and just ending to yet another horrendous kidnapping story. Most editorials sanctioned the execution, although a surprising number did not.

Perhaps Steve Trumbull of the *Brownsville Herald* summed it up best. "A young fellow," he wrote, "who had failed dismally with life tried desperately here today to turn in a masterful performance with death. The actor was Franklin Pierce McCall, and the performance fell short of its goal. For life's last act with the kidnap-slayer of little 'Skeegie' Cash was an audacious protestation of innocence, which his audience could not reconcile with fact."[43]

Bailey Cash worked at his store on the day of Franklin McCall's execution. In the past, he'd toiled to provide a better life for his son than he himself had had as a child. Now he worked to forget the pain of loss.[44]

In the nine months since Skeegie's abduction, little joy remained in Bailey's life. Rooms that once bustled with his son's exuberant play now sat empty.

He looked on others with suspicion: his boarders, the customers at his businesses, even strangers he met on the streets. Worst of all, Bailey questioned whether his own brother, Asbury, might have had something to do with the abduction. In his heart he knew better, but a poisonous doubt nagged at his soul. The relationship between the two would never be the same.[45]

It had taken Vera months to recover, and still she seemed unable to shake the horror of losing her only son. Bailey hurt for his wife's overwhelming sadness.

Occasionally, during those months before the execution, McCall's name would pop up in news articles. Seeing his name brought back all the pain. Then, friends in the killer's hometown of Jasper began a petition to spare him the death penalty. Seventy citizens signed the document.[46]

Then the appeals began. They seemed to last forever. His lawyers threw up a seemingly endless series of roadblocks designed to halt the execution. Where were those shysters, Bailey wondered, when his son, his own little Skeegie, lay in the killer's arms taking his final breath? It seemed to the father as though the whole legal system was designed to prolong his agony.

An eye for an eye, so the Good Book said. Cash wasn't overly religious, but he believed in that passage.

As darkness drifted into Princeton that day, it brought the realization that even with McCall's death, things hadn't changed. Skeegie would never again call out to his father, or race his tricycle through the house, or joke with customers at the store. All Bailey Cash had left were a few pictures and a memory.[47]

And that wasn't enough. Not by a long shot.

# Afterword

*James Bailey Cash* died in 1984. He and Vera had no children after Skeegie's murder, so he established the J. B. Cash Foundation to honor the memory of his beloved son.[1]

*Vera Cash* lived for fifty-seven years after the kidnapping and homicide of Skeegie, dying in 1995. "She was scarred for life," her accountant, Steven C. Witmer said. After the tragedy, Vera and Bailey focused much of their energies on investing in south Florida real estate.[2]

A hurricane in 1945 destroyed their general store and home, including the apartment that Franklin Pierce McCall had lived in for six months. After the hurricane, Vera opened a lunch counter and fruit stand, but it closed in the 1950s.[3]

"She was a wonderful person," Witmer said. "She worked hard. She also was a very good cook and made good corn bread and grits for their café. She was from the old South, real Southern."[4]

After the destruction of their home, the Cashes bought a rooming house once used by Drake Lumber Company. In 1983, the Dade County Historic Preservation Division informed Bailey and Vera that because of its historical status they couldn't make improvements to the home or change it in any way. Vera sued the bureaucrats. Her attorney, Robert A. Hendricks, said that "she thought this kind of thing could happen in the Soviet Union, but that it could never happen in the United States." The legal slugfest lasted for years before it finally petered out with no known decision.[5]

Before her death, Vera established the Vera Cash Foundation. While its annual donations are far-reaching, one stands out: the National Center for Missing and Exploited Children.[6]

*Arthur Rutzen* resigned from the FBI in 1942, but not before helping to break up Al Capone's gang. According to his obituary, "his efforts led to the convictions of Frank 'The Enforcer' Nitto and Paul 'The Waiter' Ricca." After leaving the bureau, he took a job with Wurlitzer Corporation and later worked for two decades at the Department of Commerce. Rutzen died at age seventy-nine in Boca Raton, Florida, just a few miles from where he had worked on the Skeegie Cash case.[7]

*Earl J. Connelley* remained with the FBI for thirty-four years. In 1940, Hoover made him assistant director of Major Investigations in the Field. During and after World War II, Connelley worked with the counterespionage unit of the bureau. He helped convict Alger Hiss, a communist spy. Connelley died in Cincinnati in 1957.[8]

In 1941, *Samuel K. McKee* became special agent in charge of the Washington field office. Three years later, the bureau transferred him, naming him SAC of the Newark field office. In that same year, controversy erupted when the United States Army rejected Frank Sinatra because of an alleged ruptured eardrum. McKee investigated the rumor that Sinatra had paid a local doctor $40,000 to falsify his medical records, thereby disqualifying him from service in the armed forces. Although G-men found no evidence to prove those allegations, FBI agents leaked information to reporters claiming that Sinatra suffered from "neuroses and emotional instability." (Journalist William Manchester, a veteran of World War II, once said: "I think Frank Sinatra was the most hated man of World War II, much more than Hitler," because Sinatra was safe at home, rolling in money and frolicking with beautiful babes, while the average man was shedding blood for his country.) McKee handled the controversy with the same grace under fire that he'd displayed in many a shoot-out. The Texan retired in the 1950s.[9]

In 1942, *C. A. Avriett* became the state representative from Hamilton County, Florida. A true fiscal conservative, his first act was to propose a repeal of laws that allow state retirement income for elected officials. He claimed this would save the state more than $46,000 per year. Just as his defense of Franklin Pierce McCall was unsuccessful, so his attempt to bring fiscal sanity to state government met with failure. He was not elected to a second term.[10]

*J. Edgar Hoover* remained director of the FBI under seven presidents. He was easily the most feared and hated man in Washington. On the day of his death in 1972, his secretary shredded thousands of documents he'd retained in his private office. The secrets contained in those files helped keep "that old cock-sucker," as Richard Nixon called Hoover, in power for a half-century.[11]

Despite Franklin's notorious crime, *Lillie McCall* loved her son. After his execution, she brought him home to Jasper, burying him in the family plot at Evergreen Cemetery. Like the Cash family, Lillie remained scarred until her death in 1963.[12]

One major question lingers about the case.

Did McCall purposely murder Skeegie, or did the child die in a tragic accident? FBI interviewers and most reporters seemed to buy into his story that the boy's death was a tragic accident. Since the state didn't need to provide proof of murder in his kidnapping trial, they never addressed the issue.

But on further examination, the notion that McCall killed the child by accident makes little sense.

In McCall's final confession, he told agents that he planned to tie Skeegie up, hide him in an abandoned house he'd found, and keep him blindfolded for two days until he received the ransom. Thereafter, he said, he would release the boy.

Given the opportunity, however, McCall seemed unable to lead FBI agents to the house.

It seems implausible that a five-year-old boy, well known to the suspect, would not recognize his abductor, even with a blindfold. Since McCall had no way to drive the child deep into the Everglades, he would have been forced to hide him within a mile or two of his home. Searchers would almost certainly have located the victim within hours.

McCall, a cold-blooded character, seemingly impervious to conscience, likely planned to kill the boy all along. That way, Skeegie could not identify him.[13]

# Notes

## Preface

1. Blaise Picchi, *The Five Weeks of Giuseppe Zangara: The Man Who Would Assassinate FDR* (Chicago: Academy Chicago Publishers, 1998), 169–70.

2. Ibid., 182.

3. "M'Call Dies with Pleas of Innocence," Panama City (FL) *Pilot*, February 24, 1939, 1.

4. Ibid.; "Miami-Dade County: Kidnapping of James Bailey Cash," http://genealogytrails.com/fla/miamidade/news_kidnapping.html, accessed June 5, 2013 (henceforth "Kidnapping Timeline").

5. Private letter, Sheriff D. C. Coleman Collection (henceforth Coleman Collection), which contains letters, news clipping, and reports regarding the careers of sheriff and state senator D. C. Coleman; in the possession of Brien D. Coleman, Miami, Florida, and Ann Coleman Hicks, Miami, Florida.

6. "M'Call Dies with Pleas of Innocence."

7. Ibid.

8. "McCall Goes to Chair for Kidnap Slaying in Florida," Lowell (MA) *Sun*, February 24, 1939, 1.

9. Ibid.

10. "M'Call Dies with Pleas of Innocence."

11. Ibid.

12. Ibid.

13. Ibid.

14. Picchi, *The Five Weeks of Giuseppe Zangara*, 188–91.

15. Ibid.; "M'Call Dies with Pleas of Innocence."

16. Ibid.

17. Ibid.

18. "Kidnapper Pays for Crime in Prison Chair," Hammond (IN) *Times*, February 24, 1939, 1. (The *Times* and many other newspapers and journals incorrectly called prison physician Dr. Walter Murphree "Dr. W. E. Murphy.")

19. "The G-men Are Awaiting Kidnap Money," Tipton (IN) *Daily Tribune*, June 6, 1938, 1.

## Chapter 1

1. Federal Bureau of Investigation, James Bailey Cash Jr. Files, June 5, 1938, 7-106, S. K. McKee, 1–14, National Archives and Records Management, College Park, MD (henceforth FBI files).

2. FBI files, 7-106, S. K. McKee, June 5, 1938, 4.

3. FBI files, 7-106, S. K. McKee, 17.

4. FBI files, 7-106, S. K. McKee, 2.

5. Ibid.

6. Ibid.

7. Ibid.

8. FBI files, 7-106, E. J. Connelley, June 13, 1938, 26–27.

9. Ibid.

10. Ibid.

11. Ibid.

12. Ibid. The events and characters in this book are real. Dialogue was recreated from primary sources, and accurately reflects the information and emotions conveyed by these sources.

13. Ibid.

14. Ibid.

15. Ibid.

16. FBI files, 7–106, S. K. McKee, June 5, 1938, 2.

17. FBI files, 7–106, S. K. McKee, 3.

18. "Only One Clue Aids G-Men in Hunt for Levine Killer," Oakland (CA) *Tribune*, May 30, 1930, 4.

19. "Abetting the Criminal," Waterloo (IA) *Daily Courier*, August 1, 1933, 4; "Kidnapping Wave Sweeps the Nation," www.nytimes.com/books/98/09/27/specials/lindbergh-wave.html.

20. "Weyerhaeuser Kidnap Suspect Arrives at End of Trail," Abilene (TX) *Morning News Reporter*, May 10, 1936, 1.

21. "Child Found Dead in Hunt for Girl Kidnapped September 1," Joplin (MO) *Globe*, November 14, 1934, 1.

22. FBI files, C. E. Weeks, 7-106, June 16, 1938, 4.

23. Frank Parker Stockbridge and John Holliday Perry, *So This Is Florida* (Jacksonville, FL: John H. Perry Publishing, 1938), 137–38.

24. FBI files, S. K. McKee, June 5, 1938, 2.

25. R. G. Dun (Business Directory), 1938, 33.

26. FBI files, 7-106, S. K. McKee, June 5, 1938, 4.

27. Bob Crossland, "Kidnapped! Florida's Jimmy Cash Horror," *True Detective*, October 1958, 16 (henceforth "Florida's Jimmy Cash Horror"). Bob Crossland is almost cer-

tainly the nom de plume for a police officer, or a federal agent, who helped in the investigation of the "Skeegie" Cash crime.

28. FBI files, 7-106, E. C. Weeks, June 16, 1938, 33.

29. Ibid., 7.

30. Ibid., 30, 42; Crossland, "Florida's Jimmy Cash Horror," 114–17; FBI files, "The Background of Franklin Pierce McCall," (radio script) (henceforth "McCall Radio Script"), July 20, 1938, 1–5.

31. FBI files, 7-106, C. E. Weeks, June 16, 1938, 129.

32. FBI files, I.C. #7-2348, "Franklin Pierce McCall with Alias 'Preacher Boy,' James Bailey Cash, Jr. Victim Kidnapping," October 20, 1938, 2–3. This is a summary of the case published by John Edgar Hoover's Office.

33. FBI files, 7-106, S. K. McKee, June 5, 1938, 3; FBI files, "Memorandum for Mr. Tamm," Re: Cash Kidnapping Case (henceforth "Memo for Tamm"), June 1, 1938, 9:25 p.m.

34. FBI files, 7-106, E. J. Connelley, 25.

35. FBI files, 7-106, S. K. McKee, 6–9.

36. Ibid.

37. Ibid.

38. Walter Winchell, "Walter Winchell on Broadway," Logansport (IN) *Pharos-Tribune*, June 18, 1938, 7.

39. "G-Men Seize Man from Crowd in Front of Where Kidnapped Boy Lived," Waterloo (IA) *Daily Courier*, June 1, 1938, 1.

40. FBI files, 7-106, S. K. McKee, June 5, 1938.

## Chapter 2

1. FBI files, 7-106, E. J. Connelley, June 13, 1938, 7; FBI files, 7-2348, no author, Memorandum, June 7, 1938, 1–2 (henceforth FBI files, June 7, 1938, MEMO).

2. FBI files, 7-106, S. K. McKee, June 5, 1938, 3, 10–11.

3. FBI files, 7-2348, June 7, 1938, MEMO, 8–9.

4. Crossland, "Florida's Jimmy Cash Horror," 17.

5. Ibid.

6. Ibid.

7. Ibid.

8. FBI files, 7-106, S. K. McKee, June 5, 1938, 1–2.

9. "Arthur Rutzen, Ex-FBI Agent, One of the Original 'G-Men,'" http://articles.sun-sentinel.com/1989-08-05/news/8902240413_1_fbi-agent-fbi-offices-fbi-operations, SunSentinel.com, August 5, 1989 (obituary), accessed June 5, 2013.

10. FBI files, 7-106, S. K. McKee, June 5, 1938, 1–2.

11. Ibid.; "The Roberts Mayfair: A Historic Hotel, History," http://www.robertsmayfairhotel.com/index.php?option=com_content&view=article&id=373&Itemid=267, accessed June 5, 2013.

12. Crossland, "Florida's Jimmy Cash Horror," 17.

13. "Faded Glory: Dusty Roads of an FBI Era," http://historicalgmen.squarespace .com/agents-of-the-30s-biographie, accessed June 5, 2013. (Even this unofficial site, taking information from early FBI in-house newsletters, has little information on S. K. McKee.)

14. K. B. Chaffin, "Jelly Bryce: The FBI's Legendary Sharpshooter," http://www .gutterfighting.org/jellybryce.html, accessed June 5, 2013.

15. FBI files, 7-2348, June 7, 1938, MEMO, 4.

16. Crossland, "Florida's Jimmy Cash Horror," 16.

17. FBI files, 7-106, E. J. Connelley, June 13, 1938, 7.

18. Ibid.

19. FBI files, 7-2348, June 7, 1938, MEMO, 3.

20. Ibid.

21. Ibid.

22. Jim Fisher, *The Lindbergh Case* (New Brunswick, NJ: Rutgers University Press, 1995), 7–12.

23. Fisher, *The Lindbergh Case*, 40–45, 109–19; 270; Evan J. Albright, "Crime of the Century and the Cape Cod Connection," http://capecodconfidential.com/ccc2-17.shtml, accessed June 5, 2013.

24. Jim Fisher, *The Ghosts of Hopewell: Setting the Record Straight in the Lindbergh Case* (Carbondale: Southern Illinois University Press, 1999), 38.

25. Ibid., xx–xxv (Lindbergh Case Chronology).

26. Curt Gentry, *J. Edgar Hoover: The Man and the Secrets* (New York: W. W. Norton, 1991), 151–53.

27. Ibid.; "Kidnapping Timeline," 2–3.

28. "The Encyclopedia of Arkansas History and Culture: Barker-Karpis Gang," www. encyclopediaofarkansas.net/encyclopedia/entry-detail.aspx?entryID=5740, accessed June 5, 2013.

29. O'Dell, Larry, "Urschel Kidnapping," digital.library.okstate.edu/encyclopedia /entries/U/UR009.html, accessed June 5, 2013.

30. Gentry, *J. Edgar Hoover*, 178–79.

31. Ronald Kessler, *The Bureau: The Secret History of the FBI* (New York: St. Martin's Press, 2002), 35.

32. FBI files, 7-2348, June 7, 1938, MEMO, 3.

33. FBI files, 7-106, E. J. Connelley, June 13, 1938, 11.

34. FBI files, 7-2348, June 7, 1938, MEMO, 3.

35. Ibid.

36. "Hope for Kidnapped Boy Wanes," Richmond *Times-Dispatch*, June 2, 1938, 4.

37. FBI files, 7-106, S. K. McKee, June 5, 1938, 4.

38. "Vera Cash, South Dade Pioneer Whose Son Was Murdered," Miami *Herald*, March 10, 1995, 4B.

39. FBI files, 7-2348, June 7, 1938, MEMO, 4.

40. Ibid.

41. Ibid.

42. Ibid.

43. Tony Poveda, *The FBI: A Comprehensive Reference Guide* (Westport, CT: Greenwood, 1998), 356.

44. Daryl C. McClary, "Ten-Year-Old Charles Mattson Is Kidnapped in Tacoma and Held for Ransom on December 27, 1936," HistoryLink.org, December 13, 2006, http://www.historylink.org/index.ctm?DisplayPage=output.cfm&fileid=8028, accessed June 5, 2013.

45. "Boy of 10 Is Kidnapped in Tacoma," Helena (MT) *Independent*, December 26, 1936, 6.

46. McClary, "Charles Mattson."

47. FBI files, 7-2348, June 7, 1938, MEMO, 10.

48. FBI files, 7-106, Letter from A. Rutzen to J. Edgar Hoover, May 30, 1938.

49. FBI files, 7-2348, June 7, 1938, MEMO, 14.

50. "U.S. Flies 14 More Men to Kidnap Probe," Canton (OH) *Repository*, June 3, 1938, 1. The article asserted, "the new agents augmented an already formidable force of FBI manpower."

51. FBI files, 7-106, S. K. McKee, June 5, 1938, 17.

52. FBI files, 7-2348, June 7, 1938, MEMO, 5–7.

53. Ibid.

54. Ibid.

55. Ibid., 9.

56. Ibid.

57. Ibid.

58. FBI files, 7-106, S. K. McKee, June 5, 1938, 17–18.

## Chapter 3

1. "Find Body of Peter Levine Near His Home," Biloxi (MS) *Daily Herald*, May 30, 1938, 1.

2. Ibid.

3. FBI files, 7-106, C. E. Weeks, June 16, 1938, 18, 20.

4. FBI files, 7-2348, June 7, 1938, MEMO, 11.

5. "Secret Burial for Levine Boy," Oakland *Tribune*, May 30, 1938, 1, 4.

6. Ibid.

7. S. T. White, "G-Men Never Forget! After Two Years of Arduous Investigation Federal Agents Are Finally Set to Crack Levine Kidnapping," Port Arthur (TX) *News*, May 5, 1940, 30.

8. Ibid.

9. Ibid.

10. Ibid.

11. Ibid.

12. Ibid.

13. "The New Rochelle Police Department, (A Brief History)," http://www.nrpd
.com/aboutus.htm, accessed June 5, 2013.

14. FBI files, 7-2348, June 7, 1938, MEMO, 4.

15. FBI files, 7-106, C. E. Weeks, June 16, 1938, 15.

16. "Top of the Charts, 1938," http://www.popculturemadness.com/Music/Charts
/1938.html, accessed June 7, 2013.

17. "List of American Films of 1938," http://en.wikipedia.org/wiki/List_of_American
_films_of_1938, accessed June 7, 2013.

18. "Jim Crow Museum of Racist Memorabilia," Ferris State University, http://ferris
.edu/jimcrow/what.htm, accessed June 7, 2013.

19. Gentry, *J. Edgar Hoover*, 182–87.

20. Ibid., 192–95.

21. Ibid.; "Karpis Captured in New Orleans by Hoover Himself," *New York Times*,
May 1, 1936, 1.

22. Kessler, *The Bureau*, 25.

23. Gentry, *J. Edgar Hoover*, 192–93.

24. Kessler, *The Bureau*, 62–63.

25. "Atrocious Revival," *Time Magazine*, June 13, 1938.

26. "Lock the Barn, Then Burn It," Alton (IL) *Evening News*, May 4, 1938.

27. David J. Krajicek, "Hoover and the Child Snatcher," http://www.nydailynews
.com/news/crime/hoover-child-snatcher-article-1.294513, accessed June 8, 2013.

28. Ibid.

29. "Three Billion Deficit Looms," Oakland *Tribune*, May 19, 1938, 7.

30. Ibid.

31. "Lock the Barn, Then Burn It."

32. "Forcing a Wage-Hour Bill upon a Nation," San Antonio (TX) *Express*, June 8,
1938, 6.

33. "$308,000 Provided by House for War on Kidnapping," Galveston (TX) *Daily
News*, June 9, 1938, 5.

34. Krajicek, "Hoover and the Child Snatcher."

35. Walter Winchell, "Walter Winchell on Broadway: Private Papers of a Cub Reporter," Waterloo *Daily Courier*, June 20, 1938.

36. FBI files, 7-2348, June 7, 1938, MEMO, 10.

37. Ibid.

38. Crossland, "Florida's Jimmy Cash Horror," 17.

39. FBI files, 7-2348, "Memo for Tamm," June 7, 1938, MEMO, 10.

40. Memorandum for the Director from E. A. Tamm, 7-2348, May 30, 1938, 5:15 P.M.

41. FBI files, 7-106, C. E. Weeks, June 16, 1938, 3.

42. Ibid.

43. FBI files, 7-2348, June 7, 1938, MEMO, 4.

44. FBI files, 7-2348, "Memo for Tamm," May 29, 1938, MEMO.

45. FBI files, 7-106, C. E. Weeks, June 16, 1938, 61–63.
46. FBI files, 7-2348, "Memo for Tamm," June 1, 1938, MEMO.
47. Ibid.
48. FBI files, 7-106, C. E. Weeks, June 16, 1938, 4–5.
49. Ibid.
50. MTT, 5.
51. "Florida Kidnapper Asks $10,000 Ransom," Canandaigua (NY) *Daily Messenger*, May 31, 1938, 1.
52. FBI files, 7-106, S. K. McKee, June 5, 1938, 13.
53. "Boyle, Kidnapper, Quickly Convicted," *New York Times*, May 7, 1909.
54. FBI files, 7-106, C. E. Weeks, June 16, 1938, 61–63.
55. FBI files, 7-106, S. K. McKee, June 5, 1938, 13.

## Chapter 4

1. Crossland, "Florida's Jimmy Cash Horror," 18.
2. Ibid.
3. FBI files, 7-106, S. K. McKee, June 5, 1938, 13.
4. FBI files, 7-2348, Memorandum (no author), June 7, 1938, MEMO, 2; Florida Military Service Records, http://www.floridamemory.com/items/show/218895, accessed June 8, 2013.
5. FBI files, 7-106, S. K. McKee, June 5, 1938, 13.
6. Crossland, "Florida's Jimmy Cash Horror," 18.
7. FBI files, 7-106, E. J. Connelley, June 13, 1938, 77.
8. Ibid.
9. Ibid., 38.
10. FBI files, 7-106, E. J. Connelley, June 13, 1938, 77.
11. Ibid.
12. Ibid., 38.
13. Ibid.
14. Ibid., 77.
15. Ibid., 38–39.
16. Ibid.
17. FBI files, 7-2348, Memorandum, (no author), June 7, 1938, MEMO, 12.
18. FBI files, 7-106, E. J. Connelley, June 13, 1938, 3.
19. Crossland, "Florida's Jimmy Cash Horror," 19.
20. FBI files, 7-106, E. J. Connelley, June 13, 1938, 78.
21. Ibid.
22. FBI files, 7-106, S. K. McKee, June 5, 1938, 13.
23. FBI files, 7-106, E. J. Connelley, June 13, 1938, 78.
24. FBI files, 7-106, S. K. McKee, June 5, 1938, 14.
25. FBI files, 7-106, E. J. Connelley, June 13, 1938, 81.

26. FBI files, 7-106, C. E. Weeks, "Statement of James Bailey Cash, Sr.", June 8, 1938, 7.

27. FBI files, 7-2348, Memorandum, (no author), June 7, 1938, MEMO, 11.

28. Ibid.

29. Crossland, "Florida's Jimmy Cash Horror," 112.

30. Cash kidnapping account, Coleman Collection.

31. "McCall Radio Script," 1.

32. Ibid.

33. Ibid., 2.

34. Ibid., 4.

35. Ibid., 3; FBI files, 7-106, E. J. Connelley, June 13, 1938, 42.

36. Ibid.

37. Ibid., 2–3.

38. Ibid., 5.

39. Ibid., 2.

40. Ibid., 1–2.

41. James Pylant, "Vintage True Crime Magazines: An Untapped Goldmine for Genealogists," http://www.genealogymagazine.com/crime.html, accessed June 9, 2013.

42. FBI files, 7-106, E. J. Connelley, June 13, 1938, 53.

43. MTT, 74.

44. MTT, 75.

45. Ibid.

46. MTT, 89–90.

47. FBI files, 7-106, E. J. Connelley, June 13, 1938, 1–2, 75–76.

48. MTT, 1.

49. MTT, 1–2, 76.

50. FBI files, 7-106, E. J. Connelley, June 13, 1938, 79.

51. Ibid., 40.

52. Ibid.

53. FBI files, 7-106, E. J. Connelley, June 13, 1938, 79.

54. Ibid.

55. Ibid.

56. Ibid.

57. Crossland, "Florida's Jimmy Cash Horror," 19.

58. FBI files, 7-2348, June 7, 1938, MEMO, 12–13.

59. Ibid.

60. Ibid.

61. "Florida Kidnappers Ask $10,000 Ransom," Canandaigua (NY) *Daily Messenger*, May 31, 1931, 1.

62. "Death M'Call's Sentence," Burlington (IA) *Daily Hawk-Eye Gazette*, May 31, 1938, 1; FBI files, 7-106, E. J. Connelley, June 13, 1938, 79.

63. FBI files, 7-106, E. J. Connelley, June 13, 1938, 79.

64. Ibid.

65. "McCall Radio Script."

66. FBI files, 7-106, E. J. Connelley, June 13, 1938, 79.

67. MTT, 4.

68. Ibid.

69. "Confesses Killing of Cash Boy," Emporia (KS) *Gazette*, June 10, 1938, 1.

70. "Father, Son Questioned in Kidnapping," Butte *Montana Standard*, June 2, 1938, 1.

71. Ibid.

72. "Man Seized In Florida Kidnap Case," Lock Haven (PA) *Express*, June 1, 1938, 1.

73. "Memo for Tamm," June 1, 1938, 9:25 P.M.

74. FBI files, 7-106, C. E. Weeks, June 16, 1938, 29.

75. FBI files, "Memorandum for the Files," E. A. Tamm, May 31, 1938, 1–2.

76. Ibid.

77. "Florida Kidnappers Ask $10,000 Ransom."

78. "Kidnap Posseman Nabbed by G-Men," San Antonio (TX) *Light*, June 1, 1938, 1.

79. Ibid.

80. FBI files, "Memorandum for the Files: Re: Cash Kidnapping Case," E. A. Tamm, May 31, 1938.

81. Gene M. Burnett, *Florida's Past: People and Events That Shaped the State*, vol. 1 (Sarasota, FL: Pineapple Press, 1996), 92.

82. Crossland, "Florida's Jimmy Cash Horror," 110.

83. Howard Kleinberg, "History of the Miami *News* (1896–1987)," 24. (This online article has no URL.)

84. "New Kidnapping Horrifies Nation—Other A. P. Wirephotos of World Events," Oakland (CA) *Tribune*, May 31, 1938, 24.

85. "Florida Boy Is Abducted, $10,000 Paid," Oshkosh (WI) *Northwestern*, May 31, 1938, 1.

86. "Confesses Slaying of Cincinnati Girl," Hamilton (OH) *Daily News Journal*, May 31, 1938, 1–2.

87. Ibid.

# Chapter 5

1. "Hope Gone for Cash Boy: Posses Launch Manhunt," Greensboro *Record*, June 3, 1938, 1; "Hundreds Join for Youth Nabbed Saturday," *State Times Advocate*, June 1, 1938, 6.

2. Ibid.

3. Crossland, "Florida's Jimmy Cash Horror," 111.

4. Poveda, *The FBI: A Comprehensive Reference Guide*, 320–21.

5. "Roosevelt Asks Kidnap Hunt Funds," Cleveland (OH) *Plain Dealer*, June 8, 1938, 1; "U.S. Flies 14 More Men to Kidnap Probe," the *Repository* notes "there was no doubt that he [Hoover] was driving his men forcefully."

6. FBI files, 7-2348-29, J. Edgar Hoover, "Memorandum for the Files," May 31, 1938, 29–30, mentions four suspects and several possible scenarios.

7. "Hope for Kidnapped Boy Wanes."

8. FBI files, 7-106, M. F. Braxton and family, June 6, 1938, 128–91 (henceforth "Braxton Files").

9. "Sure Boy Dead, Says Father but G-Men Push Hunt," San Diego *Union*, June 5, 1938, 1.

10. "Cash Voices Doubt Kidnapped Boy Will Be Returned Alive," Springfield (MA) *Republican*, June 5, 1938, 2.

11. "G-Men Seek Additional Kidnap Figures," San Diego *Union*, June 10, 1938, 2.

12. "Braxton Files."

13. Ibid.

14. FBI files, 7-106, C. W. Toulme and E. J. Connelley, "Braxton Files," 150–60.

15. Ibid.

16. FBI files, 7-106, C. E. Weeks and L. A. Newsom, (report on civilian spies), June 2, 1938, 29–30.

17. Ibid.

18. Ibid.

19. Crossland, "Florida's Jimmy Cash Horror," 110.

20. FBI files, "Memorandum for Special Agent in Charge" (US Department of Justice, New York, New York), May 31, 1938, 1–5.

21. Ibid.

22. Ibid.

23. Ibid.

24. Ibid.

25. Ibid.

26. Ibid.

27. Ibid.

28. Crossland, "Florida's Jimmy Cash Horror," 110.

29. "Vast Manhunt for Florida Kidnappers Organized," Greensboro *Record*, June 1, 1938, 1.

30. "Hope to Find Young Child Alive Fades," Marietta (GA) *Journal*, June 1, 1938, 1. See generally, Dana Ste. Claire, *Cracker: The Cracker Culture in Florida History* (Gainesville: University Press of Florida, 2006).

31. Crossland, "Florida's Jimmy Cash Horror," 111; FBI files, 7-106, C. Ray Davidson, June 7, 1938, 12. Cash is called "the best man in the community . . . and everyone held a high opinion of him."

32. "Vast Manhunt for Florida Kidnappers Organized."

33. Crossland, "Florida's Jimmy Cash Horror," 111.

34. "Vast Manhunt for Florida Kidnappers Organized"; Preston Bird, Record of Search, Coleman Collection.

35. Ibid.

36. Ibid.

37. FBI files, 7-2348, June 4, 1938, Letter from Maude E. Beckner to Hoover, 1–4.

38. FBI files, 7-106, C. E. Weeks, June 6, 1938, 44.

39. Ibid.

40. "Memo for Tamm."
41. Ibid.
42. Ibid.
43. Ibid.
44. FBI files, 7-106, C. E. Weeks and L. A. Newsom, June 2, 1938, 29–30.
45. Ibid.
46. "Memo for Tamm."

## Chapter 6

1. "Charge of Hunt for Cash Youth," *State Times Advocate*, June 2, 1938, 6.
2. Crossland, "Florida's Jimmy Cash Horror," 111.
3. Ibid.; "Hope for Kidnapped Boy Wanes."
4. "The Search Goes On," Omaha (NE) *World Herald*, June 2, 1938, 10.
5. "Cash Boy's Father Gives Up All Hope," *New York Times*, June 4, 1938, 1.
6. "Parents Give Up Hope For Boy," San Diego *Union*, June 5, 1938, 4, includes Henry Cypress quote.
7. "Florida National Guard Summary History to 1940," http://ufdc.ufl.edu /UF00047664/00001/2j, accessed June 12, 2013. See generally, Robert Hawk, *Florida's Army: Militia, State Troops, National Guard, 1565–1985* (Englewood, FL: Pineapple Press, 1986).
8. Crossland, "Florida's Jimmy Cash Horror," 111; "Aerial Search Finds No Abduction Clues," Seattle *Daily Times*, June 1, 1938, 10.
9. Crossland, "Florida's Jimmy Cash Horror," 111.
10. Ibid.
10. Ibid.
11. Ibid.
12. Ibid.; "Hoover Assumes Charge of Cash Kidnap Search," Trenton (NJ) *Evening Times*, June 2, 1938, 1.
13. Crossland, "Florida's Jimmy Cash Horror," 111.
14. Ibid.
15. Ibid.
16. Ibid.
17. Preston Bird Papers, Coleman Collection.
18. "Ransom Vain . . . Posses Ready," Seattle *Daily Times*, June 1, 1938, 10.
19. "Kidnap Clue Checked," Seattle *Daily Times*, June 3, 1938, 14.
20. "Kidnap Trail Grows Cold as Search Is Continued," Greensboro *Record*, June 3, 1938, 1.
21. "Hope for Kidnapped Boy Wanes."
22. "Hoover Takes Charge of Hunt for Cash Youth," *State Times Advocate*, June 2, 1938, 6.
23. "Hope Gone for Cash Boy, Posses Launch Manhunt," Trenton (NJ) *Evening Times*, June 1, 1938, 1.

24. "Kidnap Clue Checked."

25. "Investigators Unable to Find Trace of Child," Baton Rouge *Advocate*, June 4, 1938, 4.

26. "Searchers Find New Clews In Cash Kidnapping," Springfield *Republican*, June 2, 1938, 9; "Ransom Put in 2 Spots, $5 Missing," Cleveland *Plain Dealer*, June 10, 1938, 1, 2.

27. Crossland, "Florida's Jimmy Cash Horror," 111.

28. Ibid.; Preston Bird Papers, Coleman Collection.

29. "Hoover Assumes Charge of Cash Kidnap Search."

30. Crossland, "Florida's Jimmy Cash Horror," 111.

31. Ibid.

32. Ibid.

33. "G-Men Seek Additional Kidnap Figures," San Diego *Union*, June 10, 1938, 2.

34. "Ransom Vain . . . Posses Ready."

35. "Hoover Assumes Charge of Cash Kidnap Search."

36. "Kidnap Clue Checked."

37. Susan Butler, *East to the Dawn: The Life of Amelia Earhart* (New York: Da Capo Press, 2009) 385–91; "Hoover Assumes Charge of Cash Kidnap Search."

38. "Hoover Takes Charge in Hunt for Kidnappers," Canton (OH) *Repository*, June 2, 1938, 1.

39. "Hoover Directs Kidnap Hunt," Rockford (IL) *Register Republic*, June 2, 1938, 1; "FDR Asks Money for Kidnap Case," Augusta *Chronicle*, June 8, 1938, 1.

40. "Searchers Find New Clues in Cash Kidnapping."

41. "Numerous Breaks Rumored in Case of Kidnapped Boy," Baton Rouge *Advocate*, June 3, 1938, 2.

42. "Hoover Takes Charge of Hunt for Cash Youth."

43. "Hoover Directs Kidnap Hunt"; Crossland, "Florida's Jimmy Cash Horror," 111.

44. Ibid.

45. Ibid.

46. Ibid.

47. Ibid.; "Ransom Cash Box Found by Posses." *Dallas Morning News*, June 2, 1938, 1, 2.

48. Crossland, "Florida's Jimmy Cash Horror," 111.

49. "Hope for Kidnapped Boy Wanes."

50. FBI files, 7-2348-61, R. E. Vetterli, June 1, 1938, 1–2; FBI files, 7-106, C. E. Weeks, June 16, 1938, 224–25.

51. FBI files, 7-106, C. E. Weeks, June 16, 1938, 224–25.

52. "Hoover Takes Charge of Hunt for Cash Youth;" "Hoover Assumes Charge of Cash Kidnap Search."

53. "Cash Voices Doubt Kidnapped Boy Will Be Returned Alive," Springfield *Republican*, June 5, 1938, 1.

54. "Hoover Assumes Charge of Cash Kidnap Search"; "Hoover Takes Charge of Hunt for Cash Youth."

## Chapter 7

1. "Navy Planes Join Search for Missing Florida Boy: Press Levine Case," Augusta *Chronicle*, June 4, 1938, 1.

2. "2,000 Men Scour Snake-Infested Area for Child," New Orleans *Times-Picayune*, June 3, 1938, 1.

3. "Search for Kidnapped Boy Is Virtually Abandoned," Greensboro *Journal*, June 6, 1938, 3.

4. "Hopes for Kidnap Solution Fading," Springfield *Republican*, June 9, 1938, 4.

5. "Search for Kidnapped Boy Is Virtually Abandoned."

6. "Searchers Find New Clews in Cash Kidnapping." This account notes the danger of rattlesnakes, but the FBI files provide no clues to the bureau's reasoning for ending the search. Hoover opposed the search to begin with, likely because of the presence of attorney Fritz Gordon.

7. Ibid.

8. Preston Bird report of search, Coleman Collection.

9. "Seen in Indiana," Augusta *Chronicle*, June 4, 1938, 4.

10. "Hoover Takes Charge of Kidnap Case," Dallas *Morning News*, June 3, 1938, 12.

11. FBI files, 7-106, C. E. Weeks, (M. F. Braxton and family), June 8, 1938, 128–91.

12. Ibid.

13. Ibid.

14. Ibid.

15. Ibid.

16. Ibid.

17. Ibid.

18. Ibid.

19. Ibid.

20. Ibid.

21. Ibid.

22. Ibid.

23. Ibid.

24. Ibid.

25. Ibid.

26. Ibid.; Crossland, "Florida's Jimmy Cash Horror," 112.

27. Ibid.

28. Ibid.

29. Ibid.

30. Ibid.

31. Ibid.

32. Ibid.

33. Ibid.; Crossland, "Florida's Jimmy Cash Horror," 112.

34. Ibid.

35. Ibid.; "Paper Is Found Like That Used for Ransom Note," Baton Rouge *Advocate*, June 2, 1938, 8.
36. "Braxton Files."
37. Ibid.
38. Ibid.
39. Ibid.
40. Don Grubin and Lars Madsen, "Lie Detector and the Polygraph: A Historical Review," *Journal of Forensic Psychiatry and Psychology* 16, no. 2 (2005): 357–69; see generally, Ken Alder, *The Lie Detectors: The History of an American Obsession* (New York: Free Press, 2007).
41. "Sure Boy Dead, Says Father but G-Men Push Hunt," San Diego *Union*, June 5, 1939, 1.
42. "Two Questioned in Cash Kidnap Probe Released," *State Times Advocate*, June 6, 1938, 1, 6.
43. "Hopes for Kidnap Solution Fading."
44. "Carpenter Rejoins Family after Kidnapping Mixup," New Orleans *Times-Picayune*, June 9, 1938, 27.
45. FBI files, 7-106, C. E. Weeks, (Willard Campbell), June 9, 1938, 200–224.
46. Ibid.
47. Ibid.; "Two Questioned in Cash Kidnap Probe Released."
48. Ibid.
49. Ibid.
50. Ibid.
51. Crossland, "Florida's Jimmy Cash Horror," 113.

## Chapter 8

1. FBI files, 7-106. The bureau files contain literally hundreds of pages of tips and suspicions supplied by well-meaning citizens.
2. FBI files, 7-106, E. J. Connelley, (Willard Campbell), June 2, 1938, 200–224.
3. Ibid.
4. Ibid.
5. FBI files, 7-106, C. E. Weeks, (Walter Fisher), June 4, 1938, 90–114.
6. Ibid.
7. FBI files, 7-106, C. E. Weeks, (Beatrice Cash), June 4, 1938, 25, 107.
8. FBI files, 7-106, Walter Fisher.
9. Ibid.
10. Ibid.
11. Ibid.
12. Ibid.
13. Ibid.
14. Ibid.
15. Ibid.

16. Ibid.
17. Ibid.
18. Ibid.
19. Ibid.
20. FBI files, 7-106, Beatrice Cash.
21. FBI files, 7-106, Walter Fisher.
22. Ibid.
23. Ibid.
24. Ibid.
25. Ibid.
26. Ibid.
27. Ibid.
28. Ibid.
29. Ibid.
30. Ibid.
31. Ibid.
32. Ibid.
33. Ibid.
34. Ibid.
35. FBI files, 7-106, C. E. Weeks, ("Windy" Davis), June 16, 1938, 303–8.
36. Ibid.
37. Ibid.
38. Ibid.
39. Ibid.
40. Ibid.
41. Ibid.
42. Ibid.
43. Ibid.
44. Emily Jack, "WBT Charlotte in the Golden Age of Radio," http://www.learnnc .org./lp/editions/nchist-newcentury/5198, accessed June 11, 2013.
45. "McCall Radio Script."
46. Ibid.
47. "G-Men Seek Data on Which to Hang Kidnap-Slayer," New Orleans *Times-Picayune*, January 24, 1938, 14; "Ross Kidnapper Forfeits Life," Riverside (CA) *Daily Press*, July 14, 1938, 2.
48. Ibid.
49. Ibid.
50. "McCall Radio Script."
51. FBI files, 7-106, Franklin Pierce McCall, (First Confession), June 7, 1938, 65–68 (shows he continued his normal routine and considered himself safe); Crossland, "Florida's Jimmy Cash Horror," 112; various accounts in Coleman Collection.
52. Ibid.
53. "Carpenter Rejoins Family after Kidnapping Mixup."

54. FBI files, 7-106, McCall (First Confession), June 7, 1938, 65–68; Crossland, "Florida's Jimmy Cash Horror," 112; Coleman Collection.

55. Ibid.

56. Ibid.

## Chapter 9

1. James M. Denham and William Warren Rogers, *Florida Sheriffs: A History, 1821–1945* (Tallahassee, FL: Sentry Press, 2001), 158 (henceforth *Florida Sheriffs*); Coleman Collection.

2. Picchi, *The Five Weeks of Giuseppe Zangara*, 26–28; Barbara Garfunkel, "Sheriff Recalls Wild Miami When Shotguns Ruled City," Miami *News*, August 13, 1933, 36.

3. Picchi, *The Five Weeks of Giuseppe Zangara*, 26–28.

4. Ibid.

5. Ibid.

6. Ibid.; "Hardie Praised as Officer at Ouster Hearing," Tampa *Tribune*, November 8, 1933, 11. See generally, Merlin G. Cox, "David Sholtz: New Deal Governor of Florida, *Florida Historical Quarterly* 43, no. 2 (1964): 138–51.

7. Ibid.; "Sholtz Denies Plea for Return to Sheriff's Post," Tampa *Tribune*, December 8, 1933, 1.

8. Ibid.; Westbrook Pegler, "Boom Likely in Florida's Gaming Dens," Omaha *World Herald*, October 26, 1933, 19. The writer, who apparently wrote for the boozers and bettors, averred Hardie too honest to bribe and too upright to ignore the law, but his removal might loosen things up in south Florida. Sheriff Coleman, however, proved him wrong.

9. Denham and Rogers, *Florida Sheriffs*, 158; background data from Coleman Collection.

10. Denham and Rogers, *Florida Sheriffs*, 158; "Race Information Bureau Asks Court Protection," New Orleans *Time-Picayune*, January 16, 1937, 12; "Nuisance Suits May Bar Sheriff from Raiding Gaming Halls," San Diego *Union*, January 25, 1939, 2.

11. Denham and Rogers, *Florida Sheriffs*, 158; "Gale Victim's Bodies Burned," Omaha *World Herald*, September 8, 1935, 1; "Bodies of Hurricane Victims Cremated," Greensboro *Record*, September 7, 1935, 1.

12. Ibid.

13. Denham and Rogers, *Florida Sheriffs*, 158; Coleman Collection.

14. Ibid.

15. Ibid.

16. Ibid.

17. Crossland, "Florida's Jimmy Cash Horror," 112.

18. Ibid.; Coleman Collection.

19. Ibid.

20. Ibid.; "G-Men Seek Additional Kidnap Figures," San Diego *Union*, June 10, 1938,

1–2. This is the fullest account in a mainstream newspaper of Coleman's participation in the Cash case.

21. Crossland, "Florida's Jimmy Cash Horror," 112; Coleman Collection; "G-Men Seek Additional Kidnap Figures."

22. Ibid.

23. Ibid.

24. Ibid.

25. Ibid.

26. Ibid.

27. Ibid.

28. Ibid.

29. Ibid. There is no indication in the FBI files, Coleman Collection, or any source we checked that indicates Bailey Cash confided a premonition of McCall's guilt.

30. Ibid.

31. Ibid.

32. Ibid.

33. Ibid.

34. Ibid.; "McCall Confesses Kidnap-Slaying," Omaha *World Herald*, June 10, 1938, 12.

35. Ibid.

36. Ibid.

37. "Kidnap Suspect with Sheriff," Trenton (NJ) *Evening Times*, June 10, 1938, 25.

38. Crossland, "Florida's Jimmy Cash Horror," 112.

39. "Hoover, Sheriff 'Swap Bouquets' over Case," Omaha *World Herald*, June 10, 1938, 12.

40. FBI files, 7-106. In the four thousand plus pages of FBI files of the Cash case, Sheriff Coleman is mentioned fewer than five times. Not only did Coleman's bringing McCall to the FBI office in Miami, and explaining his suspicions to Connelley, not make the files, he was also excluded from the list of people who discovered the body of little Skeegie.

41. Coleman Collection.

42. Ibid.

43. Ibid.

# Chapter 10

1. Robert S. McElvaine, *The Great Depression: America, 1929–1941* (New York: Times Books, 1993), 132–35. McElvaine classes Roosevelt's 1932 victory in the presidential election as "overwhelming," noting FDR received the largest margin since Abraham Lincoln's second (1864) election.

2. Jean Edward Smith, *FDR* (New York: Random House, 2007), 150–52.

3. Hazel Rowley, *Franklin and Eleanor: An Extraordinary Marriage* (New York: Farrar, Straus and Giroux, 2010), 81–83.

4. Smith, *FDR*, vii, 150–52.

5. Ibid.

6. Gentry, *J. Edgar Hoover*, 206, 302.

7. Ibid., 302.

8. Rodney Streitimatter, ed., *Empty without You: The Intimate Letters of Eleanor Roosevelt and Lorena Hickok* (New York: Da Capo, 2000), 22, 54. Hickok informed the Roosevelt children that she had destroyed some of the more explicit missives.

9. Gentry, *J. Edgar Hoover*, 385.

10. "G-Men Get Aid in Mobilizing to Fight Crime," San Diego *Union*, June 9, 1938, 1.

11. Ibid.

12. "Hamstringing of G-Men Hit," Omaha *World Herald*, May 20, 1938, 9.

13. "American Crime Starts at Home, Hoover Charges," New Orleans *Times-Picayune*, December 4, 1937, 13.

14. Ibid.

15. Ibid.

16. Ibid.

17. "G-Men Get Aid in Mobilizing to Fight Crime."

18. "Last 2 Suspects Freed in Florida Kidnapping," New Orleans *Times-Picayune*, June 7, 1938, 2.

19. "Two Questioned in Cash Kidnap Probe Released," *State Times Advocate*, June 6, 1938, 1, 6.

20. Ibid.

21. Crossland, "Florida's Jimmy Cash Horror," 112–13; "Youth Is Jailed as Suspect," Modesto (CA) *Bee*, June 9, 1938, 1.

22. Literally hundreds of "leads" are contained in the files, as below.

23. FBI files, 7-2348-195, June 7, 1938, report of S. A. Guy Hottel to Hoover.

24. FBI files, 7-2348-182, June 7, 1938, report of S. A. Guy Hottel to Hoover.

25. FBI files, 7-2348-217X2, June 6, 1938, report of S. A. D. M. Ladd to Hoover.

26. FBI files, 7-2348-198, June 6, 1938, report signed E. A. Tamm; FBI files, 7-2348-182, June 6, 1938, report of S. A. Guy Hottel to Hoover.

## Chapter 11

1. Tim Weiner, *Enemies: A History of the FBI* (New York: Random House, 2012), 35–36.

2. "Cash Searchers to Comb Cape," Charleston (WV) *Daily Gazette*, June 7, 1938, 1.

3. Ibid.

4. Ibid.

5. "Roosevelt Asks Solons for $50,000 to Help Solve Florida Kidnap Case," New Orleans *Times-Picayune*, June 8, 1938, 2.

6. "Cash Searchers to Comb Cape."

7. Ibid.

8. FBI files, 7-106, C. E. Weeks, June 15, 1938, 331–36.
9. Ibid.
10. Ibid.
11. Ibid.
12. Ibid.
13. Ibid.
14. Ibid.
15. Ibid.
16. Ibid.
17. Ibid.
18. Ibid.
19. FBI files, 7-106, E. J. Connelley (summation of events), June 14, 1938, 4.
20. Ibid.
21. FBI files, 7-106, E. J. Connelley, June 14, 1938, 12–16.
22. Ibid.
23. Ibid.
24. FBI files, Franklin Pierce McCall (first confession), June 14, 1938, 62–68.
25. Ibid.
26. Ibid.
27. Ibid.
28. Ibid.
29. Ibid.
30. Ibid.
31. Ibid.
32. Ibid.

## Chapter 12

1. FBI files, 7-106, Earl J. Connelley, 7-14-1938, 12–14.
2. Ibid.
3. "Felony murder doctrine," http://dictionary.law.com/Default.aspx?selected=741, accessed June 14, 2013.
4. Ibid.
5. FBI files, 7-106, Statement of Richard Asbury Cash, 49–50.
6. Ibid.
7. Ibid.
8. FBI files, 7-106, S. K. McKee, June 8, 1938, 22–26.
9. Ibid.
10. Ibid.
11. Ibid.
12. Ibid.
13. Ibid.
14. Ibid.

15. "Kidnap Suspect Leads FBI Agents to Cash Boy's Body," Seattle *Daily Times*, June 9, 1938, 2, 5.

16. Ibid.

17. Ibid.

18. Ibid.

19. FBI files, 7-106, Earl J. Connelley, 4.

20. FBI files, 7-106, Earl J. Connelly, 16–20.

21. Ibid.

22. Ibid.

23. Ibid.

24. Ibid.

25. Ibid.

26. Ibid.

27. Ibid.

28. FBI files, 7-106, Franklin Pierce McCall (henceforth McCall first confession), 62–68.

29. FBI files, 7-106, H. B. Dill, 17–20.

30. Ibid.

31. Ibid.

32. Ibid.

33. Ibid.

34. Ibid.

35. Ibid.

36. Ibid.

37. Ibid.

38. Ibid.

39. Ibid.

40. Ibid.

41. "Dr. Thomas Otto Dies in Boston," Miami *News*, June 17, 1962, 17.

42. FBI files, 7-106, Dr. Thomas Otto, 56 and 86–87.

43. Ibid.

44. Ibid.

45. MTT, Dr. Thomas Otto, 56–59.

46. FBI files, 7-106, Dr. Thomas Otto.

47. FBI files, 7-106, Agent H. B. Dill, 19.

48. FBI files, Agent Richard G. Danner, 57.

# Chapter 13

1. FBI files, 7-106, Dr. Thomas O. Otto, 56 and 87–88.

2. Ibid.

3. Ibid.

4. Ibid.

5. Ibid.

6. Ibid.

7. "Kidnapping Timeline," 1.

8. "Seek Speedy Kidnap Trial," Rockford (IL) *Morning Star*, June 11, 1938, 1–2.

9. FBI files, 7-106, G. W. Turner, 58; Crossland, "Florida's Jimmy Cash Horror," 114.

10. Crossland, "Florida's Jimmy Cash Horror," 114.

11. Ibid.; unattributed clipping, Coleman Collection.

12. Crossland, "Florida's Jimmy Cash Horror," 114.

13. Ibid.

14. Ibid.

15. Unattributed clipping, Coleman Collection.

16. "This Is a House of Sorrows," Brainerd (MN) *Daily Dispatch*, June 9, 1938, 1.

17. "Vera Cash, South Dade Settler Whose Son Was Murdered."

18. Crossland, "Florida's Jimmy Cash Horror," 114.

19. "Compliments Swapped," Dallas *Morning News*, June 10, 1938; "Confessed Kidnapper Closely Guarded," Richmond *Times-Dispatch*, June 11, 1938, 7.

20. Edwin C. Hill, "Human Side of the News," Syracuse (NY) *Journal*, February 7, 1939.

21. FBI files, 7-106, Franklin Pierce McCall, 74–84 (henceforth "McCall Final Confession").

22. FBI files, E. J. Connelley, 21–24.

23. Ibid.

24. "McCall Final Confession."

25. Ibid.

26. Ibid.

27. Ibid.

28. Ibid.

29. "Kidnapping Trial Plans Speeded," Canton *Repository*, June 10, 1938, 2.

30. "Walter Winchell on Broadway," Waterloo *Daily Courier*, June 20, 1938.

31. Ibid.

32. Ibid.

33. "McCall's Final Confession."

34. "Kidnapping Timeline," 1–2; "Kidnapper Confesses He Killed Cash Child; Speedy Trial Sought," Richmond *Times-Dispatch*, June 11, 1938, 1.

35. "House Votes $308,000 to Aid G-Men," Dallas *Morning News*, June 9, 1938, 1; "Confessed Kidnapper Is Closely Guarded."

36. Ibid.

37. "Law and Parents," Charlotte (NC) *News*, June 9, 1938.

38. Ibid.

39. "McCall Faces Speedy Trial in Kidnapping," Omaha *World Herald*, June 11, 1938, 4.

40. "Kidnapping Timeline," 2.

41. "Mrs. McCall Is Dazed by Her Son's Arrest," Richmond *Times-Dispatch*, June 10, 1938, 3.

42. Ibid.

43. "Mother of Kidnapper, Victim Meet, Mrs. Cash Spurns Plea," Omaha *World Herald*, July 7, 1938, 1.

## Chapter 14

1. "Ransom Put in 2 Spots, $5 Missing," Cleveland *Plain Dealer*, June 10, 1938, 1.

2. Ibid.; *Miami and Dade County, Florida: Its Settlement, Progress, and Achievement* (Washington, DC: Victor Rainbolt, 1921), 227–28 (Worley biography). Several modern jurists apparently believe that scientific and medical testimony is too complex for inquest jurors.

3. "Ransom Put in 2 Spots, $5 Missing"; "McCall Confesses Kidnapping, Killing," Omaha *World Herald*, June 10, 1938, 1; "Kidnapper Confesses He Killed Cash Child: Speedy Trial Sought," Richmond *Times-Dispatch*, June 11, 1938, 1.

4. Ibid.

5. Ibid.

6. Ibid.

7. "Coroner's Jury Brands McCall as Lad's Slayer," Albuquerque (NM) *Journal*, June 12, 1938.

8. "Ransom Put in 2 Spots, $5 Missing"; "McCall Gets Chair," Augusta *Chronicle*, June 17, 1938, 2.

9. "McCall Takes Entire Blame for Kidnapping," Greensboro *Record*, June 10, 1938, 1.

10. "Pioneers of Miami, Florida," http://genealogytrails.com/fla/miamidade/pioneers html, accessed June 13, 2013; "Kidnapping Timeline," 1–5.

11. MTT, 1–115.

12. Ibid.

13. Ibid.

14. Ibid., 7.

15. Ibid., 2–12.

16. Ibid., 13–15.

17. Ibid., 15–17.

18. Ibid., 17–33.

19. Ibid.

20. Ibid., 34–42.

21. Ibid., 44–49.

22. Ibid., 52–53.

23. Ibid., 55.

24. Ibid., 55–76.

25. Ibid.

26. Ibid.

27. Ibid., 77–92.

28. Ibid., 92–95.

29. Ibid.

30. "Precautions Are Taken for Kidnapper's Safety," Greensboro *Record*, June 15, 1938, 1.

31. Ibid.

32. MTT, 92–95; "Precautions Taken for Kidnapper's Safety."

33. "Kidnapper Silent and Erect, Hears Sentence of Death," Richmond *Times-Dispatch*, June 17, 1938, 1.

34. Ibid.

35. "Kidnapper Taken into 'Death Row' to Await Chair," New Orleans *Times-Picayune*, June 18, 1938, 1.

36. "Kidnapping Timeline," 2.

37. "History of the Florida Parole Commission: Seven Decades of Service to the State," http://fpc.state.fl.us/History.htm, accessed June 14, 2013.

38. "Mothers of Kidnapper, Victim Meet: Mrs. Cash Spurns Plea," Omaha *World Herald*, July 17, 1938, 1; "Deny Leniency to Cash Killer," Rockford *Morning Star*, June 18, 1938, 2.

39. Ibid.

40. Ibid.

41. Ibid.; "Kidnapping Timeline," 2.

42. "No Grounds for Clemency," Zanesville (OH) *Times Recorder*, September 7, 1938.

43. "Kidnapping Timeline," 2.

44. "Florida Corrections: Centuries of Progress, 1932," http://www.dc.state.fl.us/oth /timeline/1932a/html.

45. Ibid.

46. McCall v. State, Florida, 1939 [Supreme Court of Florida, Division A], Fla. 1939, 135 Fla. 712, 185 So., 608 Florida State Archives, Tallahassee, Florida, 1–9 (henceforth "McCall Appeal.")

47. Ibid.

48. "Apostolic Methodist Church," http://www.encyclopedia.com/article-1GZ -3274100042/non-episcopal-methodist.html.

49. "McCall Appeal."

50. "To Save McCall," (undated, no city, clipping in FBI files), *Florida State News*; "McCall's Tale of Beating Called 'Bunk,'" Madison *Wisconsin State Journal*, February 7, 1939.

51. "McCall Appeal."

52. Ibid., 3.

53. Ibid., 9.

54. Ibid., 2.

55. "Kidnapper-Slayer of Cash Boy Loses Plea in Court Here to Escape Execution," New Orleans *Times-Picayune*, February 23, 1939, 1.

56. "Kidnapping Timeline"; "Supreme Court Judges Deny Stay for McCall," Boston *Herald*, February 24, 1939, 12

57. "Kidnapping Timeline," 2.

# Chapter 15

1. "Florida Kidnapper Granted 4-Day Stay from Chair," Marietta *Journal*, February 20, 1939, 1; "McCall Granted Stay of Execution until Friday; Appeal Set," *State Times Advocate*, February 20, 1939, 1.

2. Ibid.

3. Ibid.; "Kidnapping Timeline," 2.

4. "McCall Granted Stay of Execution until Friday; Appeal Set"; "Long Conference Held by McCall's Attorney," Greensboro *Record*, February 21, 1939, 12.

5. "Kidnapper McCall Weeps: Set to 'Ride Thunderbolt,'" Omaha *World Herald*, February 20, 1939, 3.

6. "Doomed Pair Realizes Wish: McCall Gets Stay, Other Dies," Omaha *World Herald*, February 21, 1939, 10; "Bunge Confesses Slaying Family," Augusta *Chronicle*, May 9, 1938, 1–2; "Bunge Is Convicted: Faces Death Chair," Richmond *Times-Dispatch*, May 20, 1938, 12.

7. Ibid.

8. Ibid.

9. Ibid.; "M'Call Escapes Chair as Poet Dies," Panama City (FL) *News Herald*, February 20, 1939, 1.

10. Ibid.

11. Ibid.

12. Ibid.

13. Ibid.

14. "Florida Kidnapper Granted 4-Day Stay from Chair."

15. "McCall Is Executed for Fatal Kidnapping," Greensboro *Record*, February 24, 1939, 18.

16. Carbon copy of letter from Franklin Pierce McCall to Lillie McCall, no date, Coleman Collection.

17. Ibid.

18. "Mrs. McCall on Air," Circleville (OH) *Herald*, September 26, 1938, 3.

19. FBI files, 7-106, Franklin Pierce McCall (Final Confession), June 9, 1938, 74; "McCall Dies with Protest of Innocence," *State Times Advocate*, February 24, 1939, 1.

20. Harold S. Cohn, undated article, Jacksonville (FL) *Journal*, Coleman scrapbooks.

21. Ibid.

22. Ibid.

23. Ibid.

24. Several unattributed news clippings, Coleman Collection.

25. "McCall Executed for Fatal Kidnapping"; "Doomed Pair Realizes Wish: McCall Gets Stay, Other Dies."

26. Howard Van Smith, "Warden Chapman's 25 Years at Raiford: Gunshot Changed Prison History," Miami *News*, January 6, 1956, 16.

27. "M'Call Dies in Electric Chair," Rockford *Morning Star*, February 25, 1939, 12.

28. "Father Wants to Pull Switch on Cash Killer," Dallas *Morning News*, June 28, 1938, 1.

29. Unattributed clippings in Coleman Collection. Numerous newspapers reported that Vera, Bailey, and W. P. Cash visited McCall four days before his execution "to make peace with Frank before he died." This was completely untrue. "Florida Kidnaper Given 11th Hour Stay from Death," New Orleans *Times-Picayune*, February 21, 1939, 11.

30. "Kidnapping Timeline," 4; "Florida Kidnapper Granted 4-Day Stay from Chair."

31. Ibid.

32. "M'Call Dies in Electric Chair."

33. "Kidnapping Timeline," 4.

34. Ibid.

35. "McCall Pays for Slaying Youth," Marietta *Journal*, June 24, 1939, 1.

36. "M'Call Dies with Pleas of Innocence."

37. Ibid.

38. Ibid.

39. Ibid

40. Ibid.

41. "Kidnapping Timeline," 4; "M'Call Dies in Electric Chair."

42. "Franklin Pierce McCall, Jr.," http://www.findagrave.com/cgi-bin/fg.cgi?page=gr&GRid=36652619, accessed June 13, 2013.

43. Steve Trumbull, (quoted by Walter Winchell), "On Broadway with Walter Winchell," Brownsville (TX) *Herald*, June 29, 1939, 4.

44. Unattributed news clipping, Coleman Collection. Bailey and Vera took time off to listen to a radio broadcast of the execution.

45. "Vera Cash, South Dade Settler Whose Son Was Murdered," states, "The *Cashes* never recovered from the loss of *their* son."

46. "Attorney Asks Delay in McCall's Warrant," Richmond *Times-Dispatch*, June 23, 1938, 17.

47. "Vera Cash, South Dade Settler Whose Son Was Murdered."

## Afterword

1. J. B. Cash Foundation, Inc., http://j-b-cash-foundation-inc.idilogic.aidpage.com/j-b-cash-foundation-inc/, accessed June 14, 2013.

2. Vera Cash Foundation, Inc., http://vera-cash-foundation-inc.idilogic.aidpage.com/vera-cash-foundation-inc/, accessed June 14, 2013; "Owner Fights Move to Label Boarding House as Historic," Miami *Herald*, August 11, 1983, 10; "Vera Cash, South Dade Settler Whose Son Was Murdered."

3. Ibid.

4. Ibid.

5. Ibid.

6. Ibid.

7. "Arthur Rutzen, 79; Ran 5 FBI Offices," *New York Times*, August 5, 1989 (obituary); Arthur Rutzen, Ex-FBI Agent, One of the Original 'G-Men,'" SunSentinel.com, August 5, 1989 (obituary).

8. "Former High FBI Man, Earl J. Connelley, Dies," *Pacific Stars and Stripes*, July 22, 1957, 3.

9. Lewis Erenberg, *Swingin' the Dream* (Chicago: University of Chicago Press, 1999), 197; Michael Newton, *The FBI Encyclopedia* (Jefferson, NC: McFarland, 2012), 314.

10. "State Would Save $46,589 Year under Law's Repeal, Claim," Panama City *News Herald*, April 15, 1943, 8.

11. Jeffreys Diarmuid, *The Bureau: Inside the Modern FBI* (New York: Houghton Mifflin, 1995), 73–75.

12. http://www.findagrave.com/cgi-bin/fg.cgi?page=gr&GRid=36652619, accessed June 14, 2013.

13. FBI files, 7-106, Earl J. Connelley, June 14, 1938, 16–20.

# Bibliography

## Primary Sources

Coleman Collection. Letters, news clippings, and reports contained in more than fifty scrapbooks documenting the career of sheriff and state senator D. C. Coleman. Owned by Brien D. Coleman and Ann Coleman Hicks, of Miami, Florida.

Federal Bureau of Investigation Files, 7-106 and 7-2348. Four thousand documents related to the kidnapping and murder of James Bailey Cash Jr. National Archives and Records Management, College Park, MD.

McCall v. State of Fla., 185 So. 608 (Fla., 1939).

McCall v. State of Fla., 186 So. 803 (Fla., 1939).

Transcript of the Record of the Proceedings in the Circuit Court of the Eleventh Judicial Circuit, in and for Dade County, Florida. In the Case of the State of Florida v. Franklin Pierce McCall, June 14–16, 1938, Florida State Archives, Tallahassee.

## Books

Alder, Ken. *The Lie Detectors: The History of an American Obsession*. New York: Free Press, 2007.

Breuer, William B. *J. Edgar Hoover and His G-Men*. Westport, CT: Praeger, 1995.

Burnett, Gene M. *Florida's Past: People and Events That Shaped the State*. Vol. 1. Sarasota, FL: Pineapple Press, 1996.

Butler, Susan. *East to the Dawn: The Life of Amelia Earhart*. New York: Da Capo, 2009.

Denham, James M., and William Warren Rogers. *Florida Sheriffs: A History, 1821–1945*. Tallahassee, FL: Sentry Press, 2001.

Diarmuid, Jeffreys. *Inside the Modern FBI*. New York: Houghton Mifflin, 1995.

Erenberg, Lewis. *Swingin' the Dream*. Chicago: University of Chicago Press, 1999.

Fisher, Jim. *The Ghosts of Hopewell: Setting the Record Straight in the Lindbergh Case*. Carbondale: Southern Illinois University Press, 1999.

———. *The Lindbergh Case*. New Brunswick, NJ: Rutgers University Press, 1995.

Gentry, Curt. *J. Edgar Hoover: The Man and the Secrets*. New York: W. W. Norton, 1991.

Hawk, Robert. *Florida's Army: Militia, State Troops, National Guard, 1565–1985*. Englewood, FL: Pineapple Press, 1986.

Kessler, Ronald. *The Bureau: The Secret History of the FBI*. New York: St. Martin's Press, 2002.

McElvaine, Robert S. *The Great Depression: America, 1929–1941*. New York: Times Books, 1993.

*Miami and Dade County, Florida: Its Settlement, Progress, and Achievement*. Washington, DC: Victor Rainbolt, 1921.

Newton, Michael. *The FBI Encyclopedia*. Jefferson, NC: McFarland, 2012.

Picchi, Blaise. *The Five Weeks of Giuseppe Zangara: The Man Who Would Assassinate FDR*. Chicago: Academy Chicago Publishers, 1998.

Poveda, Tony, et al. *The FBI: A Comprehensive Reference Guide*. Westport, CT: Greenwood, 1998.

Powers, Richard Gid. *Broken: The Troubled Past and Uncertain Future of the FBI*. New York: Free Press, 2004.

———. *Secrecy and Power: The Life of J. Edgar Hoover*. New York: Free Press, 1987.

Rowley, Hazel. *Franklin and Eleanor: An Extraordinary Marriage*. New York: Farrar, Straus and Giroux, 2010.

Smith, Jean Edward. *FDR*. New York: Random House, 2007.

Ste. Claire, Dana M. *Cracker: The Cracker Culture in Florida History*. Gainesville: University Press of Florida, 2006.

Stockbridge, Frank Parker, and John Holliday Perry. *So This Is Florida*, Jacksonville, FL: John H. Perry Publishing, 1938.

Streitimatter, Rodney, ed. *Empty without You: The Intimate Letters of Eleanor Roosevelt and Lorena Hickok*. New York: Da Capo, 2000.

Weiner, Tim. *Enemies: A History of the FBI*. New York: Random House, 2012.

## Magazines and Journals

"Atrocious Revival." *Time*, June 13, 1938.

Cox, Merlin G. "David Sholtz: New Deal Governor of Florida." *Florida Historical Quarterly* 43, no. 2 (1964): 138–51.

Crossland, Bob. "Kidnaped! Florida's Jimmy Cash Horror." *True Detective*, October 1958, 14–19, 110–17.

Grubin, Don, and Lars Madsen. "Lie Detector and the Polygraph: A Historical Review." *Journal of Forensic Psychiatry and Psychology* 6, no. 2 (2005): 357–69.

## Newspapers

Abilene (TX) *Morning News Reporter*
Albuquerque (NM) *Journal*
Alton (IL) *Evening News*

Augusta (GA) *Chronicle*
Baton Rouge (LA) *Advocate*
Biloxi (MS) *Daily Herald*
Boston *Herald*
Brainerd (MN) *Daily Dispatch*
Brownsville (TX) *Herald*
Burlington (IA) *Daily Hawk-Eye Gazette*
Butte *Montana Standard*
Canandaigua (NY) *Daily Messenger*
Canton (OH) *Repository*
Charleston (WV) *Daily Gazette*
Charlotte (NC) *News*
Circleville (OH) *Herald*
Cleveland (OH) *Plain Dealer*
Dallas *Morning News*
Emporia (KS) *Gazette*
Galveston (TX) *Daily News*
Greensboro (NC) *Record*
Hamilton (OH) *Daily News Journal*
Hammond (IN) *Times*
Helena (MT) *Independent*
Jacksonville (FL) *Journal*
Joplin (MO) *Globe*
Kansas City (MO) *Star*
Lock Haven (PA) *Express*
Logansport (IN) *Pharos-Tribune*
Lowell (MA) *Sun*
Madison *Wisconsin State Journal*
Marietta (GA) *Journal*
Miami *Herald*
Miami *News*
Modesto (CA) *Bee*
New Orleans *Times-Picayune*
*New York Times*
Oakland (CA) *Tribune*
Ocala (FL) *Star Banner*
Oshkosh (WI) *Northwestern*
*Pacific Stars and Stripes* (Portland, OR)
Panama City (FL) *News Herald*
Panama City (FL) *Pilot*
Port Arthur (TX) *News*
Richmond (VA) *Times-Dispatch*
Riverside (CA) *Daily Press*

Rockford (IL) *Morning Star*
Rockford (IL) *Register Republic*
San Antonio (TX) *Express*
San Antonio (TX) *Light*
San Diego (CA) *Union*
Seattle (WA) *Daily Times*
Springfield (MA) *Republican*
*State Times Advocate* (Baton Rouge, LA)
Syracuse (NY) *Journal*
Tampa (FL) *Tribune*
Tipton (IN) *Daily Tribune*
Trenton (NJ) *Evening Times*
Waterloo (IA) *Daily Courier*
Zanesville (OH) *Times Recorder*

## Electronic Sources

Albright, Evan J. "Crime of the Century and the Cape Cod Connection," http://capecodconfidential.com/ccc2-17.shtml.
Apostolic Methodist Church, http://www.encyclodedia.com/article-1GZ-3274100042/non-episcopal-methodist.html.
"Arthur Rutzen, Ex-FBI Agent, One of the Original 'G-Men,'" http://articles.sun-sentinel.com/1989–08–05/news/89022404131fbi-agent-fbi-offices-fbi-operations-SunSentinel.com.
Barker-Karpis Gang. The Encyclopedia of Arkansas History and Culture, www.encyclopediaofarkansas.net/encyclopedia/entry-detail.asp?entryID=5740.
Chaffin, K. B. "Jelly Bryce: The FBI's Legendary Sharpshooter," http://gutterfighting.org/jellybryce.html.
"Faded Glory: Dusty Roads of an FBI Era," http://historicalgmen.squarespace.com/agents-of-the-30s-biographe.
"Felony murder doctrine," http://dictionary.law.com/Default.aspx?selected=741.
"Florida Corrections: Centuries of Progress, 1932," http://www.dc.state.fl.us/oth/timeline/1932a/html.
"Florida Military Service Records," http://www.floridamemory.com/items/show/218895.
"Florida National Guard Summary History to 1940," http://ufdc.ufl.edu/uf00047664/00001/2j.
"Franklin Pierce McCall, Jr.," http://www.findagrave.com/cgi-bin/fg.cgi?page=gr&GRid=36652619.
"History of the Florida Parole Commission: Seven Decades of Service to the State," http://fpc.state.fl.us/History.htm.
Jack, Emily. "WBT Charlotte in the Golden Age of Radio," http://www.learnnc.org./lp/editions/nchist-newcentury/5198.

"J. B. Cash Foundation, Inc.," http://j-b-cash-foundation-inc.idilogic.aidpage.com/j-b-cash-foundation-inc.

"Jim Crow Museum of Racist Memorabilia," Ferris State University, http://ferris.edu/jimcrow/what.htm.

Kleinberg, Howard, "History of the Miami *News* (1896–1987)." This online article has no URL.

Krajicek, David J. "Hoover and the Child Snatcher," http://www.dailynews.com/news/crime/hoover-child-snatcher-article-1.294513.

"List of American Films of 1938," http://en.wikipedia.org/wiki/List_of_American_films_of_1938.

McClary, Daryl C. "Ten-Year-Old Charles Mattson Is Kidnapped in Tacoma and Held for Ransom on December 27, 1936," http://www.historylink.org/index.cfm?DisplayPage=output.cfm&fileid=8028.

"Miami-Dade County: Kidnapping of James Bailey Cash," http://genealogytrails.com/fla/miamidade/news/kidnapping.html.

"The New Rochelle Police Department (A Brief History)," http://www.nrpd.com/aboutus.htm.

O'Dell, Larry. "Urschel Kidnapping," digital.library.okstate.edu/encyclopedia/entries/U/UR009.html.

"Pioneers of Miami, Florida," http://genealogytrails.com/fla/miamidade/pioneers.html.

Pylant, James. "Vintage True Crime Magazines: An Untapped Goldmine for Genealogists," http://www.genealogymagazine.com/crime.html.

"The Roberts Mayfair: A Historic Hotel, History," http://www.robertsmayfairhotel.com/index.php?option=com_content&view=article&id=373&Itemid=267.

"Top of the Charts, 1938," http://www.popculturemadness.com/Music/Charts/1938.html.

"Vera Cash Foundation, Inc.," http://vera-cash-foundation-inc.idilogic.aid.page.com/vera-cash-foundation-inc/.

# Index